The Pavlova Story

THE PAVLOVA STORY

A slice of New Zealand's culinary history

Helen Leach

With classic pavlova recipes
updated and photographed by Mary Browne

Otago University Press

Otago University Press
PO Box 56 / Level 1, 398 Cumberland Street, Dunedin, New Zealand
Fax: 64 3 479 8385. Email: university.press@otago.ac.nz
Website: www.otago.ac.nz/press

ISBN 978 1 877372 57 5

First published 2008
Reprinted 2009
Published with the assistance of the
History Group, Ministry for Culture & Heritage

Book design by Jenny Cooper
Printed through Condor Production Ltd, Hong Kong

Contents

6 Pavlovas from 1935 to 1950

7 Pavlovas come of age, 1950–59

8 Pavlovas consolidate, 1960–79

9 Pavlovas paramount, 1980–99

10 Some sticky issues

11 Why pavlovas are important

Classic pavlova recipes, revised and illustrated by Mary Browne

Acknowledgements

AS EXPLAINED in Chapter One, I became entangled in the pavlova debate in 1995, and wrote up my initial findings in the paper I delivered at the Oxford Food Symposium in 1996. The collection of New Zealand cookbooks that I had started decades earlier continued to grow, and although I used it as a source of material for my subsequent encounters with the media and occasional public talks, it was not until 2004 that I was able to give the collection the attention it deserved. The award of a Marsden grant by the Royal Society of New Zealand for 2005–7 provided the opportunity to investigate the development of New Zealand's culinary traditions in much greater depth. My research team consisted of Michael Symons, Janet Mitchell, Raelene Inglis, Jane Teal, and Sophia Beaton. Fiona Crawford, Renée Wilson, and Miang Lim also became associated with the project in 2006. To the Marsden Fund and my extended research team, I wish to express my sincere gratitude for allowing me to make a systematic study of a topic that has suffered from too many superficial investigations in the past.

The research underpinning my second conference paper on pavlovas, delivered in Adelaide in 2006, and then subsequently expanded into this book, depended on detailed analysis of a very comprehensive collection of pavlova recipes from cookbooks, newspapers, and periodicals. I am especially grateful to Jane, Raelene, and Janet who tirelessly forwarded me recipes to enter into my pavlova database, and looked up archives. Michael Symons, Duncan Galletly, and André Taber have also been active contributors of useful ideas and references, as have Colin Bannerman, Joan Bishop, Margery Blackman, Tony Carrell, Lois Daish, Elizabeth Driver, Des Hurley, Barbara Keen, Louis Leland, Clare Phipps, Perrin Rowland, Charmian Smith, and Murray Thomson. I will remember my discussions with the late Elizabeth Hinds, Harry Orsman, Phyl Robinson, and Kathleen Fountain very appreciatively. Thanks are also due to people who answered requests for information: Sheree Littlewood (Griffins), John Fenby and Wayne Dixon (South Otago High School), Phyllis Aspinall and Martin Chamberlain (St Peter's College). Many others took the time to contact me with memories and information, including M. Black, Delia Cook, Jean Kissel, Penny Milne, Beverley Morris, Willy Munro Hoen, Freda Trevethan, and R. Way. Brian Romeril sent me his jazz CD entitled 'Pavlova' while Miriam Vollweiler gave me a smart pavlova apron.

Many people have provided books for my research collection over the years. Particular thanks are due to Frank Leckie for buying cookbooks for me at countless auctions and fairs. Others who have sent me recipe books include Erena Barker, Beverley Shore Bennett, Reva Calvert, Logan Coote, Yanbin Deng, Anne Dix, Nola Easdale, John Fairweather, Judith Ferguson and Kevin Hayward, Elizabeth Hanan, Dena Henderson, Alice Hunt, Duncan Galletly, Mary Green, Francie Haslemore, Chris Hendry, Jane Hulst, Raelene Inglis, Lorraine Isaacs, Fay Jewell, Weihong Ji, Ann Kirwan, Margaret Lane, Garry Law, Gillian Lewis-Shell, Joy McNicoll, Colin Marshall, Clare Maynard, Geoffrey and Rosalie Mehrtens, Alison Middlemiss, Ron Murray, Elizabeth Niven, Kathryn Parsons, Barbara Smith, Rod Stace, Jane Teal, Judith Thompson, Andrea Ward, Barbara Withington, and Connie Wood. I am indebted to all of you, as well to those whose names escaped my filing system, for preserving old cookbooks not for their appearance but for what they tell us about home cookery in the past.

Permission to reproduce illustrations from other publications, and assistance in scanning or copying them, has been generously given by Greg Clarke, Lily Binns, and *Saveur*; Les Gibbard; Mary Lewis and all the helpful staff of Hocken Collections Uare Taoka a Hakena; Glenys Christian and the *New Zealand Dairy Exporter*; Julian Smith of Allied Press; Tim Corballis and the Alexander Turnbull Library; Linda McInnes and the National Library of Australia; Esther Read, Jo Boyle, Dan Taylor, and the Lower Hutt Plunket Society; Tui Flower and Penguin Books; Janet Mitchell, and Jane Teal.

Finally I must express my deepest gratitude to colleagues, friends and family who helped to turn this quest into a book. My research team and family read and commented on the manuscript. My sister Mary Browne adapted the classic pavlova recipes and made (and remade) them until they could be successfully produced in a modern kitchen. Mary also took the delectable photographs of the finished products. My publisher Wendy Harrex, copy-editor Linda Pears and designer Jenny Cooper brought the book to fruition. Thank you all for your help and support.

HELEN LEACH

The Pavlova Wars

The Pavlova Wars break out

In 1999, seventy years after the first pavlova cake was made in New Zealand, a war broke out with Australia – a war of words, of course, but the rhetoric was as jingoistic as the real thing. On 28 January *The Press* of Christchurch announced under the headline 'Pav-pretenders bowl an under-arm' that 'the great trans-Tasman row over the origins of pavlova is raging once more'.[1] A day later the *Sydney Morning Herald* reported that 'the Kiwis have bitten back'. Their headline was still relatively restrained: 'Pav whips up storm'.[2] The New Zealand Press Association then elevated the row into a war. On 2 February they declared 'Passions run high over pavlova war'.[3] New Zealand newspapers liked that concept and the pun on the passionfruit topping, which had become the centre of the argument, and many repeated the story that 'the trans-Tasman pavlova wars are raging again'.[4] For variety, Wellington's *Evening Post* came up with the punchy headline on 3 February: 'Food fight erupts over Kiwi pavs'.[5]

Wellington had a special role in the outbreak of these hostilities because it was Te Papa, the National Museum of New Zealand in the capital city, that fired the first shots. To celebrate their first birthday, they baked a 45-metre-long 'Pavzilla' that spokesman Paul Brewer proudly referred to as a 'great Kiwi icon'.[6] This was reported in Sydney on 26 January, a date that few New Zealanders recognised as important, but that all Australians knew as Australia Day. There was an immediate response from the Australian press, who called in Margaret Fulton, the doyenne of Australian food-writers. She insisted to Reuters that, as everyone knew, the pavlova was created in Western Australia by Bert Sachse in 1935, and its Australian-ness also came from its passionfruit topping. New Zealanders used kiwifruit on their version – in her opinion, a 'dreary' fruit.[7]

New Zealand journalists responded with obvious glee that a book entitled 100 *Things Everyone Needs to Know about Australia*, written by David Dale of the *Sydney Morning Herald*, accepted the pavlova's origin in New Zealand.[8] Then a Blenheim freelance journalist, John Adeane, revealed the existence of a 1927 recipe for a Pavlova Cake in a Christchurch publication, as well as recipes for meringue cakes with similar ingredients dating back to the year of Pavlova's first visit to Australasia in 1926.[9] The argument subsequently widened to include other contested icons as well as the merits of passionfruit versus those of kiwifruit.

Some historical context was provided by the *Illawarra Mercury* on 4 February, which pointed out that although in both countries sports had previously provided the 'battle grounds on which the war for national pride has been waged', the latest 'in this long line of epic contests is a dispute over who really invented the pavlova'. Putting dispassionate analysis to one side, they let fly with 'These bloody New Zealanders are trying to nab our national dish'.[10] Sarah-Kate Lynch, food editor of the *New Zealand Herald*, had expressed the same sentiment two days earlier: 'Those bloody Australians. It's so typical. They're always trying to steal our best ideas.'[11] Obviously the possibility of New Zealand pavlova recipes predating 1935 was worrying the Australian press. What their journalists didn't know was that the 1926 meringue cake recipe was printed in a book written by an Australian (Emily Futter), and that John Adeane's 1927 pavlova recipe was actually a four-layered gelatine dish, probably developed in Australia by Davis Gelatine.

Little attention was paid to a statement on 3 February by David Burton, food and wine editor of Wellington's *Evening Post*, that there were two recipes called 'pavlova' in New Zealand recipe books in 1933.[12] One of these had come into my possession in 1996 and I had referred to it in a volume of conference proceedings published in England in 1997.[13] Somehow my name came to the attention of Channel 9 in Sydney as a suitable person to interview. In fact what they had in mind was more of a confrontation. On Tuesday 2 February I was in my office at the University of Otago preparing a course outline for the new semester, when Bernadette from Channel 9 rang to ask whether I would debate the origins of the pavlova live with Margaret Fulton the next morning. She presumed I would have to travel to Wellington, since Dunedin no longer had a local television station. 'Dunedin is the headquarters of the world-famous Natural History New Zealand,' I replied. We were offered use of a corner of the unit's furniture store, the former Mastermind studio, and an independent cameraman (Ray Collins) was engaged. At this stage Bernadette suggested that I bake a pavlova and pretend to throw it at Margaret Fulton. 'Absolutely not,' was my response. Every New Zealand and Australian home cook is familiar with Margaret Fulton's name, and many have her recipe books. In 1999 she was seventy-four years old, and had just been elected one of the hundred Australian Living Treasures.[14] Have they no respect for their senior food-writers? I asked myself. In retrospect I wondered if they wanted to start a real war. As an academic, I replied that I dealt with facts not insults. I would bring along the recipe for the first true pavlova cake, dated to 1933.

On Wednesday I was at the television studios in Dunedin at 10.10 a.m. ready for the live debate. Margaret Fulton began by repeating her argument about the true pavlova having a passionfruit topping, to which I replied that I had a 1934 pavlova cake recipe from Wellington that stipulated a passionfruit topping, and that kiwifruit toppings were not popular until after World War 2. Then I used her momentary hesitation to advance my point that no-one creates recipes from scratch. They evolve and are passed from person to person, even across the Tasman. There was, I continued, so much similarity in cooking in Australia and New Zealand that it would not be surprising to find that the pavlova had evolved in both countries. She agreed wholeheartedly and we left the interviewer uncertain where to go next. I had tried to tell the Channel 9 researcher the previous day that my published paper on the pavlova had emphasised evolution not creation, but was quickly given to understand that such academic findings don't interest viewers or interviewers. Within a few days, pavlovas were old news and the rivalry subsided. I doubt if many readers noticed a letter from an Aucklander, published in the *Sydney Morning Herald* on 11 February, saying that her mother's generation (now in their nineties) had used passionfruit toppings on their New Zealand pavlovas.[15]

Meanwhile in New York, an expatriate Australian journalist, who wrote for the American food magazine *Saveur*, decided that she would look deeper into the evidence. *Saveur* has a commitment to 'authentic cuisine'. Not surprisingly the journalist, Chloe Osborne, contacted me by e-mail in late April 1999 with a string of detailed questions. I replied with even more detail, prompting her to write, 'I think you may be the only other person out there who knows how complicated meringue, cream and fruit can get.' The *Saveur* test kitchen was commissioned to make a pavlova, and that prompted more enquiries about toppings. Cartoonist Greg Clarke prepared an accompanying picture of a cross kiwi (New Zealand's iconic bird) with a wooden spoon facing off against an angry kangaroo (Australia's iconic animal) with rolling pin (Fig. 1.1). Chloe Osborne's article, entitled 'Pavlova wars', was light-hearted but gave the facts as we then knew them. She even repeated my view that 'pavlova ... wasn't the work of one chef, but a gentle evolution, the result of years of recipe swapping and baking between women. Women from New Zealand'. She finished her article by saying that she would always think of Australia when eating a pavlova and of Anna Pavlova, who hadn't lived to sample the cake named after her.[16] In her e-mails she joked that she might never be allowed home, but that it was important 'to get beyond the silly squabble'.

1.1   Greg Clarke's iconic cartoon in the American magazine *Saveur* (No. 36, p. 17) accompanied Chloe Osborne's 1999 article on the Pavlova Wars.

Reproduced with permission from Greg Clarke and *Saveur*, www.saveur.com

PAVLOVA WARS

Margaret Fulton had observed a certain periodicity in the pavlova argument; in her experience it heated up every ten years. However, I had already participated in a previous trans-Tasman pavlova debate in 1995–6, and was to become involved in two more episodes, in 2005 and again in 2006. Perhaps, like volcanic magma, it had reached a period of more intense activity. In the meantime the Australian newspapers recorded Bert Sachse's invention of the dish every year on its anniversary (3 October). On 4 July 1999, Bert Sachse's niece gave his original recipe to Jan Oldham of the *Sunday Times Perth*, who published her article under the headline 'The pavlova is ours'.[17] It was no surprise to me that the descendants of the Hotel Esplanade staff involved in the birth of the Australian pavlova should be so passionate about their reading of its history. I had encountered the same feeling in elderly New Zealand cooks.

New Zealand franchisees of the American fast-food chain McDonald's took the dispute into consideration when launching the McPav, a mini soft-centred pavlova, on 10 March 2000, admitting that it was a Kiwi icon but using a passion-fruit sauce topping in deference to Australian tradition.[18] They were clearly unaware of the frequent use of passionfruit in New Zealand pavlovas of the nineteen thirties and forties. In April that year, another giant pavlova was baked in Wellington, this time to celebrate 160 years since the local signing of the Treaty of Waitangi. On this occasion there was no reaction from the Australian press.[19] An account of a pavlova for twenty-five guests made in New Zealand from a single emu's egg also went unremarked.[20]

After the live 'confrontation' with Margaret Fulton on Sydney's Channel 9 in 1999, I was weary at the thought of further television exposure on the issue. When an e-mail arrived on 11 June 2004 from a researcher for the *George Negus Tonight* history programme on Australia's ABC television, asking me to appear as an expert on New Zealand food history, I should have been alerted by the proposed name of the segment, 'The Pavlova Wars'. I was, however, assured that this programme had a reputation for in-depth and balanced treatment of historical debates. Besides, they also intended to interview Michael Symons, who had written the most thorough investigation of the Australian origins of the pavlova in his 1982 book, *One Continuous Picnic*.[21] Michael (then resident in Wellington) was in frequent contact with me as we were planning a major research project on the development of New Zealand's culinary traditions, including some research on Australian and New Zealand iconic dishes such as the pavlova. The interviewer was Jeremy Boylen and he sent us both a series of questions that he intended to ask. Once again Ray Collins was to be the local cameraman, and once again I was to bring in the 1933 cookbook containing New Zealand's first single-layer pavlova recipe. I was also ready to talk about a new find – a pavlova cake recipe published in a New Zealand rural magazine in 1929.[22] On 20 July the interview was filmed in the same studio we'd used in 1999. All the questions were covered and I came away satisfied that there was genuine interest in the details.

The programme went to air in Australia on Monday 30 August 2004, but I didn't receive a recorded copy for several weeks. On Tuesday morning, there was an irate phone call from Paul Plowman, a descendant of Elizabeth Paxton in Perth, who thought I had trivialised his family's involvement with the pavlova – according to family tradition Elizabeth had named Bert Sachse's pavlova. It was the first of many calls, most requesting radio or television interviews. I found the transcript of the George Negus show online, and realised that what had taken me more than ten minutes to explain had been cut to thirty-five seconds. Michael's words had been spliced around mine, giving him a total of forty-four seconds. George Negus had introduced the item as a food fight and 'pav stouch', and after Jeremy Boylen concluded that the 'Kiwis have it', George Negus added that it was a lot of fuss over egg white and sugar. Why then did he ask Michael and me to appear as experts? I agreed wholeheartedly with Paul Plowman that the story had been trivialised, but this was neither Michael's fault nor mine. My recommendation to Paul was to check local Western Australian community cookbooks of the period, since such books had proved so useful in determining the history of the pavlova in New Zealand. I also told him that it was possible the Perth pavlova had developed quite independently, a point made in the original interview but edited out.

Paul Plowman clearly felt a sense of injustice, and I shared his feeling. It was hard not to be short with the television and radio reporters who wanted a share of what they saw as a Kiwi victory. On Wednesday 1 September, I gave an interview to Radio Pacific at 8.15 a.m., was filmed by a TV3 cameraman with the 'evidence' at 12.30 p.m., recorded a taped radio interview during the afternoon, and finally Radio New Zealand rang for a more searching interview at 5.45 p.m. A local television crew arrived at my office at 1.30 p.m. the next day and I had a bizarre interview with The Rock radio station. Media attention tailed off over the weekend, during which the violent end of the Beslan school hostage crisis in Russia was brought live to our living rooms. From the bizarre to the brutal, I thought, convinced that some of the media swing from the trivial to the sensational with no middle ground allocated to serious analysis. My neighbour reported that she had heard an interview in which some Australian travel agents, asked about my pavlova findings, had commented that I obviously didn't have anything better to do. I don't think this was simply sour grapes. My words had been edited to suggest that I was a willing mercenary in the pavlova wars. The Southland Times referred to the 1929 recipe as my 'knockout blow' delivered to 'those pav-pinching dingo wranglers'.[23]

Less than a year later, research published in 2004 by Jane Teal (one of the members of my research team investigating the development of New Zealand's culinary traditions) led to a feature article in The Press.[24] Jane had used her skills as an archivist to tell us about Laurina Stevens, the contributor of the 1933 pavlova recipe found in the Rangiora Mothers' Union Cookery Book, and about community where she lived. The article included a photo of a pavlova cake made from Mrs Stevens' recipe. Australian and New Zealand journalists picked up this story, with no apparent memory of the press coverage of exactly the same evidence in September 2004.[25] Given that they had online access to electronic indexing and full-text newspaper resources, it seemed to me that researching the history of the debate was not important to them. However, one Australian newspaper, the Courier Mail, invited Australian readers who had evidence that the pavlova was made in Australia before 1929 to e-mail them the details.[26] Even the online BBC news service featured the 'Antipodean palaver over pavlova', soliciting comment from around the world. I particularly liked the view of Yoko, a Japanese expatriate living in the United States: 'Who cares! We've got the Iraq war ... terrorist attacks ... poverty the world over. ... And the Aussies and Kiwis are concerned who invented a dessert.'[27]

Quite right! This story is not about invention, but how humans link their identity to certain dishes they cook, and how they constantly modify those dishes, adding new meanings each time they make them. I would not deny for a minute the importance to Australians of Bert Sachse's experiments with meringue cakes or Elizabeth (Plowman) Paxton's choice of name. I have, however, found that there are many pavlova stories, each as important as the Sachse story, each contributing to the complex history of pavlovas. If the media persist in seeking a single act of pavlova creation, then there can be only one original creator, and only one victor in the 'pavlova wars'. Other people with legitimate memories will feel disbelieved and dispossessed. That is not the history that I wish to promote.

The origin of the Pavlova Wars

Can we identify the origins of the pavlova wars? Wars, even of the verbal variety, usually follow a period in which boundaries are disputed, and issues become polarised. When did Australians and New Zealanders start to identify with this particular dish? How long was it before they became hypersensitive to each other's statements of ownership and provocative in their choice of words?

In 1950 Auckland's Medical Officer of Health, Dr A.W.S. Thompson, complained that 'New Zealand housewives expend far too much energy and thought on afternoon teas'.[28] He called for a competition for a national dish, to lead these housewives away 'from their cakes and pastries, which are admittedly excellent,' to true gastronomy, by which he meant meals. Dr Thompson does not seem to have allowed for the possibility that a national dish might already be emerging within the afternoon tea items, which of course included the pavlova.

There is a suggestion that this process was underway in Robin Howe's book *Cooking From the Commonwealth* (1958), which draws on her experience of travelling through Commonwealth countries over the previous twenty-five years. Mrs Howe inserted a recipe for 'Meringue Cake or Pavlova Cake' within the New Zealand recipe section, but she made a comment that in Australia, as in New Zealand, 'a good deal of housewives' cooking ingenuity goes into the baking of cakes, especially pavlova cake'.[29] It is likely that as New Zealanders and Australians enlarged their horizons in the 1950s, each group increasingly came to see their pavlovas as distinctive of their home country.

A year or so before Robin Howe's book, a two-volume work entitled *Home Management*, edited by Alison Barnes, had been published in London for the British market. It included a section on 'Cookery at Home and Abroad'. The recipes from abroad were supplied by named food-writers, home economists and marketing boards representing twenty-five countries. The Australian section of twelve pages was contributed by Nancy Gepp. In addition to recipes for Anzac Biscuits, Gem Scones, and Lamingtons ('a national favourite'), she included a recipe for a Passionfruit Pavlova.[30] In contrast, New Zealand was limited to two pages, containing only six recipes supplied by the Butter Information Council and by Catherine Macfarlane, a lecturer in foods at the University of Otago Home Science School (1951–61). All but one were sweet items. The Kiwi Crisps were recognisably New Zealand, but Anzac Nutties appeared to be a new name, perhaps because the preceding Australian section already featured Anzac Biscuits. The recipe was for the wheatmeal variant of Anzac Biscuits, without rolled oats, a concept that was common in New Zealand only in the 1940s.

For New Zealanders, the response to an official request in 1961 for three New Zealand recipes to appear in a revised edition of *Favourite Recipes from the United*

1.2 *New Zealand Dishes and Menus* (1960) was written by the Otago University Association of Home Science Alumnae for Price Milburn's series of recipe books featuring international cuisines for New Zealanders. Other books in the series introduced Chinese, American, and French cookery.

Nations, confirms the pavlova's position as an acknowledged national dish. The choice of recipes was left to the president of the University of Otago Home Science Alumnae, Mrs M. Ratley. The earlier edition (1956) had recipes for Oyster Soup, Pavlova, and Queen of Puddings. For the revision, the pudding was replaced by a recipe for Roast Lamb with Mint Sauce. Significantly the pavlova recipe was altered from a six-egg-whites version cooked in a tin to a more up-to-date three eggs type cooked on a tray.[31] The new recipe was identical to that published in 1960 in the Home Science Alumnae's book *New Zealand Dishes and Menus* (Fig 1.2).[32]

Soon after this request, Mrs Ratley and a Miss Manning were asked by the New Zealand Embassy in Paris to prepare an article on New Zealand foods and wine for the magazine *Cuisine et Vins de France*. Under a section entitled 'Dishes Especially Liked' was an entry for the pavlova: 'Pavlova is a meringue cake covered with whipped cream and decorated with either fresh or cooked fruit, and is served as a sweet or as a cake at tea parties. This is regarded as a national sweet.'[33] Did the Australians feel the same way about their pavlova? Judging from their selection of recipes to represent Australia in books like *Home Management*, the answer is yes. Observers in the Northern Hemisphere could probably see what was happening well before New Zealanders and Australians realised that their national dessert had dual citizenship.

As an outsider, Austin Mitchell's description of the New Zealand he encountered while a lecturer in political science at the University of Otago in the mid 1960s probably did more than any other publication to confirm iconic status for the pavlova. In the book's title *The Half-Gallon Quarter-Acre Pavlova Paradise* (1972), he lined the pavlova up with two unquestioned Kiwi icons of the time: the half-gallon jar (to be filled with beer) and the quarter-acre section (the typical size of a suburban landholding). The fact that he mentioned the pavlova in just one sentence of the text can be read as confirmation that the pavlova was a national symbol, a fact that needed no justification. Referring to the Kiwis' need for reassurance, he wrote 'Kiwis bludge praise. Internationally they stand waiting for pats – for their race relations, butter, efforts in Vietnam or Pavlova cakes'.[34] On the dust jacket, the talented Les Gibbard drew a New Zealand 'home-maker' carrying a tray of afternoon tea, with a plate of pikelets, and a pavlova tucked behind the teapot (Fig. 1.3).[35] If a Yorkshireman tells us that the pavlova is a Kiwi icon, who are we to doubt it?

With the death of the Australian 'inventor' of the pavlova cake, Bert Sachse, in 1974, the isolation that kept the two stories apart started to break down. Dunedin's *Otago Daily Times* ran an editorial under the headline 'Sweet and light'

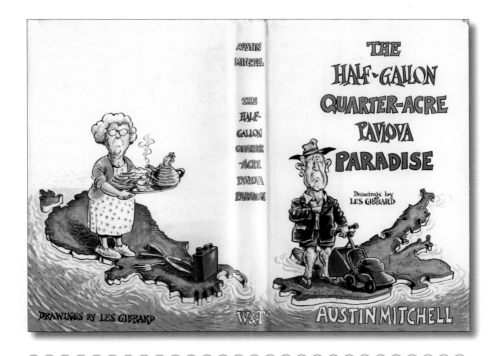

1.3 The dust jacket of Austin Mitchell's *Half-Gallon Quarter-Acre Pavlova Paradise* (1972) was drawn by the young New Zealand-born artist, Les Gibbard, who later became political cartoonist for the *Guardian*. Reproduced with permission from Les Gibbard.

on 6 April 1974. After outlining the story of Anna Pavlova and the cake named after her, the writer observed:

> New Zealanders have in the past claimed the distinction, but an obituary item from Australia gives a Mr Herbert Sachse the honour of producing the first Pavlova cake, in 1935. It is said to be the only indigenous dish in Australia. But the same claim has been made in New Zealand. If there is room for a counter-claim, it might be difficult to settle definitively who invented the Pavlova. Perhaps the matter might have to be settled statistically – the credit going to the country which could claim that its people ate more Pavlovas per head than any other nationalities do. No prizes would be offered to contestants.[36]

The writer included a most revealing and prescient remark, predicting the course of the debate over the next quarter century: 'any controversy that might be generated about the Pavlova cake might develop into an international argument about who did originate the Pavlova.'

While the people of Australia and New Zealand assumed before 1974 that their national dessert was theirs alone, after Bert Sachse's death they had to justify their ownership at an international level. Readers were quick to respond to this editorial, and the 'Talk of the Times' column on 24 April reported that 'many people were convinced it was a New Zealand creation.' Doubt was raised over the accuracy of the Australian claim:

> The wife of a Mosgiel man clearly remembers – because she was pregnant at the time – being invited to the home of a friend who was an excellent cook and being unable to eat the beautiful Pavlova served at supper. The date was July–August 1932.[37]

A longer article appeared in the 'Mainly for Women' page in the *Otago Daily Times*, on 2 May, under the headline 'Australian claim on pavlova unsupported by N.Z. evidence'. The mock shock-horror style was even more apparent than before: the idea that the pavlova was indigenous to Australia was 'truly galling to any New Zealand housewife worthy of the name' and has 'led an army of quiet peaceable homemakers to take up arms and, probably for the first time in their lives, start writing to the paper.'[38] Judging from the choice of metaphor, a war was clearly brewing.

Most of the evidence submitted was anecdotal, such as that of three women who worked together in a local Dunedin cake shop from the end of the 1920s into the early 1930s. They remembered baking, filling, and selling pavlovas. Nevertheless the women's page editor was well aware that 'memory can play funny tricks' and she reported that 'when pushed, they cannot be sure they actually called them 'pavlova cakes'. What was needed was printed evidence, clearly dated. An Oamaru woman using the pseudonym Urumoa (later written as Urumao) sent in a personal memory of eating a mulberry-and-cream-filled pavlova in Napier, in the summer that followed the disastrous 1931 earthquake, but she realised that a printed recipe would be more definite proof. She began searching through the recipe books she had inherited from her mother, coming up with a 1934 recipe for a meringue cake copied from the *Otago Daily Times* of 26 June 1934; a Meringue Sponge or Pavlova Cake recipe in the third edition of *Miss Finlay's Cookery* (Miss Finlay demonstrated for the Dunedin City Gas Department); and pavlova cake recipes in two privately published church recipe books from Invercargill. At the time it was thought that Miss Finlay's book was published in 1933. The church recipe books were even earlier. The writer said that these 'must be pre-1933, as we left the city in that year'. She also asked why it took nine years after Pavlova's triumphant tour of Australasia 'for a cake to be named after her'.[39]

Her question remained unanswered. I'm not sure whether I was aware of the pavlova controversy then. Though I was living in Dunedin in 1974, I was busy as a lecturer in the anthropology department at the University of Otago, trying to finish my doctoral dissertation on ancient Maori gardens before the birth of my daughter Katie at the end of the year. I did read the women's page from time to time, and cut out recipes for my scrapbooks, but Urumao's observations went unnoticed. I had no idea that I would meet her in 1995, and that she would hand on the 'torch' by giving me her mother's old recipe books.

In Nina and Jim Munro's *A Taste of New Zealand in Food and Pictures* (1977), the question of New Zealand's 'national' dishes was confronted for the first time in a book-length work. Jim Munro was Director of the Hawke's Bay Art Gallery and Museum, and Nina was an experienced teacher of homecraft. They had the benefit of seeing New Zealand cuisine through British eyes. In their considered opinion, the pavlova was probably developed in 1926, the year of Pavlova's visit to New Zealand, or soon after, by an unnamed benefactress. They were inclined to accept the claim that the 'pav' is New Zealand's sole contribution to international cuisine.[40] No reference was made to Australia's rival claim.

Through the 1980s expatriates from other English-speaking countries kept newspaper readers aware that pavlovas were internationally contested, often by writing in a letter of protest after a journalist confidently attributed the dish to New Zealand or to Australia. Some new versions of the origin story emerged, such as that it was invented by an infatuated chef in Sydney in 1926 when Pavlova was on tour there, and then spread to New Zealand.[41] One journalist, quoting the chairman of the Sydney-Auckland pavilion at a Toronto food festival, wrote that it was created by a Melbourne chef, during Pavlova's visit 'at the turn of the century'.[42] Canadian food-writers usually noted that both countries claimed the honour of creating the dessert, before moving on to the recipe, which was becoming increasingly popular in Canada.

Michael Symons' close analysis of the origins of the pavlova in *One Continuous*

Picnic (1982) had given the Australians the first scholarly treatment of the available evidence, including an assessment of the New Zealand counter-claims. He began with Bert Sachse's story of the pavlova's origins as told to a reporter in 1973, the year before Bert died. With encouragement from the Hotel Esplanade's licensee, Mrs Elizabeth Paxton, and her manager, Harry Nairn, Bert Sachse had worked for a month on a recipe for a soft-centred meringue cake, discovering that cornflour and vinegar added to the whipped whites gave the marshmallow centre. When he presented the result to them, Mrs Paxton or Harry Nairn described it as being 'as light as Pavlova'.[43] The year was 1935. As Michael Symons showed, economic conditions in Western Australia provided a convincing background to this story.

Yet Symons was aware that the Munros' 1977 book proposed a much earlier origin for the New Zealand pavlova. With help from New Zealand librarians, he found that meringue cakes were commonly made in the early 1930s in New Zealand and some were 'to all intents and purposes what we know as a "Pavlova",' including vinegar and/or cornflour among their ingredients. The one pre-1935 recipe found that was actually called 'Pavlova Cakes' was for small meringues, coincidentally named for their lightness.[44] There was a possible connection between New Zealand meringue cakes and Bert Sachse, in that Bert might have seen a recipe contributed by Rewa of Rongotai to the Australian Woman's Mirror of 2 April 1935. His wife revealed that he read women's magazines. With the concept of the marshmallow-centred cake established in New Zealand before 1935, Michael Symons concluded that Bert Sachse's role was to distil or codify a New Zealand idea, to which someone at the Hotel Esplanade in Perth added the memorable name.

In 1988 the debate became fully international, involving a third country: the Sydney Morning Herald took offence at the publication of a low-calorie pavlova (foolishly attributed to New Zealand) by the Los Angeles Times. The Australian response was clearly designed to reprimand the Californians and annoy New Zealanders: 'We are prepared to graciously acknowledge that the Land of the Long White Shroud has produced some famous sheep, even some very distinguished sheep. But the pav?'[45] Reference was made to the Macquarie Dictionary of Australian English (1981) which repeated what had now become the orthodox creation story for the Australian pavlova: it was invented in Perth in 1935 by Australian chef Herbert Sachse and named by Harry Nairn. Michael Symons had used the words 'distil, codify, crystallize' rather than invent, but it was a while before his book was cited by Australian journalists. They preferred the Macquarie's tone of certainty.

I became involved in the debate in late 1995. Once again the Otago Daily Times picked up some provocative statements in the Sydney Morning Herald of 17 November. An Australian had been horrified to discover a tearoom in Jerusalem selling pavlova as 'originally from New Zealand'. Again the Sydney Morning

Herald cited the *Macquarie Dictionary* that it was an Australian invention, though they wondered if New Zealanders might claim the kiwifruit-topped variety. On Saturday 25 November, Robin Charteris of the *Otago Daily Times* replied that New Zealand claimed all varieties, supplying some details on the history of the debate, including material published in the *Sydney Morning Herald* in 1994 supporting a New Zealand claim.[46] Mention was made of a 1926 Aunt Daisy recipe book containing a three-egg pavlova cake. That caught my eye because as a collector of New Zealand recipe books, I knew that Aunt Daisy's long series of cookbooks didn't start until the mid-1930s, but I didn't have her earliest compilations. Intrigued, I hurried to the Hocken Library, which has a better collection of cookery books than most other New Zealand libraries. First I checked the c. 1926 meringue cake recipe by the Australian writer Emily Futter. Then I requested Aunt Daisy's books. In *The N.Z. 'Daisy Chain' Cookery Book* I found one meringue cake recipe, and two for pavlovas. The first was for a large meringue cake cooked so that it sank in the middle providing a hollow for the cream and fruit. The second was for small meringues, flavoured with coffee essence and speckled with chopped walnuts.[47] Though the book carried no formal date, there was a note from the printing firm that from January 1935 they would be occupying new premises.[48] At last here was real evidence of a pre-1935 pavlova.

To set the record straight I rang Robin Charteris early on Monday 27 November. He had been researching the 1974 controversy and wanted me to check whether 'Urumao' had been correct in dating Miss Finlay's *Cookery* with its recipe for 'Meringue Sponge Sandwich or Pavlova Cake' to 1933. He would hold back his next column on the pavlova until I could get more information. I knew that my friend Elizabeth Hinds, the late Director of the Otago Settlers' Museum, had an early copy of Miss Finlay's book in her office, dated to late 1932 or early 1933 by its advertisements. She checked it and found the words 'or Pavlova Cake' had not yet been added to the meringue cake recipe – but without more editions, we couldn't be sure when the addition was made.

By Wednesday 29 November, several elderly ladies had rung the newspaper with memories of early pavlovas but nothing definitive. However, the Oamaru correspondent 'Urumao', who in 1974 had provided the best evidence and a research plan, was keen to get involved again. She was now eighty-six and living in a retirement home, but had kept a file of clippings related to pavlovas, as well as her mother's earliest cookbooks. Robin Charteris asked me if he could pass on my address to her. I willingly agreed. Just over a week later, I received a letter (Fig. 1.4) from Miss Noeline Thomson ('Urumao'). After introducing herself she said that she had 'been very interested in the origin of the Pavlova since reading some years ago, in an Australian magazine, claims that an Australian chef Henry [sic] Sachse had invented it in 1935, when I knew perfectly well that my mother had made them when I was at Otago University (1928–32) and that I'd eaten a slice of Pavlova, peaked at the corners with the centre filled with mulberries and cream at a 21st birthday party at Napier in Jan. 1932.'[49]

Like most of us at the time, Noeline believed that the pavlova derived its distinctive soft-centre from the addition of vinegar and cornflour:

> What we really need to know or rather, authenticate, is the date of the inclusion of the teaspoon of vinegar and also of cornflour in the three-egg recipe that gives the N. Z. Pavlova its characteristic firm exterior and soft, marshmallow centre that I saw my mother make in Invercargill about 1931–2, when I was home on holiday from university. She had got the recipe from her sister who got it from a member of her croquet club. Where did the latter get it? That is the mystery that needs solving.[50]

I could tell that Noeline found researching into the pavlova was even more engrossing than reading a detective novel. Unfortunately her health was not the best – she had a painful hip and used a walking frame, and the slanting handwriting on her letters confirmed her failing vision. Would I like to add her mother's cookbooks to my collection to carry on the investigation, she asked, setting out a list of their titles. It included one of the undated church fund-raising books, the *Girls' Auxiliary Recipe Book*, mentioned in 1974. She later told me that her sister Eileen had belonged to the group responsible for compiling the book before the family left Invercargill in March 1933. I replied that nothing would please me more than to continue the research. We arranged that I would visit her in Oamaru just before Christmas. In the meantime I found from her letters that she had taken an MA in English and French at Otago, followed by a postgraduate Diploma in Education.[51] This enabled her to become a secondary teacher. She remembered teaching Janet Frame at Waitaki Girls' High School.

1.4 This excerpt from Miss Noeline Thomson's first letter to the author set out her unwavering belief that she had eaten a slice of pavlova in Napier in January 1932 (letter dated 6 November 1995).

My sister Mary Browne, a food-writer, and I made the trip to Oamaru together on Sunday 24 December. Noeline had a list of items she wanted to discuss with me, but these were almost forgotten as we shared details of our backgrounds. From an earlier letter we knew that she had grown up in New Plymouth. So had our late mother, Peggy Watkins. 'I was at school with her, and visited their house,' said Noeline. 'Your mother had a mass of curls, and there was a parrot too.' Mary and I felt very moved. Noeline had known our mother before we did. We gave Noeline a watercolour calendar for 1996 by our sister, Nancy Tichborne, and came away with a dozen mostly coverless cookbooks.

Two days later, after spending Christmas night absorbed in the computer manual, I set up a database to record the details of my collection. Noeline was just as busy: 'When asking around locally, I have been surprised to discover that some use cornflour, some vinegar and still get the marshmallow centre. I thought both were needed.'[52] Some commentators on the pavlova still believe that cornflour is the necessary ingredient. Perhaps they too should ask around a community of pavlova makers whether this is true in practice.

Noeline and I continued our correspondence until December 1998. Throughout that period she wrote stories to send to Jim Sullivan's oral history radio programme 'Sounds Historical', as well as poetry. She continued to ask her friends about old recipe books. Two comments in her later letters summed up her motives in the pavlova quest. In February 1996 she wrote, 'I've still got my hopes on a 1931–2 printed recipe even if just to prove I've got a good memory!'[53] A year later she said, 'I'm still asking round about old recipe books as I want to validate my claim re my mother's Invercargill pavlovas pre 1932. Some day I'm sure it will turn up.'[54] We found the 1929 pavlova cake recipe in 2005, but could not share it with Noeline. She had died in 2001, aged ninety-two.[55] It was not a sense of wounded national pride that spurred Noeline's efforts to find the origins of the New Zealand pavlova, but faith in her own memory. It was as powerful a force for Noeline Thomson as it was for Elizabeth Paxton's descendants.

Pavlovas and the Oxford connection

When I became actively involved in the pavlova debate in 1995, I was finalising my plans to spend part of my 1996 research and study leave in Cambridge, United Kingdom. From 1980 to 1981, I had spent two years as a Rhodes Visiting Fellow at St Hilda's College, Oxford, and had given a paper on traditional Polynesian cookery methods at the 1981 Oxford Food Symposium.[56] This international symposium on food history is held annually and in the intervening period grew in numbers attending and in prestige. I decided that it would be a valuable experience to attend in 1996 when the theme was to be 'Food on the Move'. What was intriguing me in my research on the pavlova was the chain of transmission of the recipe and concept within New Zealand, and between New Zealand and Australia. Pavlova recipes had travelled fast, and apparently across the Tasman, though there was clearly some disagreement about the direction. By January 1996 I had enough data on the pavlova to write a short paper.

On 3 January 1996 I confirmed that the earliest pavlova recipe cited in the *Oxford English Dictionary* was actually for a layered jelly.[57] The recipe was accompanied by a signed illustration but a search of the New Zealand Post Office directories of the time could not provide a match for the signature. I suspected that the recipe and illustration may have originated outside New Zealand. I had also located the source of the second pavlova recipe to be mentioned in the *Oxford English Dictionary*, a cookbook produced by Katrine McKay in 1929.[58] There was a copy at the Otago Settlers' Museum. To my surprise these pavlovas were small meringues containing coffee essence and walnuts. Their contributor was a Dunedin woman. It was ironic to think of all the people who had used the dictionary entries as evidence of the New Zealand origin of the pavlova cake, without realising that these first two 'pavlovas' were quite different to our modern version.

It proved much more difficult to pin down the first appearance of the meringue cake that took the name 'pavlova'. There were a few dated recipes for meringue cakes, starting with Emily Futter's Meringue with Fruit Filling about 1926.[59] The pavlova cake recipes that I found in 1995 and early 1996 were from cookbooks that were officially undated – that is to say the printers hadn't inserted a date of publication – but this did not mean that they were undatable. The books were full of advertisements containing phone numbers and addresses. Since businesses open and close, and rise and fall, changes in premises are common. These can be picked up and dated by reference to post office and trade directories. The same method can be applied to the recipe books that have lost their front and back pages where the critical information about editions and dates is normally found.

I had already dated the pavlova recipes in the second of Aunt Daisy's compiled cookbooks, *The N.Z. 'Daisy Chain' Cookery Book*, through the printer's advance notice of a change of premises in January 1935.[60] This was sufficient evidence of the existence of a pre-1935 pavlova cake for me to include it my Oxford Symposium paper. The date was, however, of much less importance in my overall scheme than the concept of recipe evolution. Working through the early editions of Miss Finlay's *Cookery* (published by the Dunedin City Gas Department), I found progressive alteration of the recipe for 'Meringue Sponge Sandwich', including addition of the words 'or Pavlova Cake' to the recipe title in the third edition.[61] Using the advertisements, I concluded that this edition appeared between 1934 and 1936 (Fig. 1.5). The series provided nice documentation of the evolution of the meringue cake into the pavlova cake. In my paper I pretended to go along with the 'heated nationalistic debate' over the 'invention' of the pavlova cake, declaring that with a pre-1935 recipe, New Zealand had won, and that perhaps Bert Sachse had 'borrowed' a New Zealand recipe. I even thought up a mock headline containing 'all the ingredients ... to stir up national outrage yet again, with the added spice of gender exploitation, and of rivalry between professionals and amateurs. The imaginary headline "AUSSIE CHEF STEALS KIWI WOMEN'S CREATION" expresses the divisive and polarizing potential of my findings'.[62]

Having stirred the pot, I then turned off the heat. Recipes, I said, are not created, but evolve. The name 'pavlova' was so popular that it had been applied to three quite different dishes. It could easily have been applied independently to meringue cakes being made in Australia and New Zealand. I blamed national rivalry for promoting the idea of a single 'creation'. In fact many cooks contributed to the evolution of the various pavlovas. I considered the question of their nationality to be much less relevant than the multi-step process that brought us our modern pavlova cake. This is not to say that invention has played no part in culinary history. Variants of well-established dishes can follow active experimentation, and they are often given new names, especially where the experimenter is a professional chef with a reputation to build. In such circumstances the concept of the heroic inventor dominates, at the expense of the evolutionary scenario.

The Oxford Symposium took place on 6–8 September 1996. I delivered my short paper on the pavlova at one of the Saturday afternoon sessions. Over a tea break,

No. 452.—MERINGUE SPONGE SANDWICH OR PAVLOVA CAKE.

Ingredients :—

Whites of 3 eggs
7 or 8 ozs. Sugar
Pinch of Salt

1 Teaspoon vanilla essence
1 Teaspoon vinegar
Suitable tins, 8in. diam. Sandwich tins or special Pavlova cake tin

Method.—Add salt to egg whites. Whisk them stiffly; add sugar gradually and continue beating for a few minutes. Carefully mix in vinegar and essence. Place in greased tins and cook in a slow oven for 1 to 1½ hours.

When cooked, turn out carefully. Fasten cakes together with a filling of whipped cream. Some tart fruit, such as raspberries or loganberries, may be added to cream. Cream may also be piled on top, finishing off with fruit used in centre.

1.5   Isabella Finlay added the word 'Pavlova' to the title of her recipe for Meringue Sponge Sandwich when she prepared the third edition of *Cookery* for the Dunedin City Gas Department (Recipe No. 452, p. 125). Although there was no date of publication, advertisements indicated that it was issued between 1934 and 1936.

the editor of the forthcoming *Oxford Companion to Food*, Alan Davidson, and his assistant, Helen Saberi, came up to congratulate me on the paper and to say that they would use it as the basis of their entry on the pavlova. This duly appeared in print in 1999,[63] and provided a more user-friendly source of information than the misleading entry in the *Oxford English Dictionary*.

Soon after my return from study leave, I had the chance to present my paper again, this time to the New Zealand Guild of Food Writers' annual conference being held at the University of Otago. Canterbury food-writer Mavis Airey was present and her report on my findings appeared in *The Press*, under the headline 'The Great Pavlova Controversy'. The article began: 'For more than half a century, Australia and New Zealand have been at war over a bit of froth and bubble...'.[64] This was a slight exaggeration – as I have shown, there was little awareness of a disputed claim to the pavlova cake until after Bert Sachse's death in 1974, and at this stage there was no sign of the strong language that emerged in the late 1990s.

Little over a week after *The Press* report, the *Otago Daily Times* ran a half-page article that I wrote exclusively for them, with the latest results of my research.[65] The headline was 'Evolution of the Pavlova'. I described how four editions of Miss Finlay's *Cookery* (1934–50) had been used to show the transition of the name from meringue cake to pavlova cake, the changing proportions of sugar, the introduction of cornflour, the shift from a multi-layer to single layer cake, and from cooking the meringue in a cake tin to baking it on a paper-covered tray. Then I introduced some new evidence: a recipe for a single layer pavlova in the *Rangiora Mothers' Union Cookery Book*.[66] My book collector friend Frank Leckie had bought this rather drab, Depression-era recipe book for me in one of the many fairs he attended. As I entered its details in my database, I spotted the pavlova cake recipe, and the printed date 1933. In my article I once again rejected the simplistic view that Bert Sachse had borrowed the recipe from New Zealand, even though we were finding evidence for more and more pre-1935 pavlovas.

A copy of my article was sent to Harry Orsman, who was finalising the *Dictionary of New Zealand English*. He wrote to me on 18 January 1996:

> It's curious how the word [pavlova] seems to generate more mistaken and often heated comment on both sides of the Tasman than any other Australasian shared word except perhaps for POMMIE. At least that is my experience over the last 45 years. I've found (as you may already have) that public statements about 'pavlova', no matter how well researched, generate letters and phone calls insisting that the word was used by grandmother in WWI, or the confection was invented by an aunt in such and such a place at such and such a date. People most often confuse the history of the name with the history of the confection, and the Australians don't realize that the earliest Australian use found by the prime authority, the *Australian National Dictionary*, after thorough searching was 1940. The AND

acknowledges the earlier NZ datings. *The Macquarie Dictionary*, otherwise an excellent dictionary, has for many years now been red-faced over its derivation. I'd thought the Sachse thing had been laid to rest a long time ago. But urban myths hang around so on their eternal gallows.'[67]

With his letter, Harry Orsman included his draft pavlova entry for me to read. I replied that the date for his example from Miss Finlay's *Cookery* should be changed from c. 1933 to sometime between 1934 and 1936. I also supplied two early examples he hadn't used, the Aunt Daisy one of late 1934 and the new 1933 find from Rangiora. The Rangiora example was especially important as at that time it was the earliest pavlova recipe of the modern type, and I enclosed a photocopy of all the details. Where Harry Orsman and I differed was in our attitude to the Sachse story. As a lexicographer, Harry dealt with dated and printed examples of word usage. To him the Sachse claim to have invented the pavlova was not backed up by printed evidence. To me, as an anthropologist, oral tradition is just as deserving of study and explanation as printed 'evidence'. I was trained to ask the question: what does Bert Sachse's memory of an event in Perth about 1935 tell us about the context in which the renaming occurred there, and how does it compare to the application of the name to various dishes in New Zealand?

Despite ten years of research, writing, and lecturing about the pavlova debate, I have found it very hard to shift the public assumption that the pavlova cake was created just once, on a certain date and in a certain place, and that these details are worth arguing about for the sake of national pride. I don't believe that the simplistic version of the story prevails because the journalists who promote it and the public who read it aren't open to the concept of independent evolution. On the contrary, to those who are not involved personally, the periodic skirmishes provide an excellent opportunity for redressing the imbalances created by sports encounters, and generating a comfortable feeling of national identity. They do not want the question 'who invented the pavlova?' to be answered once and for all, and certainly don't want to be told that the question is invalid.

I discovered early in my involvement that this question is asked because it divides people, elevates individuals beyond their actual contribution, and is in fact unanswerable – since we can never be sure that the very first recipe has been found. As the public engage in their mock pavlova wars, the casualties are ignored, especially those whose memories are treated as unreliable, or whose ancestors are accused of plagiarism. This book is dedicated to those who have been doubted, and to those who are genuinely interested in the complicated history of all the different sorts of pavlovas.

Why pavlova?

THERE IS a significant difference between a dish named after its originator, such as Aunt Maude's Meat Paste, and one named in honour of a famous person, such as Pêches (Peach) Melba, which was devised by the equally famous chef Escoffier in 1893 when Nellie Melba was beginning to shine as an opera star.[1] While there is usually only one Aunt Maude's Meat Paste, handed down to family and friends by the original Maude, it is quite common for a celebrity to be honoured in more than one dish. Poires (Pear) Melba is another of Escoffier's tributes to the opera singer.[2] If a performer is so outstanding that several separate dishes are named after her by one chef, isn't it possible that other people will also name dishes in her honour?

No-one has ever suggested that Anna Pavlova devised any of the dishes that were named after her. The various pavlovas were all the product of cooks who wanted to celebrate her stardom, both during her lifetime and after her premature death in 1931. In New Zealand we know that there were at least three dishes named pavlova in the second half of the 1920s, all three circulating in recipe books and/or newspaper columns. Though two are based on meringue, they differ in concept and origin; and since there are three that we know about, there may even be more awaiting discovery. This is a good reason why the question 'who invented the pavlova?' is simplistic and misleading. However, for the question 'who invented the earliest pavlova?' I will provide an answer, but it will surprise and perhaps even disappoint some readers, for the first dish named pavlova is not the familiar meringue that started the 'pavlova wars'.

What then are the right questions? I have already answered the important one, 'how many dishes that we know of were named after Anna Pavlova?' and will describe each of the three types in the following chapters, along with the details of their first known appearance and the subsequent spread of these recipes. I will also answer the question 'did these dishes formerly exist under other names?' In this chapter I want to address two questions: 'how common was it to name dishes after famous people?' and 'what qualities of Anna Pavlova as a person and performer were being recognised?'

How common was it to name dishes after famous people?

Turn to the index of Auguste Escoffier's massive *Guide to Modern Cookery*, and you will find the names of many European notables, from members of royal families (e.g. Edward VII and the Czarina), to statesmen (e.g. Talleyrand and Metternich), *demi-mondaines* (society women of dubious reputation), and stage performers (e.g. Sarah Bernhardt the actress, and Adelina Patti the opera singer).[3] Some of them would have been patrons of the various hotels at which Escoffier worked with hotelier César Ritz, such as the Savoy Hotel and later the Carlton Hotel in London.[4] Significantly, Ritz is credited with making it acceptable for women to dine in public.[5] The sight of the names on the menus would have encouraged patronage both by those already so honoured, and by those who had hopes of being immortalised in a dessert or soup. Names of famous opera characters such as Tosca, Aïda, and Carmen were also included. In his choice of names, Escoffier may have been celebrating the London seasons of these operas, since it was customary to go to the Savoy or Ritz for a late supper after the opera; this would also explain his use of the names of composers like Rossini and Gounod.

Encouraging patronage, however, was not Escoffier's only motivation. In his index there are also many names of historical figures, like Joan of Arc, Madame Pompadour, and Nero. A possible explanation for the profusion of names lies in the way restaurant and hotel menus were written. The ice-cream dessert known as a *bombe* provides an example. Escoffier provided eighty-seven recipes for these elaborate and highly fashionable dishes, made originally in spherical dome-shaped moulds.[6] In order to list on the menu the particular variation to be served that evening, Escoffier had to find a distinctive name, anywhere between *Bombe Américaine* and *Bombe Vésuve*. His naming system was oriented to specific rather than generic dishes, and it required him continually to come up with new names.

For the mistress of the household who required a menu for a dinner party, or the lady who had been invited to dine in a high-class hotel, remembering the characteristics associated with the burgeoning number of specific French names became a challenge. To aid them, Nancy Lake wrote a book entitled *Menus Made Easy: or how to order dinner and give the dishes their French names*. By 1915 it was into its twenty-fifth edition. This is what she had to say about celebrity naming:

> Neither are such dishes enumerated as owe their name to a passing interest, such as the visit of some foreign royalty, a prominent statesman or general, or some

social event or ceremonial. These dishes have no culinary importance. They often hardly differ from those already well known. Such interest as they have would be purely historical, and even were the event worth recording, the study of history is not profitably pursued in the kitchen![7]

Escoffier would have been incensed, and were I to adopt her view, there would be no need to write this book. However, her words give a strong indication that the practice of recording important people and events in recipe naming was widespread in high society at the start of the twentieth century.

Escoffier's *Guide Culinaire* 'became the bible of chefs trained in the classical French tradition',[8] and this was the tradition that underpinned the haute cuisine of restaurants and hotels of many countries in the first half of the twentieth century. Not only were the professional chefs quite used to attaching famous names to their dishes, but the public who dined at their establishments became familiar with some of the variations. Most were very elaborate dishes. Take Peach Melba, for instance. When originally served at the Savoy, it consisted of poached peaches on a bed of ice cream resting in a swan carved from ice, in recognition of the swan in Wagner's opera *Lohengrin*, which Nellie Melba was currently singing at Covent Garden.[9] Later Escoffier thought up the raspberry topping:

> It is made by lining a silver dish with a fairly thick layer of the best vanilla ice cream, and placing on top peeled peaches which have been steeped in a syrup flavoured with vanilla, and left until they are quite cold. The peaches are then covered with *Raspberry purée*.[10]

Peach Melba is one of the few examples of celebrity-named haute cuisine that trickled down into middle-class domestic kitchens. In the process the dish was reinterpreted. An example is the recipe for Peach Melba contributed by 'Summer Breeze' in 1934 to 'Aunt Daisy' (the name by which Mrs Daisy Basham was known to her radio listeners). A serving consisted of a square of sponge cake, topped with a half cooked peach, with its cavity filled with strawberries or raspberries, the whole covered with custard, decorated with a strawberry or cherry and served with cream.[11]

The history of chefs combining famous names with their trademark dishes can be traced back to the seventeenth century, when French chef François Pierre de la Varenne was one of the first to do so. He is credited with developing the recipe for *duxelles* of mushrooms, named after his employer, the Marquis d'Uxelles.[12] By the eighteenth century, French aristocrats who hosted the king increasingly had their name attached to particular dishes. Rather than celebrating the nobility, names like *soubise* (applied to a classic onion purée) are more like Aunt Maude's meat paste, in that they reflect the origin of the dish, in this case in the kitchen of the Prince de Soubise.[13] In contrast, the writers of English cookery books of the eighteenth century seldom attached people's names to their recipes. Search the

2.1 The elegant spine of *Soyer's Standard Cookery* (1912) suggests that its readers would have been impressed by a recipe named after the Rothschilds.

contents pages of Hannah Glasse's *The Art of Cookery Made Plain and Easy* (first published in 1747) and you will find just one dish that is associated with a person's name: 'To jar Cherries Lady North's Way'. This is clearly a reference to the way cherries were bottled in Lady North's kitchen.[14] Hannah Glasse honoured her subscribers by printing a list of their names at the start of the book, not by naming recipes after them. More often Hannah marked variations by reference to the region of origin, such as 'To boil a Rump of Beef the French Fashion', 'Portugal Beef', 'To dress Mutton the Turkish Way', or 'A Cheshire Pork-Pye'. In the nineteenth century, food-writers addressing the needs of middle-class households seldom indulged in naming their recipes after famous people. Mrs Beeton includes a small number of recipes attributed to professionals such as Brillat-Savarin and Soyer, along with Prince of Wales Soup, and puddings named Baroness, Royal Coburg, and Empress, but these are offset by Aunt Martha's, Aunt Nelly's and Vicarage puddings.[15]

Were the books written by Escoffier's contemporaries as prone to the practice of celebrity recipe naming? *Soyer's Standard Cookery* (1912) written by Nicolas Soyer, a former chef and grandson of the great chef Alexis Soyer, is a little more restrained than Escoffier (Fig 2.1). However, his consommés and egg dishes have a sprinkling of proper names, such as Rothschild and Demidoff.[16] It seems that two trends in the later nineteenth and early twentieth centuries contributed to the appearance of dishes named in honour of celebrities and important occasions: the rise of high-class public dining establishments, and the social imperative to adopt the French system of classifying dishes and writing menus. As this penetrated private homes, along with the recipe books written by the chefs, possibilities opened up for innovative home cooks to think up their own recipe names. Even if they lacked the facilities and time to make the elaborate named dishes that characterised haute cuisine, there was nothing to stop them naming some dishes in their own repertoire after famous people or events.

Since my prime purpose is to track the history of a New Zealand dish, it is necessary to survey a sample of local recipe books from the early twentieth century to check whether what was true of recipe naming in England was also the case in this country. I looked at the *South Auckland Queen Cookery Book* first published during the World War 1; it contained recipes for Gallipoli Steak, Melba Peaches, Mafeking Cake, and Anzac Toffee.[17] At the other end of the country, the *Southland Red Cross Cookery Book* published about 1917 or 1918 included Anzac Pudding, Allies Bread, Red Cross Cakes and Buns, Ladysmith Cake, and Belgian Biscuits (formerly named German Biscuits).[18] In Palmerston North, the *Town and Country Patriotic Women Workers' Cookery Book* (1917) contained a boiled meat pudding called War Gelatine, a Soldier Cake, and the widely known Khaki Cake (Fig. 2.2).[19] Where new names have been coined, in all three books they are predominantly war-related, and refer not just to the current war but also to the earlier Boer War (1899–1902).

If you were to ask, in the light of this history, 'who was more likely to name a dish after Pavlova?' I would have to reply a chef-cum-food-writer, rather than a housewife-cook. There is an unconfirmed story that a Wellington chef named a new type of meringue cake 'pavlova' at the time of Pavlova's visit in 1926. While working on his New Zealand dictionary, Harry Orsman was told this story by a woman who had been in the Wellington Ballet Company in 1926. Having heard that Pavlova liked meringues, they consulted a chef who came up with three versions. Eventually a soft-centred variety was selected, named pavlova, and presented to the ballerina. Because there is nothing to link this story with any of the printed pavlova recipes of 1927, 1928 or 1929, it is not recorded in the dictionary; yet it is quite plausible. Similar stories have been recorded for

2.2 The *Town and Country Patriotic Women Workers' Cookery Book* (1917) is typical of many New Zealand fundraising recipe books from World War 1, containing contributed recipes and numerous advertisements.

Melbourne and Sydney (see Chapter One). There were receptions for Pavlova wherever she travelled in New Zealand, and in view of the social importance of these occasions great efforts would have been put into the catering. Take, for example, this account of her Wellington visit that appeared in a Dunedin newspaper on 22 June 1926:

> A well-arranged reception was given at the Midland Hotel, inspired by the J.C. Williamson firm, with Mr Bert Royle directing, as a welcome to Madame Pavlova, and attended by many leading citizens of Wellington. The Mayoress, Mrs C.J. Norwood, was hostess, and later the Mayor made a speech of welcome, which was replied to by Madame Pavlova herself. Tea was much enjoyed, the tables being set with beautiful narcissi and autumn leaves ....
>
> Another very pleasant reception was that given by Mrs J. O'Shea for Miss Thurza Rogers who is her guest. The party was given on Tuesday afternoon at the Jacobean Room at Kirkcaldie's, the tables being decorated with Iceland poppies and large sprays of maidenhair fern. Madame Pavlova was present and she and Miss Rogers had charming posies of flowers presented to them.[20]

Thurza Rogers was a young New Zealand dancer touring with Pavlova (Fig. 2.3). If only the degree of detail given to the reporting of the flowers at her reception had been extended to the food!

On the evidence we have at present, the first dish to be published as a pavlova was the product of the Davis Gelatine Company in 1926, and was named by someone associated with the company, perhaps a director or employee. So, for now, the naming of the pavlova by a New Zealand chef, following in the footsteps of Escoffier, must remain an unverified family memory.

2.3 Dame Anna Pavlova and Miss Thurza Rogers on their arrival in New Zealand, from the *Otago Witness*, 8 June 1926, p. 48.

Hocken Collections, Dunedin, reproduced with permission from Allied Press.

MADAME PAVLOVA ARRIVES AT AUCKLAND.
M. Lucien Wumser, Miss Thurza Rodgers (New Zealand), Madame Anna Pavlova, and Mr Bert Royle.

How did dishes named after Anna Pavlova symbolise her special qualities?

Three distinct types of pavlova – a four-layered jelly set in a mould, small meringues with walnuts and coffee essence folded in, and the meringue cake that we now consider to be the 'true' pavlova – will be described in later chapters. First, however, we consider what these dishes have in common, other than their name, and whether they reflect a specific quality of the famous ballerina or whether they are just a celebration of the admiration in which she was held.

There is no doubt that Pavlova was the most publicly acclaimed ballerina in the world during the first three decades of the twentieth century. As often happened with film stars who achieved similar international fame, her background was romanticised to almost fairytale proportions. This is how she was introduced to the readers of the *Otago Witness* in the weeks leading up to her Dunedin visit:

> There once lived in St. Petersburg a simple Russian peasant girl. Sometimes her clothes were old and worn, but even the rags she wore could not disguise the slim beauty of her figure, nor detract from the peculiar grace of her movements. She lived with her mother in a tiny flat, and they were very poor, as her father had died when she was only two, and there was not much sympathy for widows in Russia in the days of the Czars. Nevertheless, on feast days, her mother always managed, no matter at what sacrifice to herself, to give her child a little pleasure. When she was eight years old she was taken to see a performance of 'The Sleeping Beauty' at the Marinsky Theatre. As they were coming out the child said: 'One day I shall be the princess and dance on the stage of this theatre.' At the time her mother laughed at the idea, but she lived to see her daughter gain her ambition .... Anna did not rest till she had induced her mother to allow her to join the Imperial Ballet School. The merciless discipline there had no terrors for her, as her one fixed idea was to be a ballerina, and she was willing to endure anything in order to become one.[21]

Much of this information was supplied by Pavlova's own account of her origins, though with selective omissions that made her career seem even more remarkable. Pavlova recalled that, at Easter, her mother would provide 'some pretty toys enclosed in a gigantic egg,' and at Christmas 'we always had our Christmas tree, a little fir adorned with golden fruit shimmering with the reflected light of many little candles'.[22] Anna and her mother spent their summers at a cottage in the countryside, a fact that seems inconsistent with the life of a peasant child forced to wear rags. The phrase 'merciless discipline' was indeed in Pavlova's own account, but she also recorded that at the School of the Imperial Ballet, they were roused at eight, went to prayers, had breakfast at nine, and then began dancing lessons. Lunch was served at noon, followed by a walk and then more lessons until dinner was served at four. After a period of leisure there might be rehearsals in the early evening or a performance. Supper was at eight, and at nine they were sent to bed.[23] It was a well-ordered but hardly merciless existence.

The publicity that surrounded Pavlova suggests that a very effective management team underpinned her tours. This is where the term 'merciless' might be applied more aptly. In one tour to the United States in 1925, her company appeared in seventy-seven towns during twenty-six weeks, and gave 238 performances.[24] In five days in Dunedin in 1926 she danced in five evening performances. Such exposure filled the theatres and enhanced her reputation. Her death just short of her fiftieth birthday shocked her fans, but keen observers suspected that by 1929 her touring schedule was wearing her out. To the public, her reputation was such that even when she dropped her most demanding roles, audiences continued to idolise her in a way described as 'uncritical and monotonously enthusiastic'.[25] Under the circumstances it is not surprising that food items were named after her – but were they simply honorific namings, or did the dishes have a particular similarity?

If the dishes celebrated Pavlova the person, then we might expect to find somewhere in the many countries in which she toured, a Sauce à la Pavlova, or Oysters Pavlova, or Consommé à la Pavlova, in the fashion of Escoffier. However, the only pavlova dishes that I have encountered are the desserts and cakes recognised in Australia and New Zealand. Perhaps there was something specific that provides the link between the dancer and these dishes. The pavlova jelly is brightly coloured and when inverted on its serving plate is a fluted, shimmering shape. The top layer is spring green, the second layer milk-white, the third layer bright orange with inset slices of orange, and the base layer is red jelly. What possible connection could this moulded jelly have to Pavlova? In contrast the small meringues are pale fawn while the cake is white, both the meringue and the cream topping. Here the connection is not hard to make. A widely held belief is that the cake celebrates Pavlova's exceptional lightness as a ballerina. This quality was certainly emphasised in newspaper accounts of her performances:

> Madame Pavlova regards her achievements as part of a harmonious scheme, in which music and scenery are allied with the dance. But who can think of anything else but the dance as he watches this peerless artist, ethereal as a fairy, flashing as a diamond, light as thistledown?[26]

> She appeared in His Majesty's theatre before an audience which sat spellbound, entranced, as she showed through the medium of the dance how beautiful is the beauty of posture and line, of colour and motion, and of expression and music. She was a snowflake scintillating in a world of moonlight, so swift and light and sparkling that the eye was dazzled at the sight.[27]

It is also possible that the pavlova cake imitates Pavlova's appearance in one of her famous roles. Two stand out: *Snowflakes* and *The Swan (Le Cygne)*. The first was a one-act ballet, first performed in 1915, derived from the snowflake scene in the first act of Tchaikovsky's *Nutcracker Suite*. Pavlova's costume was a very stiff horizontally oriented white tutu, representing fallen snow. She performed

this ballet in several centres on her Australasian tour in 1926, including Sydney, Auckland, and Dunedin.[28] *The Swan* was an older role (usually referred to as a divertissement), first danced in 1907. For this Pavlova wore the traditional white costume, designed by Léon Bakst, associated with the ballet *Swan Lake*. It consisted of layers of white tulle underlying a feathered bodice and surmounted with swan's wings.[29] A reviewer ('Phillida') described it as 'tufted plumy white ... [while] down nestled in her hair; but the drooping, curving, palpitating wings were drawn from her marvellous arms'.[30] Hundreds of photographs were taken of Pavlova in this costume, and one was used on the front of the programmes printed for the New Zealand performances (Fig. 2.4). It became the prime souvenir of her tour, a memory reinforced every time the programme was brought out. Only five years later, as she lay dying from pleurisy on the evening of 22 January 1931, she is said to have whispered these last words to her personal maid: 'Marguerite ... prepare my Swan costume'.[31] The public well understood the significance of this remark because the famous dance portrayed a dying swan.

In one biography, we read that she

> won the adulation of the world through her romantic and emotional interpretations of short and well-known pieces. It seemed that the more familiar audiences became with such works as *Le Cygne* and *Papillon* the more exciting they found them ...[32]

Le Cygne was the most famous of all Pavlova's dances, though one commentator thought it 'was in essence nothing more than a pretty sentimental trifle, accompanied by hackneyed, sugary music' – from Saint-Saëns' *Carnival of the Animals*.[33] Such criticism occurred nowhere in the New Zealand reviews of her performances, which were uniformly ecstatic.

I propose that the meringue pavlovas not only exemplify Pavlova's exceptional lightness on her toes, but actually imitate one of her costumes, either that portraying the snowflake or the dying swan. This, however, leaves the colourful jelly pavlova unexplained. It shimmers but is not light, and it lacks any sense of ethereality. If only colour photography had been available to record her costumes. With few exceptions we have to rely on verbal descriptions and monochrome images. From these we know that some of her dresses were both layered and very bright, especially those that were associated with her roles as a Russian peasant girl and as Amarilla, the gipsy girl, both of which she danced in Australia and New Zealand. A coloured postcard (Fig. 2.5) in an Australian collection featuring 'Anna Pavlova. The Dancing Revelation of the Age' provides a possible model for the jelly pavlova; however, its date of 1912 precedes the Australasian tour.[34] If the meringue cake celebrates a famous tutu and the performer who wore it, then it is possible that Davis Gelatine Pavlova was based on the postcard or another of Pavlova's memorable costumes.

ANNA PAVLOVA
THE DANCING REVELATION OF THE AGE
Photo by Ellis & Walery D. A. & S. Ltd.

2.5 This postcard (1912) from the Geoffrey Ingram Archive of Australian Ballet depicted the young Pavlova in a multicoloured, layered costume.

Reproduced with permission from the National Library of Australia, nla.pic-vn3409827, PIC P348/AP/35 LOC Album 810/4.

3

The first pavlova

WHEN I tell people that the first known printed recipe with the name 'pavlova' was a showy, four-layered moulded jelly requiring time-consuming preparation, they show little interest in the circumstances of its origin, and quickly ask 'but what about the real pavlova?' If I reveal to New Zealanders that this tremulous multicoloured jelly was probably developed and named in Australia in 1926, they appear unperturbed that the Australians had it first. Even those Australians who are keen participants in the 'pavlova wars' don't seem to regard this as a victory worth celebrating. To be honest, if this jelly pavlova hadn't been the earliest yet documented, I would have been tempted to relegate it to a footnote, for it is the pavlova that nobody wants to own. My goal, though, is to tell the story of all three types of pavlova in New Zealand's culinary history, and as I researched this unloved first-comer, I discovered its history was as fascinating as that of the other two pavlovas.

What's wrong with the gelatine pavlova?

My question is designed to explore our prejudices and establish why this particular pavlova is unappreciated. Is it the particular recipe that is unappealing, or is it something to do with jellies or gelatine desserts? I should examine my own attitudes first. Back in the 1950s, I often made desserts for our family of six. In summer I enjoyed preparing Lemon Snow, a gelatine dish into which you whip the beaten egg whites just as it is about to set. Without a refrigerator, I would place the enamel basin to cool in the pantry's meat safe, built so that air from the shaded south wall of the house blew through its zinc mesh-covered vents. Judging the moment to start beating in the whites took some experience. On other occasions I rose to the challenge of lining a jelly mould with fruit such as banana slices, cooked apples, pears or peaches, and then pouring in the jelly without disturbing the pattern. Unmoulding it was even more risky, for the hot water the mould was dipped in might dissolve too much of the jelly and dislodge the fruit.

These puddings combined plain granulated gelatine with fruit juices or, for blancmanges, with milk. The gelatine desserts known as 'creams' were often enriched with eggs and sometimes up to two cups of whipping cream. All were sweetened with sugar. Flavouring ingredients ranged from vanilla or lemon essence, to coffee or chocolate. Looking back, there was nothing in the dessert section of the Davis Gelatine Company's recipe books that I would consider unappetising today, except the food colouring. But in the 1950s, I avoided recipes that specified cochineal, carmine, saffron yellow or sap green not because I was suspicious of food colours – we simply didn't have any in the pantry.[1] As a result I never made the Davis pavlova.

Occasionally I made up fruit jellies marketed by other food manufacturers. Our family bought the Lushus brand – the tastes of the strawberry, raspberry and lime variants linger in my memory, but they also offered orange, lemon, wild cherry and pineapple (Fig. 3.1). There was a hollow sugar cone referred to as the 'flavour bud' in the centre of the triangular packet, surrounded by the other ingredients, all ready mixed.[2] They were so quick to make – you just poured on boiling water – but this left an aspiring cook with little sense of achievement. These pre-mixed jellies were the type that I associate with children's birthday parties. As an adult, I came to consider them over-sweet, too vividly coloured, and spoiled by what I suspected were imitation fruit flavours. Somehow the jelly pavlova became associated in my mind with these packet jellies, quite erroneously in fact, because the pavlova was made from plain gelatine, not from fruit-flavoured pre-mixes.

3.1 Lushus jellies appealed to children for their bright colours, unusual triangular packet and the hidden 'flavour bud'. Made by Shirriff's (later by N.W. Stevens & Co. Ltd), they were advertised from the 1930s through to the 1950s.

This unhappy association between pre-mixed jellies and gelatine has also been observed by food-writers and historians in Britain and the United States. Peter Brears, the author of an excellent essay on the history of jellies in England, believes that their decline in reputation is a 'direct result of the wide availability of packet jellies'.[3] In his opinion the pre-mixed artificially flavoured jellies eclipsed the homemade jellies, creams, snows, and aspics on which cooks of many previous generations had invested their time and talents. In the United States, the most famous of all the brands of pre-mixed fruit jellies was first marketed in 1897 under the name Jell-O.[4] Eventually the brand achieved iconic status, and in America the word came to stand for jellies in general.

That very status has now led to mockery. An American researcher, Kathleen LeBesco, reported suffering from Jell-O monotony by the age of ten. As an adult she went on to study the roles that the product has played in relation to social class and gender in American society. Many of the women she interviewed felt that the product's image was no longer one of elegance, modernity, or convenience, but had become a mark of unsophisticated rural tastes and low socioeconomic status. Feminists read the Jell-O recipe books as supporting old-fashioned views of the ideal wife and housewife, while supporters of natural foods regard these jellies as highly processed, industrial in origin, and ultimately derived from the bits of dead animals that were formerly boiled down to make glue. Postmodern artists set up an annual Jell-O-Rama contest in the 1990s in which the jelly became the medium for tacky or grizzly sculptures.[5] Several websites mock the product with subversive new recipes.[6]

Along the way, the makers of plain gelatine have seen their products lose the fashionable status they once possessed. Indeed, looking back at their old recipe books, we are only too ready to show our distaste – perhaps unfairly. After all, gelatine is derived from collagen. Before extraction, gelatin molecules are 'woven tightly together to form the fibrous connective-tissue protein called collagen ..., which gives mechanical strength to muscles, tendons, skin, and bones'.[7] We pay high prices for collagen-containing skin creams, and cosmetic surgeons sometimes inject purified bovine collagen to enlarge human facial tissue.

Let's have a closer look at the Davis Gelatine Pavlova (Fig. 3.2). The recipe starts with plain gelatine dissolved in one and a half cups of hot water, sweetened with sugar.[8] To one third of this liquid, a cup of freshly squeezed orange juice is added; one third is coloured red with cochineal, and sap green is used to colour the remaining third. A separate quantity of gelatine is prepared as a milk jelly. The green jelly is poured into a fluted mould and left to set, followed by the milk jelly. When it is firm, orange slices are arranged around the inside edge of the mould, and the orange jelly poured over them. When this layer has set, the red jelly is added to complete the dish. It becomes the base of the pavlova. With the help of

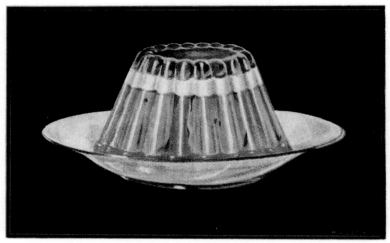

Pavlova

Ingredients.

1½ cups hot water
1 cup orange juice
½ cup milk
3 dessertspoons
   Davis Gelatine
6 dessertspoons
   sugar
Flavouring
Cochineal—sap green
   colouring

Directions.

Dissolve all but a teaspoonful of Gelatine in the hot water, and all the sugar except a dessertspoonful. Take half a cup of the mixture and add to the orange juice; of the remainder flavour with essence of lemon and divide and colour one portion with a few drops of cochineal and the other with sap green. Wet a mould and pour in the green mixture. While it is setting dissolve the teaspoonful of gelatine and dessertspoonful of sugar in a little hot water; when it is cool stir into the milk, add a few drops of flavouring essence. If the green layer is quite firm, pour over. When the milk layer is set arrange orange circles (or any fruit in season) round the mould and add the orange jelly, which should be thickening, a little at a time. When this layer is firm, pour over red jelly and leave to set. Serve with cream or custard.

3.2 The recipe for the first pavlova known in New Zealand appeared in the sixth New Zealand edition of *Davis Dainty Dishes* (1927, p. 11), one year after its publication in the fifth Australian edition.

Page Eleven

a refrigerator, it is possible to accelerate the setting of the layers, but without one making this complicated dish would have taken a long time, especially on a hot summer's day. Even with a fridge, you would be constantly checking to see if the layer had gelled. So time is another reason, to add to my unwillingness to buy food colours, why I have never made the Davis Gelatine Company's Pavlova, or their three-layer Carrington Mould, the Bi-coloured Pudding, the Black and White Coffee Jelly, or their multicoloured Rainbow Jelly.[9]

Where, when, and why was the gelatine pavlova devised?

There are fifty-two desserts in the sixth New Zealand edition of *Davis Dainty Dishes* (1927) (Fig. 3.3), and only one is named after a famous performer. Something must have prompted the Davis Gelatine Company's decision to create a new jelly in honour of Anna Pavlova. The recipe first appeared in the fifth Australian edition of *Davis Dainty Dishes* in 1926, the year Anna Pavlova visited Australia and New Zealand. It is likely that the recipe was developed at the Botany Bay factory opened by Davis Gelatine in January 1919. The New Zealand factory had been established at Woolston, Christchurch in 1913, after the Davis family took over older glue works on the site. For some years, the Woolston plant made gelatine for the Australian, Canadian, and New Zealand markets.[10] By 1926 the impetus had shifted to the New South Wales factory, and the presence of some Australian-sounding

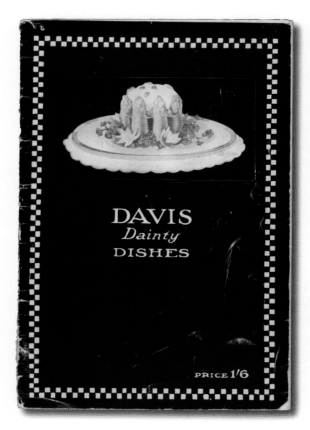

3.3 In order to promote gelatine use, *Davis Dainty Dishes* (1927) was distributed free to housewives who sent in stamps to cover the cost of postage.

recipes in both the Australian and the New Zealand editions of *Davis Dainty Dishes* argues that recipe development was taking place in Botany Bay. Recipes such as Austral Trifle (containing passionfruit), Plantaine Cream (bananas), and Paw Paw Dessert (papaya)[11] suggest an Australian array of fruits, while Kosciusko Fluff is unquestionably a reference to Australia's highest mountain.

The most convincing evidence that the gelatine pavlova came from the Australian branch of the firm involves the name of the illustrator of the pavlova in *Davis Dainty Dishes*, M.V. Leith. I had sought this artist's name in New Zealand directories, without success. However, when looking through some 1926 copies of the *Australian Woman's Mirror*, I found a full-page picture on one back cover advertising Bushells Blue Label tea, signed by Mabel V. Leith. This magazine was published by the owners of *The Bulletin*, in Sydney. It seems highly likely that the gelatine pavlova was first made, and illustrated, in New South Wales.[12]

In style the Davis Gelatine Company's recipe books are very similar to those issued by the famous American companies that manufactured gelatine during the second half of the nineteenth century (for instance the Charles B. Knox Company) and pre-mixed fruit jellies from the beginning of the twentieth century (especially the Genesee Pure Food Company, which produced Jell-O). These companies employed talented graphic artists to illustrate their products in colour, and presented the dishes as masterpieces of purity,[13] achieved through 'Science and Research'.[14] The 1927 New Zealand edition of *Davis Dainty Dishes* displays great similarities with one American book in particular, *Knox Dainty Desserts for Dainty People* (1915). Not only are the titles similar, but both booklets also have an art deco border around each page with the company badge top centre. The concepts embodied in the dessert recipes cover a similar range, from fruit juice jellies to fruit set in jellies, and from blancmanges and Bavarian creams to whipped gelatine sponges and Charlotte Russe. One recipe in the Davis 'Party Sweets' section even appears to be a direct borrowing: the Davis Christmas Plum Pudding seems to be derived from the Knox Chocolate Plum Pudding.[15]

The American manufacturers of gelatine and flavoured jellies led the way in marketing in the early twentieth century. The promotional activities of the Genesee Pure Food Company included branded rigs for the salesmen, free coloured recipe brochures, and large advertisements in women's magazines.[16] In New Zealand and Australia, the Davis Gelatine Company drew on American models for their recipe books and on British examples for their prize-winning factory gardens. This was a most effective form of publicity in Christchurch, by then known as the 'Garden City'. In 1924 all that cooks had to do to get their free copies of the third edition of *Davis Dainty Dishes* was to send twopence worth of stamps to the Woolston factory, along with their name and address. There were 10,000 copies to give away, according to their advertisement in a

Dunedin newspaper, despite the price of one shilling and six pence printed on the front cover of the booklet.[17] The Davis family was international in outlook and inspiration, and multinational in their company structure, eventually having subsidiary companies in Australia, South Africa, Canada, and New Zealand. Naming a recipe after a contemporary celebrity was a way of showing that they were fashion-leaders in an international arena. Starting with Australia in 1926, their pavlova recipe was in their New Zealand edition of *Davis Dainty Dishes* by 1927, and in the Canadian by 1932.[18]

The long tradition of multi-layered and other jellies

What surprised me most as I researched the Davis Gelatine Pavlova was the fact that the concept of a layered jelly was by no means a novelty, but has a history extending back at least to the eighteenth century. Recipes for simpler sorts of jellies go back to the late fourteenth-century medieval manuscript cookbooks of the royal courts of Western Europe. When you consider how commonly the juices of cooked meat and fish set into a jelly when cooled, and the fact that these gelling cuts usually have skin, bone or cartilage in them, it seems likely that cooks knew about natural gelatine sources hundreds if not thousands of years earlier, from the time they invented vessels to hold left-overs. Most of the medieval jellies were spiced and made more piquant with wine or vinegar; they were then strained, and poured over the meat or fish cuts that had produced the gelatine-bearing stock in the first instance. Plant dyes were frequently added to these aspics, to suit medieval taste for brightly coloured food.[19] The fourteenth-century cooks knew that the feet of calves and pigs made particularly strong jellies, and they and their successors developed techniques for removing the farmyard flavours and meat fragments by filtering and clarifying the liquid until it was perfectly clear and suitable for use in sweet jellies. Instructions for making calves' feet jellies by these laborious techniques can still be found in recipe books right to the end of the nineteenth century, decades after commercially prepared gelling agents became available.

Considering the amount of work involved, it is a testimony to the eighteenth century cooks' love of elegant decorative dishes that their recipe books have some of the most complex gelatine recipes ever developed – they make the gelatine pavlova look like child's play in comparison. Imagine a jelly in the form of a hemispherical fishpond with large and small fish enclosed within it, each made from flummery.[20] A celestial jelly scene might include a suspended moon and stars. Floating islands were popular, complete with sheep, swans, and even snakes. Other jelly desserts took the form of desert islands, rocky islands, replicas of Solomon's temple, cribbage cards, and even a plate of bacon and eggs made out of stiffly jelled flummery.[21] There was also a plum pudding made of jelly, perhaps the prototype of the Knox and Davis Gelatine versions of the early twentieth century. However, the eighteenth-century version set the fruit in multiple layers of blanched almonds, raisins, currants, and candied lemon and citron peel.

The concept of a 'Hen and Chickens in Jelly', sitting on a nest of shredded lemon peel, proved very long lasting. Elizabeth Raffald's (1782) version included the hen and chickens within a globe of clear jelly that magnified the tableau; a hundred years later, the recipe appeared in a simplified form in American cookery teacher Maria Parloa's cookbook. The hen and chickens had gone and the dish consisted of eggs in nests. Her mini-nests were made from orange peel strips, and the eggs were actual shells filled with blancmange. They were set on a bed of broken jelly flavoured and coloured with orange juice. Miss Parloa's 1882 recipe was taught by Dunedin cookery teacher Mrs Elizabeth Brown Miller, and was printed in slightly modified form in her first cookery manual (1890). Mrs Miller gave the option of making the orange peel straws into one large nest or three small ones, commenting, like Mrs Raffald, that it was 'a pretty table decoration'.[22]

Another long lasting jelly 'conceit' can be traced back to the seventeenth century. A manuscript cookbook dated by its owner, Rebecca Price, to 1681 contained a recipe for lemon halves, with the pulp removed, which were filled with different coloured jellies: red was achieved with syrup of clove gillyflowers (pinks), blue with syrup of violets, and yellow with saffron. When set, the lemon halves were cut into quarters to expose the glistening jelly, then arranged on a silver dish.[23] In their 1927 version, Davis Dainty Dishes used orange skins and filled some with cochineal-coloured jelly and the rest with plain jelly. Instead of using the juice of the oranges, they added a tablespoon of brandy or sherry to the mixture. Though they called the recipe Orange Quarters, they forgot to tell cooks that the orange halves were to be cut into quarters when their contents had set.[24]

In the eighteenth-century jelly repertoire, the closest in concept to the gelatine pavlova was a recipe entitled 'To make Ribbon Jelly' which Eliza Smith included in her book The Compleat Housewife (1734). Having prepared the jelly the day before, and clarified it with beaten egg whites, she instructed her readers as follows:

> then run the Jelly into little high Glasses; run every Colour as thick as your Finger; one Colour must be thorough cold before you put another on, and that you run on must not be blood warm for fear it mixes together; you must colour red with Cochineel, green with Spinage, yellow with Saffron, blue with Syrup of Violets, white with thick Cream, and sometimes the Jelly by itself.[25]

With each tall glass revealing a rainbow of colours, through which the candlelight glowed on the dinner table, the resulting dessert should have been both decorative and delicious.

In due course, the concept of a multilayered, multicoloured jelly was established in New Zealand. A recipe for a ribbon blancmange can be found in *Brett's Colonists' Guide*, published in Auckland in 1883.[26] Cooks were instructed to divide a blancmange mixture (made with milk, sugar, and gelatine) into as many portions as there were colours available. As with the later Davis Gelatine Pavlova, the layers were built up within a single mould, rather than individual glasses. With an opaque jelly as the starting point, this dessert would have lacked the sparkle of the pavlova. Whitcombe and Tombs' *Colonial Everyday Cookery*, first published in 1901 (Fig. 3.4), offered a simpler version of the ribbon jelly, with cochineal and saffron-coloured layers of clear jelly layered in a mould.[27] The recipe was repeated in several subsequent editions, so the method and concept of the Davis pavlova would have been familiar to most New Zealand cooks, even though the name was new.

3.4 Whitcombe & Tombs' first edition (1901) of their long-running series *Colonial Everyday Cookery* was one of several New Zealand cookbooks providing recipes for Ribbon Jelly, a forerunner to the Davis Gelatine Pavlova.

Discovering the recipes for the elaborate jellies of the seventeenth and eighteenth centuries, prepared in what we would consider primitive kitchens, made me reconsider my opinion of the early twentieth-century jelly recipes found in the manufacturers' cookbooks. They were more derivative than I had ever imagined and most had been simplified for their audience of busy middle-class housewives. Their success was not due to novelty, but to the removal of the many preparatory steps necessary in earlier centuries. In the fourteenth and fifteenth centuries, what cooks referred to as 'gely' or 'gelye' was usually extracted from the bones of young animals (especially the feet) by a long boiling and filtering process, or from freshwater fish such as eels. By the sixteenth century, the exceptional gelling properties of the swim bladders of sturgeons and other members of the *Acipenser* genus were known, and the product was sold under the name isinglass. In 1681 Rebecca Price used isinglass to make her recipe for Leech, a spiced almond and milk jelly. She soaked the isinglass slices for an hour in water and then dissolved them by boiling them in milk.[28] Rasped hartshorn (red deer antler) was another jelling product available in the seventeenth century, but like calves' feet it required long boiling and filtering. Eliza Smith used all three products in her beautiful ribbon jelly, starting with four calf's feet, three ounces of hartshorn, and three ounces of isinglass, boiled in ten quarts of water. When this had been reduced to a mere two quarts, it was strained through a fine flannel bag and left over night so the fat could be removed next day.[29]

If well made, isinglass was more convenient to use than homemade liquid gel extracted from calves' feet, but isinglass was imported (chiefly from Russia) and expensive. By 1880, when both isinglass and powdered animal gelatine were commercially available, isinglass sold for twice the price.[30] In America, manufacturers had turned to other species of fish. The resulting isinglass was sometimes of poor quality and had a pronounced 'piscatory smell'.[31] Another gelling agent, referred to as 'ivory dust', was also mentioned in some recipes, but I have no idea what unfortunate animal contributed the ivory.[32] One pound of the ivory dust was required to make two quarts of jelly, and the process involved four to five hours' simmering followed by straining.[33] Consumers were ready for a substitute.

Peter Cooper, an American inventor and owner of a glue factory, is credited with the development of food-quality gelatine in 1845.[34] Up till then, tanners had supplied the collagen products that were boiled down into glue, extracting them from hides and associated 'offal' (trimmings and feet). To make edible gelatine, manufacturers needed fresher raw materials without contaminants from the tanneries. Calfskins and mature cattle bones became the most important source, and underwent a long process of purification. Cooper's product, sold as a gum, was at first called 'Gelatine, or American isinglass', or 'Cooper's isinglass'.[35] Soon it was known simply as gelatine. In 1869 Mrs Beeton's second edition warned readers that isinglass was sometimes sold adulterated with animal gelatine. She advised them to test what they had purchased – when dropped into cold water, true isinglass turns white and cloudy whereas animal gelatine becomes clear and jelly-like.[36] By the 1870s American cooks submitting recipes for jellies to the earliest fund-raising cookbooks were recommending Cox's gelatine, purchased in boxes, more often than home-made calf's foot jelly or isinglass.

In New Zealand, judging from the recipes in our earliest cookbooks, jellies, moulds, blancmanges, and creams were just as popular as in America and Britain. The cookery book issued by the Women's Christian Temperance Union in Dunedin in 1889, one of the first to be published in New Zealand, contained fifteen recipes for cold desserts, and such was the popularity of jelly that twelve called for the use of gelatine. Only one gave the option of an ounce of 'isinglass or gelatine'.[37] Such dishes were considered 'dainty', a very popular word among those who considered themselves genteel in the late nineteenth century and the early twentieth. Mrs Murdoch of Napier titled her cookbook *Dainties; or how to please our lords and masters*.[38] The subtitle suggests that these dainty dishes were designed to appeal to men as well as women (Fig. 3.5).

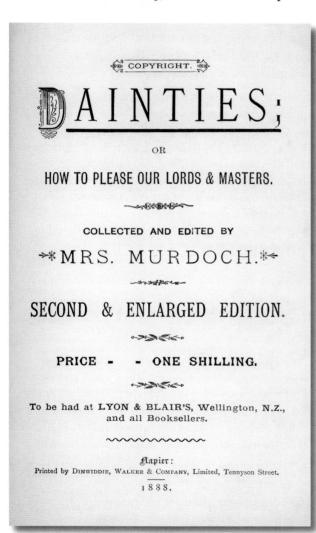

DAINTIES;

OR

HOW TO PLEASE OUR LORDS & MASTERS.

COLLECTED AND EDITED BY

MRS. MURDOCH.

SECOND & ENLARGED EDITION.

PRICE - - ONE SHILLING.

To be had at LYON & BLAIR'S, Wellington, N.Z., and all Booksellers.

Napier:
Printed by DINWIDDIE, WALKER & COMPANY, Limited, Tennyson Street.
1888.

3.5 Mrs Murdoch's cookbook is one of several published in New Zealand in the 1880s. Before then, most cooks appear to have used imported recipe books.

She provided the recipes for thirty-two cold desserts, seventeen of which used gelatine or isinglass. Judging from an advertisement at the back of her book, Mrs Murdoch may well have obtained her supplies of isinglass or gelatine from the local chemist, H. Owen, who also stocked essences, curry powder, baking powder, and citric and tartaric acid, but we can't be sure whether his isinglass was the 'real thing', derived from fish bladders, or the gelatine imitation. I suspect Mrs Murdoch was using gelatine, since her instructions apply to both products; for example, she tells us to set the fruit juice in her fruit jelly with two and a half ounces of 'isinglass or gelatine'. We might expect different mixing instructions if the isinglass had been made from fish swim bladders, as with the Isinglass Jelly in *Brett's Colonists' Guide*, which had to be clarified using two egg whites and their shells.[39] However, even this isinglass may have been an imitation, for the editor states:

> Nelson's patent refined isinglass produces a jelly with all the good qualities of calves' feet without their impurities. It can also be got ready in a few minutes.[40]

To complicate the investigation, there were two gelatine purveyors with the name Nelson in the late nineteenth century: George Nelson of Warwick in Britain, and his son William who emigrated to New Zealand in 1863, and set up his own gelatine plant in Hastings in 1880.[41] Here in New Zealand, there would have been a ready market for his product. The Davis family, like the Nelsons, started as glue manufacturers in Britain and expanded their business into gelatine. George Davis oversaw the conversion of the Woolston glue factory in Christchurch after it was purchased in 1909, and it was making gelatine soon after 1913 when George returned from a trip to the gelatine factory run by his mother's relatives in London, where he learned the necessary skills.[42]

Serving the gelatine pavlova

When Davis Gelatine produced their 1927 New Zealand edition, jellies were very popular, especially those featuring several colours. In the late 1920s, 'Katrine', the lady editor of Christchurch's *Weekly Press*, wrote:

> no supper table seems complete without vari-coloured jellies which give such a pretty, cool effect; and trifles and tipsy cakes seem also to demand a place in the scheme. Jellies, I think, look much more dainty broken up, and served in custard glasses, with a dab of whipped cream on top surmounted by a half glacé cherry. Grouped about the table with teaspoons handy, they strike a very effective decorative note. Fruit salad will naturally have a place, with a server and sweets dishes alongside.[43]

Katrine was talking about stand-up suppers at dances and twenty-first birthday parties. Such a social occasion might be invoked for Davis Gelatine's pavlova.

PAVLOVA
8-10 Servings

Ingredients

3 dessertspoons (¾ oz.) Davis Gelatine
1½ cups (¾ pint) hot water
1 cup (½ pint) orange juice
½ cup (¼ pint) milk
6 dessertspoons (1½ oz.) sugar
Slices of orange
Flavouring
Cochineal
Green colouring
Citric acid

Method

First Layer.—Dissolve 1 dessertspoon gelatine and 1 dessertspoon of sugar in one cup of hot water. Add a pinch of citric acid and lemon essence to flavour. Divide and colour one half green and the other red. Place the green mixture in a mould.

Second Layer.—Dissolve 1 teaspoon of gelatine in two tablespoons of hot water. Add 1 teaspoon of sugar to milk, stir until dissolved. Flavour with vanilla essence. Add gelatine. Carefully pour on to green layer, which must be firm.

Third Layer.—Dissolve remainder of gelatine and sugar in ½ cup hot water, add orange juice. When the milk jelly layer is set, arrange orange circles (or other fruit in season) round the mould, and add the orange jelly, which should be thickening, a little at a time.

Fourth Layer.—Remelt the red jelly if it has set, by standing in hot water, and when cool pour over the orange layer, which must be quite firm. Serve with cream or custard.

Page Thirty-nine

3.6 Davis Gelatine commissioned a new illustration to accompany their pavlova recipe in the 1930s – this is from their twelfth New Zealand edition of 1937 (p. 39).

Less showy types of jelly were commonly served as cold sweets during the summer months, either with luncheon or dinner. In her recipe book, Katrine provided recipes for fifteen 'Lighter Sweets': five used plain granulated gelatine, one stipulated a packet of lemon or orange jelly, and another used a packet of pineapple jelly.[44] The pre-mixed packet jellies were beginning to compete with plain gelatine in the preparation of these dainty desserts, and they were available in an increasing range of flavours. By 1930, Gregg's of Dunedin offered sixteen different flavours, and soon after, Edmonds were promoting twelve flavours of Sure to Set jelly crystals, at sixpence per packet.[45]

Of course we don't know how often the Davis Gelatine Pavlova was served up at parties, dances or dinners. There was a lot of competition from jelly recipes that did not require layering, as well as from the convenient packet jellies. Katrine's 1929 book contained one pavlova recipe selected from those sent in by readers of the *Weekly Press*, but it was not the gelatine pavlova. Instead it was a recipe for small meringues and was placed in the 'Cakes and Sponges' section of the book. These pavlovas will be the subject of my next chapter.

The fate of the gelatine pavlova

The gelatine pavlova recipe and its accompanying illustrations reappeared in several further editions of *Davis Dainty Dishes* until the early 1950s (e.g. Fig. 3.6). Though the recipe occurred in some fund-raising cookbooks compiled between 1927 and the 1950s, this does not mean that it had been adopted by the community, for with one exception it formed part of advertising pages paid for by Davis Gelatine and inserted into the recipe books. Even the exception cannot be used as indication of public acceptance, for it was published by Aunt Daisy in a Christmas section of her international recipe book and was carefully rewritten and renamed by her as 'Pavlova Jelly'.[46] It was not contributed by a member of her 'Daisy Chain' of readers and listeners who sent in their favourite recipes. In fact there is no convincing evidence that this first pavlova had much impact in New Zealand kitchens, for it is a complicated and time-consuming jelly to make, and many others in *Davis Dainty Dishes* looked as dainty but involved fewer steps. Yet even if only one dedicated jelly maker adopted it, it played the important role of introducing the name 'Pavlova' into the realm of food in New Zealand and Australia. The printers of the sixth New Zealand edition of *Davis Dainty Dishes* produced 20,000 copies, which were distributed and sold throughout the country. Although some home cooks may have made nothing from the book, it was hard to miss the picture, and the recipe's striking one-word name, as they leafed through the pages. At the very least, the Davis Gelatine Company should be credited with preparing the way for the next pavlovas.

Rose Rutherford's little pavlovas

THE CREDIT for the second type of pavlova, the first to be made from meringue, must go to Miss Rose H. Rutherford of Dunedin, who had come up with the recipe and its name by 1928. How do we know it was her idea? I haven't found a diary or letters in which she declares her ownership of these little pavlovas, but there is some good circumstantial evidence that she was in the kitchen when they were developed. But first I should tell you what I have learned about this innovative cook.

Who was Rose Rutherford?

Before I did some serious searching into her background, I imagined Rosie Rutherford as a devout Presbyterian, born and bred in Dunedin, and working as a cook or housekeeper. My evidence was rather flimsy: she contributed to two cookbooks published in Dunedin by the Presbyterian Church, wrote very methodical and interesting recipes, and lived (or so I thought) in parts of North Dunedin where sections were small and the cottages and villas were built to house workers and tradesmen and their families. In fact Rose was born Rosina Henrietta Rutherford in Ireland in 1869. Her parents, James (originally from Caithnesshire, Scotland) and Jane (née Somerville) arrived in New Zealand in September 1879 as saloon passengers (the equivalent of first class) on the *Waitangi*, along with their family of ten: Katherine, William, John, Jane, Ellen, Jennetta, Mary (known as Georgina), Rosina (Rose), James Bennett and Anna (known as Elizabeth).[1] James Rutherford senior bought an estate, Summerhill, at Kaitangata in South Otago in December 1879, and erected a suitable house for the family. After involvement in local government, he was elected to the House of Representatives, but attended only one session of Parliament before his sudden death in May 1883, aged only fifty-eight years.[2] His son William had died only two years earlier aged twenty-six years.[3]

In 1885 we find James's widow living in Hereford Street, Christchurch, and from 1890 in upmarket Cranmer Square, presumably with her unmarried daughters. From 1892 she was a resident of Timaru where her daughters Rosina, Elizabeth, and possibly Georgina were the 'Misses Rutherford' who ran a kindergarten.[4] By 1902, records show her established in Dunedin, with Rose and Georgina, at 196 Leith Street, a house directly opposite one of the founding professorial houses at the University of Otago. The street numbers were subsequently altered – leading to my mistaken assumption that the widowed Mrs Rutherford occupied a worker's cottage. Her son James Bennett is listed at that address in 1905, and by 1908 we know that he was working as a bank clerk. In 1911, Elizabeth is shown as living at the family's next home, 772 Cumberland Street, overlooking the tree-lined square known as North Ground.

Rose's mother died in September 1915, aged eighty-five. Elizabeth stayed in Rose's home when James moved to a wooden villa at 854 Cumberland Street, where Mary and Rose joined him. By 1922 all four had moved to one of Dunedin's most desirable locations overlooking Dunedin's main street. Their new home at 28A (then 28) Royal Terrace was just around the corner from Olveston, arguably Dunedin's finest private home. By 1928 Rose and James, now described as a bank officer, were the only listed occupants at this address. It seems likely that Rose, a spinster, kept house for her brother. She moved with him and Elizabeth to their final Dunedin address in Lawson Street, Belleknowes by 1932.[5] Rose outlived her brothers and sisters, reaching the age of ninety-four.

I found out enough of the Rutherford family history to show that, contrary to my earlier impressions, they arrived in New Zealand with a sound financial foundation and high social status. Whether Rose kept house for her mother and siblings on her own or had the help of a servant, she was clearly actively involved in cooking throughout the early Dunedin period. We can assume that along with her sisters she learned to cook at Summerhill as a teenager, and developed her skills further as her mother became older. From 1905 Rose laid a trail of recipes for us to follow. Under the name 'Rosie H. Rutherford', she contributed three recipes to Dunedin's first fund-raising cookbook, the St. Andrew's Cookery Book. This was one of the most long-running and successful community recipe books ever published in New Zealand. Thirteen editions appeared between 1905 and 1932, with 66,000 copies sold.[6] Rosie's recipes can be found in the first edition, and two were reprinted in all later editions: Egg Cutlets and Date Cake (Original) (Fig. 4.1). The word 'original' was Rosie's way of communicating that this recipe was new, and her idea. The cake batter is a standard creamed mixture, but Rosie hid a layer of almond-filled dates in the middle. When cooked, the cake was iced with Vienna icing and 'cut through the lines of dates so as to halve them and show the almonds'.[7]

Date Cake (Original).

4.1 Rose Rutherford
devised this recipe
for Date Cake and
contributed it to the
*St. Andrew's Cookery
Book* in Dunedin
(reproduced from
fourth ed. c. 1908,
p. 135).

Rose H. Rutherford.

The weight of 4 eggs in butter, flour, and sugar, 2oz
dates, almonds.   Mode: Cream the butter; add the
sugar and eggs (well beaten) gradually with the flour;
pour into a flat cake-tin.   Have ready about 2 dozen
dates, from which remove the stones, and place a
blanched almond in the centre, taking care to keep the
dates a nice shape.   Put the dates thus prepared in rows
in the cake, about 1 inch apart, smoothing the mixture
a little over them; bake in a well-heated oven.   This
cake should not be more than 2 inches in depth.   When
cold, ice with Vienna icing, and cut through the lines of
dates so as to halve them and show the almonds.

In 1919, as 'Miss Rutherford', she provided a Christmas cake recipe for the
eighth edition of the *St. Andrew's Cookery Book*, replacing the previous, rather
abbreviated, recipes of M.M. Hooper and Miss Burn. We know that Miss
Rutherford is our Rose, because of the unusual way she wrote out the recipe,
inserting the heading 'Mode' between the ingredients list and the instructions in
both the Date Cake and Christmas Cake recipes.[8] St Andrew's Church was not the
closest Presbyterian church to the various Rutherford family dwellings, but it was
the most actively involved in church missionary work and philanthropy, under
the dynamic leadership of social reformer the Rev. Rutherford Waddell. Many
Dunedin women of other denominations contributed to the St Andrew's recipe
book, including Mrs Saul Solomon, wife of a leading Jewish barrister.

We shouldn't assume the Rutherfords were members of Waddell's congregation,
but the fact that Rose contributed to another Presbyterian recipe book in 1928
suggests an affiliation with that denomination. This book was called *Dainty
Recipes*, and it was published under the auspices of the North-East Valley
Presbyterian Church in Dunedin. Rose had no recipes under her name in the first
two editions of 1926 and 1927, but she was a major contributor, as 'Miss Rose
H. Rutherford', to a new section added to the third edition of 1928. Her two cake
recipes stand out for their inviting and unique names: Ecstasy Cake and Hidden
Bliss. The first was a large fruit cake containing twelve eggs, almonds, raisins,
mixed peel, and cubes of tinned pineapple. The second was a cake that used thick
cream instead of butter. She also provided a recipe for a Devonshire dish called
Squab Pie in which pre-cooked layers of apple, onions and bacon are served under
a pastry topping. The result, she stated, 'tastes like duck'.[9]

In that same year, Rose sent away another of her innovative recipes to the 'Cooking
for the Family's Mutual Help Column', published in Christchurch's *Weekly Press*.

This recipe, called Pavlova Cakes, was printed on 5 September 1928, less than two months before the *Weekly Press* ceased publication. The 'Cookery Editress' of this paper was Katrine McKay, and she marked the passing of the weekly by publishing her columns, along with contributed recipes, in *Practical Home Cookery Chats and Recipes*, printed in 1929 (Fig. 4.2). This book had a wide circulation and brought Rose Rutherford's Pavlova Cakes to a much greater audience than just the *Weekly Press* subscribers. Rose seems to have been a regular contributor, for Katrine selected several of her recipes for the book – Mutton Pie, Tringles (savoury biscuits), and the previously mentioned Ecstasy Cake – besides Pavlova Cakes.[10] When these recipes were published, Rose Rutherford was aged sixty and was an experienced and accomplished cook. Despite the butter, cream, and pastry in her recipes, she lived for another three decades.[11]

4.2 After the *Weekly Press* ceased publication, Katrine McKay assembled her columns and a selection of readers' recipes in *Practical Home Cookery Chats and Recipes* (1929). This book included Rose Rutherford's recipe Pavlova Cakes, first published in September 1928.

PAVLOVA CAKES.

The whites of 2 eggs beaten stiffly with a pinch of salt, add 5 tablespoons of ordinary sugar, 1 small dessertspoon of cornflour, and same of coffee essence, 2 tablespoons of chopped walnuts. Cook like meringues. Time about ½ an hour. This makes three dozen little cakes. They are delightful and simple to make besides being a novelty.—Rose H. Rutherford, 28 Royal Terrace, Dunedin.

The little meringues known as Pavlova Cakes

This is how the recipe for pavlova cakes first appeared in 1928:

> The whites of 2 eggs beaten stiffly with a pinch of salt, add 5 tablespoons of ordinary sugar, 1 small dessertspoon of cornflour, and the same of coffee essence, 2 tablespoons of chopped walnuts. Cook like meringues. Time about $^1/_2$ an hour. This makes three dozen little cakes. They are delightful and simple to make besides being a novelty. – Rose H. Rutherford, 28 Royal Terrace, Dunedin.[12]

Just as she did in 1905, Rose reminds us that these are new, and even without the word 'original' attached to the recipe, we can detect her pride in her culinary innovations. Not only did she come up with new ingredients and methods, but she also had a flair for choosing catchy names.

Katrine's book appeared in 1929, but Rose's Pavlova Cakes recipe was circulating in Dunedin before then. In October 1928 someone who identified herself as 'Auntie Lils' handwrote the recipe 'Pavlova's' on a blank sheet and pasted it inside the front cover of a copy of the second edition of the North-East Valley Presbyterian Church's *Dainty Recipes*,[13] when she gave it to her niece Sheila (Fig. 4.3). She too commented that they were 'something new'. Although we

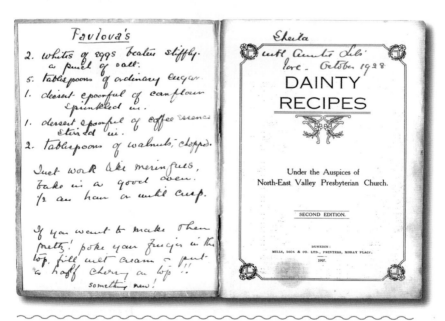

4.3 In October 1928 'Auntie Lils' carefully wrote out and pasted this version of Rose Rutherford's little pavlovas into a copy of the North-East Valley Presbyterian Church's *Dainty Recipes* (2nd ed., 1927), as a gift to 'Sheila'.

How to make Rose Rutherford's Little Coffee and Walnut Pavlovas *(1928)*

This recipe produces 30 small meringues. Delay filling until just before serving to retain their delightful crisp texture.

- **½ cup finely chopped walnuts (use freshly shelled walnuts)**
- **½ cup caster sugar**
- **2 egg whites from large eggs**
- **pinch salt**
- **¼ teaspoon cream of tartar**
- **2 teaspoons coffee essence**

Filling or topping

- **whipped cream**
- **glacé cherries**

Position two oven shelves, one above the centre and one below. Preheat oven to 120°C. Cut 2 pieces of baking paper to cover two oven trays. Grease corners to adhere to trays and prevent rolling.

In a small bowl combine the nuts and half the sugar (¼ cup).

Using an electric mixer beat whites at medium speed until opaque and frothy. Add the salt and cream of tartar. Increase speed to medium–high and beat until thick, glossy and smooth. Slowly sprinkle in the remaining quarter cup of sugar and continue to beat until just combined. Reduce the speed to low, sprinkle in the sugar and walnut mixture and the coffee essence and mix until incorporated.

Spoon or pipe the mixture onto the prepared trays to make approximately 30 small meringues. Bake for 1½–2 hours. Turn the oven off and leave to cool in the oven for several hours.

Just before serving, top each with a little whipped cream and a glacé cherry, or sandwich together in pairs with a cream filling.

will probably never know whether she obtained the recipe directly from Rose Rutherford, or read it in the *Weekly Press* a month earlier, thanks to Auntie Lils we have a clue to how little pavlovas were presented. Although Rose's recipe did not provide any hints for serving these bite-sized pavlovas, Auntie Lils' handwritten version suggested using a finger to poke a hole in the top of each meringue, inserting cream and topping the pavlova with half a cherry. In this she was building on a long-established tradition, as we will see below. Auntie Lils' pavlovas either had a hollow centre or were still soft-centred when they came out of the oven. Two later versions of Rose Rutherford's recipe (1954, 1964) suggested sandwiching them together with cream, a return to a much older practice.

The recipe for Rose Rutherford's pavlovas reappeared in at least six national publications during the 1930s: the cookbook produced by the Women's Division of the Farmers' Union about 1930 or 1931,[14] an issue of the *New Zealand Truth* in 1931[15] and the *New Zealand Woman's Weekly* early in 1934,[16] in Aunt Daisy's second cookery book published late in 1934,[17] the popular *Tried Recipes* from Auckland's Victoria League,[18] and in the sixth edition of Edmonds' 'Sure to Rise' *Cookery Book* published about 1936.[19] These were by far the most influential and widely circulated New Zealand cookbooks in the 1930s. With this nationwide publicity, Rose Rutherford's Pavlova Cakes were clearly a popular form of pavlova throughout this decade.

Three recipe books of the 1940s and another three in the 1950s included the recipe, still with the name Pavlovas, or in one case, Little Pavlovas, but the recipe name changed to Coffee Meringues in one recipe book published about 1956[20] and Pavlova Biscuits in another published in 1964.[21] The final appearance in 1966 was as Coffee Pavlova Cakes.[22] It seems that communities were rapidly forgetting the original name and identity of Rose Rutherford's meringues. What is interesting about these pavlova recipes is this lack of variation and their prolonged co-existence with the large meringue cake that we now accept as the pavlova. Indeed from 1928 to 1966 (a span of thirty-eight years) the recipe was essentially the same, with the only variation introduced being a pinch of cream of tartar (three times), and a tablespoon of boiling water (once).

A strong case has been made that the recipe name for this second type of pavlova was an original contribution by Rose Rutherford – but what about the content? Meringues in their simplest form are an amalgamation of beaten egg whites and sugar dried out in a slow oven. They do not require cornflour, flavouring or any inclusion such as nuts. Rose's pavlovas are meringues with three added ingredients: cornflour, coffee essence, and chopped walnuts. Were these extras Rose's idea? The best way of answering this question is to review the development of meringues in the culinary traditions of Western Europe.

A brief history of meringues

For many years most food-writers accepted the *Larousse Gastronomique* version of the origins of the meringue. Quoting un-named 'historians of cookery', this authoritative work states that the meringue was 'invented' in 1720 by a Swiss pastry-cook called Gasparini, who worked in a small town called Mehrinyghen, after which this little patisserie was named.[23] However, the claim that the meringue was 'invented' was treated with some suspicion by the author of the *Larousse Gastronomique*, who was well aware that egg whites were used in making pastry and confectionery before this date. He was absolutely correct, and we now know that the word 'meringue' was in use in France by 1691 when François Massialot's *Le Cuisinier Roial et Bourgeois* was first published. The word was introduced into the English language when the book was translated for an English audience in 1702.[24]

Both the concept and the name may have already reached England by the time the translation appeared, however. In 1681, at the age of twenty-one, Rebecca Price of Buckinghamshire compiled a large manuscript book of recipes, to which she added more until her death in 1740. As the daughter of a country squire, she would have expected to be a hands-on housewife when she married in 1683, supervising a cook and kitchen maids but also preparing food and medicinal mixtures herself. Among the numerous recipes she transcribed was one entitled 'To Make Melindes: a French Recipe: given me by Monsieur le Marqui Achiolier'. This called for egg whites and sugar to be beaten in a copper or silver skillet over hot embers, before the 'melindes' were laid 'upon white paper (strewed with suger) in what fashion and bigness you please to have them'. Rebecca preferred them to be about one and a half inches long and one inch wide.[25] As meringue recipes of the eighteenth and nineteenth centuries often recommended cooking them on a sheet of paper, and forming them in the shape of an egg, this recipe looks like an early version. In addition, the method of mixing over heat was one of the common ways of preparing meringue in Italy.[26] Unfortunately we cannot be sure that Rebecca wrote down this recipe before 1702.

Massialot's book therefore stands as a more definitive source. He began with a glossary of the French terms used in the recipes, describing meringues as

> a sort of Confection made of the Whites of Eggs Whipt, fine Sugar and grated Lemmon-peel, of the bigness of a Walnut. They are proper for the garnishing of several Dishes.[27]

Two recipes were provided and introduced with the comment that 'Meringues properly belong only to the Confectioner's Art' but deserved to be included because cooks sometimes used them as a garnish. Readers were instructed to whip the whites of three or four fresh eggs 'till they form a rocky Snow', then to add grated lemon peel and three or four spoonfuls of sieved fne sugar. The mixture was whipped together and placed in round or oval shaped pieces about the size of a walnut on a sheet of white paper on the table. After dusting the tops with powdered sugar as a form of glazing or icing, the cook was instructed to place the preheated domed lid of a 'Campain-oven' over the meringues.[28] Presumably this was hot enough to dry out and 'ice' the meringues but not to burn the paper or underlying table! As a finishing touch, cooks 'may also put in a little Fruit, as a Rasberry, Strawberry or Cherry, according to the Season, and joyn other *Meringues* to them, to make Twins.'[29]

Attached to *The Court and Country Cook* was a separate book by Massialot entitled *New Instructions for Confectioners*. It repeats the original recipes with a little more detail. Of particular interest is the comment that the meringues rise under the heated oven lid, 'leaving a void space in the middle; which may be fill'd up, with a grain of preserv'd Fruit'.[30] These bright red fillings were used for the next three centuries, and from the early 1800s usually in conjunction with cream. Massialot was aware that meringues could develop hollow centres as they cooked, providing a vacant space for a filling. From the 1820s the practice developed of removing meringues from the oven before the centres had dried out; they were turned upside down and the soft parts were scraped out, to be replaced at serving time with whipped cream or a bright-coloured preserve such as raspberry jam, or by 1880, candied cherries. The cherry popped into Auntie Lils' version of the little pavlovas belongs within this long tradition.

The idea of joining meringues with a soft, sweet, and colourful filling was an integral part of the concept that was brought to England from France in the early eighteenth century and from there transferred to North America. It is evident in the array of names that meringues were given as they left French-speaking kitchens, for not all English cooks chose to use the French names of the dishes they borrowed from their rivals (and occasional enemies). Elizabeth Raffald was one of those Anglophile cooks. In her book *The Experienced English Housekeeper*, meringues appeared as Cream Cakes, a name that survived in use till the 1840s.[31] Since there is not a single reference to cream in the recipe, we must assume that cream was inserted into the hollow centres prior to serving or used to sandwich two of the little cakes together. When the concept of meringues reached North America, the name 'kisses' was frequently applied, no doubt because the two halves were pressed close together and tasted sweet. The earliest kisses that I have found are from Sarah Josepha Hale's book *The Good Housekeeper*, published in Boston in 1839.[32] Mrs Hale was the lady editor of a fashionable women's magazine. Americans liked the name so much that virtually all meringues that were sandwiched together in this way were referred to as kisses. As late as 1945, home economics students in Kansas were still taught how to make kisses, distinguished from meringues by their smaller size (less than two inches in diameter).[33] From the late nineteenth century, a much sharper distinction was made between single meringues that were filled, and kisses that were meringues joined in pairs.

To find out if any of these eighteenth- and nineteenth-century meringues were embellished with nuts we have to go back to 1702. The second meringue recipe in Massialot's book was called *Pistachoes*-Meringues. The recipe was the same as for the plain meringues, except for the addition of blanched pistachio nuts – one of the two versions specified that these were to be ground, while the other is unclear on this point. So Rose Rutherford's idea of adding walnuts to little meringues also had an historical precedent, though she was probably unaware of it. While ground nutmeats (pistachios or more usually almonds) were added to meringue mixtures in the eighteenth century, chopped nuts did not appear till the late nineteenth century. Fannie Merritt Farmer, the most famous of the principals of the Boston Cooking School, published her recipe for nut meringues in 1896.[34] She gave the option of almonds, hickory nuts or English walnuts.

Was the addition of coffee essence an original contribution by Rose Rutherford? From the time of Massialot (1702), lemon was common in meringues, continuing into the first half of the nineteenth century, to be replaced by vanilla in the second. At the turn of the twentieth century, coffee essence appeared in recipes originating in New York and London.[35] Combining the walnuts and the coffee essence may have been Rose Rutherford's special contribution, besides the name. Coffee was a popular flavour in the 1920s with many coffee cake recipes appearing in New Zealand fund-raising books, but none included walnuts.

Was the dessertspoon of cornflour Rose Rutherford's idea? Standard meringue recipes from Britain and North America do not include cornflour at this time. Closer to home, however, is the cornflour-containing Meringues recipe in the Wellington fund-raising book *Terrace Tested Recipes* (Fig. 4.4).[36] The idea of adding cornflour to meringues may have spread to Dunedin from Wellington, and ultimately from Australia where it was present by 1896.[37]

In writing out her recipe, Rose Rutherford assumed that her readers knew how to make and cook meringues, so she didn't bother to give mixing or cooking instructions. Mixing is relatively straightforward once you learn to judge when the egg whites are ready to incorporate the sugar, but cooking is more tricky since meringues tend to stick to the surface they are cooked on. Historically meringues and kisses were placed on paper, usually white writing paper, but occasionally brown or grey paper. Sometimes the paper was pre-wetted, but more commonly it was placed on a thick wooden board and then directly into the oven. By the end of the nineteenth century, it became common practice to pre-soak the board, an idea promoted by the influential chef and writer Alexis Soyer in 1847.[38] During the early decades of the twentieth century, it was realised that a greased (and sometimes also floured) oven tray worked even better than paper and boards. In New Zealand,

Terrace Tested Recipes

Collected by the Ladies of the Terrace
Congregational Church, Wellington, N.Z.

4.4 *Terrace Tested Recipes*
was a fund-raising recipe book
produced by members of The
Terrace Congregational Church
in Wellington (1927).

early meringue recipes were cooked using both methods,[39] so Rose Rutherford
should have been familiar with both. By 1934 cooks who reproduced Rose's
recipe recommended putting the little pavlovas on 'exceptionally well greased
greaseproof paper', which was newly available.[40]

When were the little pavlovas served?

At the time of their introduction to England, meringues must have been served at
meals such as dinners or formal suppers, for the afternoon tea had yet to emerge.
People were drinking tea from the second half of the seventeeth century, but the
idea of combining tea with food between meals did not become established until
the later years of Queen Victoria's reign. By the turn of the twentieth century, the
English upper class had made afternoon tea an occasion for display of wealth and
rank. In the words of Arnold Palmer, who first researched the changing pattern of
English meals,

> In big houses tea was by now a formal affair, with cake-stands, hot dishes, and
> small trays borne to and fro by footmen who remained in attendance throughout

the meal. Five o'clock was a fashionable hour, or even later. When there was company, ladies dressed for tea before dressing for dinner.[41]

This was not high tea, a term which referred to a sit-down meal taken by families who had dined in the middle of the day. The English food historian Laura Mason thinks that high tea evolved out of the eighteenth-century meal pattern, and was preserved in many homes well into the twentieth century.[42] Growing up in the 1950s in New Zealand, I well remember dinner at midday on Sundays, followed by a light tea in the evening. Now the only occasion on which members of my family eat dinner in the middle of the day is Christmas.

Afternoon tea was quite different from this sit-down high tea. It was not a meal, merely the addition of some food to a cup of tea taken during the afternoon. The degree of formality and location depended on the size of the gathering. My treasured 1920 guide, *Etiquette for Women* (Fig. 4.5), states that if there are fewer than ten guests, I should serve tea in my drawing room:

> This can either be done by having tea set out on a table at one end of the room, over which a maid presides and pours out tea, bringing round a cup to each guest as they arrive, on a tray, with milk and sugar, to which they help themselves, while cakes, bread & butter, &c., are handed afterwards; or else the hostess presides at her own tea-table, which is brought in and set immediately in front of her for her to pour out tea, the guests helping themselves to cakes, &c., which are displayed on plates and silver cake dishes arranged on the tea-table or on three or four-tier cake stands specially designed for this purpose.[43]

Whether one took tea at home or at a tea shop or tearooms, the basic accompaniments of an English afternoon tea in the early twentieth century were 'very thin bread and butter, with either a Madeira, Seed, or Dundee cake; a slightly superior form included cucumber sandwiches in summer and buttered toast or Sally Lunns in winter.'[44]

In New Zealand a similar format was followed at the Theomins' home, Olveston, just round the corner from where the Rutherfords were living in 1928. The Olveston drawing room has two doors, side by side. Miss Brenda Bell, of Shag Valley Station, who was a frequent guest at Olveston after 1909, provided an explanation which links this layout to occasions such as formal afternoon teas:

> when there are large parties it is essential that staff carrying trays of tea things, empty cups and so on do not have to push through arriving and departing guests. The second door is the service door. Tea was arranged at that end of the room and could be serviced without mixing guests and staff.[45]

There are many newspaper accounts of the dinner parties, balls, suppers, and musical 'At Home' afternoon teas held at Olveston. They describe the table settings and flowers in minute detail, but never mention the dishes that were served. There was an unwritten social convention not to refer to food items, it seems. The only comment I could find was that at a musical 'At Home' held in 1910, tea, coffee and cakes were served in the dining room, while fruit salad was available in an adjoining room.[46] Fortunately New Zealand cookbooks fill in the gaps in our knowledge, revealing the increasing elaboration of the dainties that accompanied afternoon tea. In 1888 Mrs Murdoch of Napier provided recipes for twenty-one assorted cakes (large and small), two sorts of biscuits, three buns, and two gingerbreads.[47] By 1921 the ninth edition of Dunedin's *St. Andrew's Cookery Book* had recipes for fifty-six large cakes, twenty-six small cakes, twenty-four scones and breads, thirteen eggless cakes, and twenty-two different sorts of biscuits.[48] Since there had been little change in luncheon and dinner courses over this period – they usually included a hot pudding or cold sweet – the most likely outlet for this profusion of baked goods was afternoon tea.

4.5 In the early twentieth century, books on etiquette spelt out how to behave at social occasions, including afternoon tea (from G. Devereux's *Etiquette for Women*, 1920).

Small meringues could be used to garnish a cold sweet, but the instructions that accompany Auntie Lils's version of Rose Rutherford's Pavlova Cakes suggest that they were a dish in their own right. We can imagine them on a tier of the cake-stand, or on a silver or glass dish with their cream filling protruding appetisingly around the bright red cherry on top. Like Anna Pavlova, they were light, diminutive, and exquisite. Given their long period of popularity, it is hard to dismiss them as a false start or trial run for the 'real' pavlova, though the hostess had less opportunity to show her flair with these than she did with the larger pavlova cake, to which the meringues eventually gave ground.

Making a small meringue beautiful was limited by the fact that the cream and fruit (glacé or jelly) were mostly hidden within the meringue shell. At best the top of the meringue offered space for a single dab of whipped flavoured cream. In contrast, a meringue cake or pavlova with an eight-inch (20 cm) diameter offered a blank canvas of fifty square inches (314 cm^2) of cream, on which the afternoon tea hostess could display her skills. Cutting the cake provided further opportunities for showing her good taste: a silver-plated cake slice might be employed to transfer the pieces to the bone china plates, each matching the teacup and saucer; silver-plated cake or pastry forks were on hand to avoid any messiness. Large pavlovas offered more scope for the rituals of afternoon tea than Rose's little meringues.

The first large pavlovas

$\mathbf{F}$OR THOSE of you who think that Davis Gelatine's pavlova and Rose Rutherford's little meringue pavlovas were imposters, this chapter will describe the first examples of what you consider to be the real pavlova. I should warn you, though, that there is no single foundation recipe, invented by some Kiwi kitchen genius and then dispersed all over New Zealand. The truth is that the birth of the large pavlova was essentially the renaming of an existing dish, the meringue cake. There were several versions of the meringue cake in circulation in New Zealand in the late 1920s and early 1930s, and a handful of cooks renamed their favourite version 'pavlova'. We shouldn't forget that most of them would have been familiar with the gelatine pavlova – after all, thousands of copies of the sixth and seventh editions of *Davis Dainty Dishes* had been printed and distributed, all containing the coloured illustration and recipe for the pavlova. Readers of the cookery columns of Christchurch's *Weekly Press*, and those who bought the book put out in 1929 by its 'Cookery Editress', Katrine McKay, may have been equally familiar with Rose Rutherford's recipe for little pavlova cakes. Renaming the large meringue cake a 'pavlova' was simply jumping on the bandwagon. What New Zealand cooks did with their large, newly named pavlova cake is what made it one of the most popular dishes of the twentieth century.

Early New Zealand pavlova cakes 1929–34

Since chronological disputes are at the heart of the pavlova wars, giving the details of the first New Zealand pavlovas, published before 1935, could provide ammunition for those who want to continue the campaign – but that is not my intention. I want to demonstrate that at this time there were many pavlovas, and the only pavlova fashion travelling through New Zealand was the idea of calling meringues and meringue cakes 'pavlovas'. Of course, we cannot be sure that the large pavlova published in 1929 is indeed the earliest. The search will continue as long as missing issues of women's magazines go unchecked, and while countless newspaper recipe columns remain unread. Indeed given that Pavlova the ballerina was in New Zealand in 1926, there may be earlier examples.

'Festival's' Pavlova Cake, 1929 (Fig. 5.1)[1]

As you will see when I review the history of meringue cakes, they had a variety of names that on the whole were neither catchy nor memorable. With other examples of dishes called 'pavlova' already circulating, it is not surprising that the meringue cake also underwent the renaming process. 'Festival's' cake was made with four egg whites, and four large tablespoons of sugar – such tablespoons held one ounce (28 g) of sugar when level, or up to 40 g when heaped. Half a tablespoon of cornflour was added to the beaten mixture, and then the cake was cooked in two greased sponge sandwich tins – eight-inch (20 cm) diameter tins were commonly used (Fig. 5.2). Festival finished her recipe with the instruction 'make filling of cream chopped nuts and cherries'.[2]

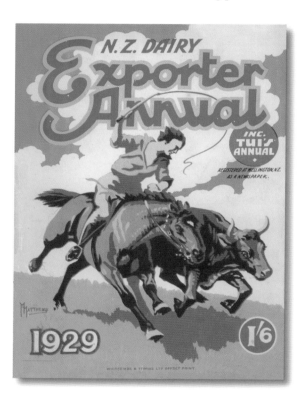

5.1 Cover of the *N.Z. Dairy Exporter Annual (Inc. Tui's Annual)* for 1929.

Reproduced with permission from the *New Zealand Dairy Exporter* and the Hocken Collections, Dunedin.

Pavlova Cake.

WHITES of 4 eggs beaten very stiff, add 4 large tablespoons sugar. Beat and lastly add ½ tablespoon cornflour.
Bake in very slow oven in greased sandwich tins, and make filling of cream chopped nuts and cherries.—**Festival.**

5.2 'Festival's' recipe for the earliest known pavlova cake was chosen by 'Tui' for publication in the *N.Z. Dairy Exporter Annual (Inc. Tui's Annual)* in October 1929.

Reproduced with permission from the *New Zealand Dairy Exporter* and the Hocken Collections, Dunedin.

How to make 'Festival's' Pavlova *(1929)*

Serves 8–10

This pavlova consists of two crisp
meringue layers without the soft
centres typical of later types. To
retain the crispness, do not fill more
than an hour before serving.

- **4 egg whites**
- **160 g sugar**
- **40 g cornflour**

Filling

- **300 ml cream**
- **½ cup toasted almonds, chopped
  (no need to remove skins)**
- **½ cup glacé cherries, chopped**
- **½ teaspoon vanilla**

Prepare two sponge sandwich pans, each 22–23 cm in diameter. Spray the sides with non-stick cooking spray and line the base of each with a circle of non-stick baking paper (see Hint 7, p. 146.) Preheat the oven to 120°C and position a rack in the centre.

Beat the egg whites until stiff. Continue beating, adding the sugar gradually, a spoonful at a time. Lastly beat in the cornflour.

Divide the mixture evenly between the two pans and spread gently to touch the sides all round. Bake for 2 hours, turn the oven off, and leave the meringues in the closed oven for a further hour.

To loosen, use a table knife to cut around the edge of each meringue. Invert each onto a cooling rack and gently remove the paper. Allow to cool completely before filling.

Whip the cream and then fold in the nuts, cherries, and vanilla. Use half the cream mixture to spread on one meringue. Position the second one on top and then use the remaining cream to cover the surface.

How to make Laurina Stevens' Pavlova *(1933)*

Serves 6

This early pavlova lives up to the standard of more modern recipes – the shell is crisp but not too brittle and the centre remains slightly soft. Mrs Stevens' suggested topping is delicious! Use freshly shelled walnuts and for a pleasant contrast with the sweetness of the meringue use fresh pineapple or canned pieces in natural juice (not in syrup).

- **2 egg whites**
- **1 cup sugar**
- **1 teaspoon cornflour**

Topping

- **½ can of pineapple pieces, drained or equivalent in fresh pineapple**
- **¼ cup walnut quarters**
- **200 ml cream**

Prepare one 18–20 cm diameter sponge sandwich pan. Spray the sides with non-stick cooking spray (see Hint 7, p. 146) and line the base with a circle of non-stick baking paper. Preheat oven to 120°C with a shelf in the centre position.

Beat the egg whites until very stiff, add the sugar and cornflour and beat again for 8–10 minutes with an electric mixer, or 12–15 minutes by hand with a rotary beater. Spoon the mixture into the prepared pan and spread evenly right out to the sides. Bake for 1 hour. Turn the oven off and leave the pavlova inside to cool for at least another hour.

Use a sharp knife to carefully cut around the sides to separate the pavlova from the pan. Turn out on to a rack and peel off the paper. Invert onto a serving platter.

Drain the pineapple. Whip the cream until stiff. Spread over the pavlova. Top with the walnut pieces and pineapple. Serve within an hour or cover and store in a fridge for up to 24 hours.

Whipped cream and candied cherries had long been popular fillings for small meringues. The nuts were a new addition. Who was 'Festival'? Judging from the readership of the *New Zealand Dairy Exporter*, which published her recipe, this *nom de plume* was likely to be that of a rural woman living in a dairy-farming area of New Zealand. The editor, 'Tui', proudly introduced the 'Cookery Notes' section as representing a selection of well-tried recipes 'from our farm kitchens'.[3] There is a possibility that 'Festival' submitted her recipe on a second occasion, this time to a weekly magazine that required its contributors to have their name or initials and district published with their recipe. In the *New Zealand 'Truth'* of 23 July 1931, a pavlova recipe identical to that of 'Festival' was sent in by two women in the 'Replies to Correspondents' section: Mrs G. of Frankton Junction and Mrs A.J.P.H. of Hastings. Mrs G. submitted the recipe to the *New Zealand 'Truth'* again on 17 April 1935. She had clearly made this recipe her own. Perhaps she was the mysterious 'Festival'.[4] After 1935, pavlova recipes moved on, and no further examples of this particular recipe have been found.

Laurina Stevens' Pavlova Cake, 1933 (Fig. 5.3)[5]

The next meringue cake recipe to be named Pavlova Cake emerged from Rangiora, a rural town in Canterbury, and was contributed to the *Rangiora Mothers' Union Cookery Book of Tried and Tested Recipes* by Laurina Stevens, the wife of the borough

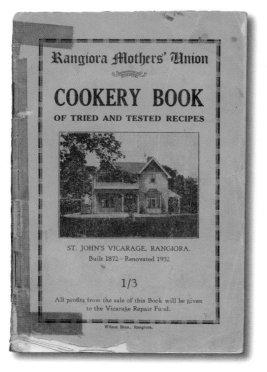

engineer, W.H. Stevens.[6] Though she was not a farmer's wife, she would have mixed with them in her community activities and undoubtedly shared recipes acquired in several places in New Zealand where her husband had worked as an engineer.[7] Born Laurina Bennett in 1896, she attended Helensville Primary School, then moved to Otahuhu and trained as a dressmaker before her marriage in 1913. Two sons were born in 1914 and 1916. The family moved to Rangiora in 1929 when Laurina was thirty-three years old. There she joined the Mothers' Union. Archivist Jane Teal, who has researched

5.3 Cover of *Rangiora Mothers' Union Cookery Book of Tried and Tested Recipes*, dated by the printers (Wilson Bros) to 1933 (p. 39).

"PAVLOVA CAKE."
Mrs. W. H. Stevens, East Belt, Rangiora.

2 Whites of Eggs	1 teaspoon Cornflour
1 cup Sugar	

Method: Beat egg whites very stiff, add sugar and cornflour; beat again. Pour into sandwich tin and bake in very slow oven for one hour. When cold, put whipped cream, pineapple, and chopped walnuts on top.

5.4 Laurina Stevens contributed her Pavlova Cake recipe to the *Rangiora Mothers' Union Cookery Book of Tried and Tested Recipes* (1933, p. 17).

her background, found evidence that 'she was among a group of women who dispensed afternoon tea at the Mothers' Union meeting in December 1931'.[8] By 1933 she was a member of both the Mothers' Union and Plunket committees.

When the Rangiora Anglicans needed to renovate St John's vicarage, Laurina contributed four recipes to the fund-raising recipe book: American Cookies (also known as cornflake meringues and found in New Zealand cookbooks from the late 1920s), Cream Puffs, Fudge Cake (a new and fashionable recipe) and Pavlova Cake. She was obviously a good cook, interested in the latest dishes. Her pavlova recipe appeared with double quotes around the title, indicating perhaps that it was a novelty, or that it was copied from another publication (Fig. 5.4). However, it did not use the same proportions or method as 'Festival's' Pavlova Cake. While the 1929 recipe was based on four egg whites and four large tablespoons of sugar, this 1933 pavlova used two whites and a cup of sugar. The earlier pavlova was baked in two sandwich tins and filled, while Laurina's smaller pavlova was cooked in a single sponge sandwich tin and topped with whipped cream, pineapple, and chopped walnuts. It is the first known single-layer pavlova cake. What these two recipes had in common was the addition of cornflour, and the absence of vinegar. Laurina's recipe was not reproduced in any other publication that I have found, and Laurina herself, after following her husband to Milton in March 1934, has not been traced after 1935.

'A Successful Pavlova-Maker's' Pavlova Cake, 1934[9]

In 1934 Maud Ruby Basham was conducting the popular 'Aunt Daisy's Mail Bag' for the newly launched *New Zealand Woman's Weekly*. One of her readers, 'Margery of Remuera', had written in complaining that her pavlova cake 'always "looks like a million dollars" when I take it out of the oven, but it then *always* goes down in the centre.' Aunt Daisy asked readers to send in their recipes for a 'reliable Pavlova' and received one from regular correspondent 'Summer Breeze'. It was identical to Rose Rutherford's little pavlovas, but 'Constant Reader' of

Cambridge wrote, 'I am anxiously awaiting further particulars of the Pavlova cake, as I have tried and tried, and just can't get it right.' Then came the reply from 'Successful Pavlova-Maker' who told Aunt Daisy that she had 'made the Pavlova cake for a long time, but my recipe differs from yours'.[10] It consisted of the whites of four eggs and a breakfast cup of sugar. When the mixture was very stiff, one teaspoon of vinegar was beaten in (but no cornflour). The cake was cooked in a round cake tin, lined with brown paper twice the height of the sides of the tin. The paper was thoroughly wetted before the meringue was put in. This cake was cooked in a gas oven, preheated to very hot and then turned very low (Regulo 1) as soon as the pavlova went in. After an hour and a half, the gas was turned off and the cake left in the oven till cold. For the topping, whipped cream and mashed strawberries were recommended as 'delicious'. Aunt Daisy closed the correspondence with the interesting remark: 'But isn't your recipe *very nearly a meringue cake?*' She was quite right to notice the similarity, for indeed the pavlova cake was a renamed meringue cake, but she might equally have noted that the pavlovas in Summer Breeze's recipe were very nearly small meringues. I suspect that Aunt Daisy had accepted Rose Rutherford's pavlova cakes as *the* pavlova, and was disconcerted to find her readers calling large meringue cakes by the same name. When her second book appeared later in 1934, Aunt Daisy inserted 'Successful Pavlova-Maker's' recipe under the title Pavlovas No. 1, while Rose Rutherford's appeared as Pavlovas No. 2. Under the title Meringue Cake, Aunt Daisy gave an almost identical recipe to No. 1, but with a teaspoon of vanilla added, and greaseproof paper as the tin liner rather than brown paper.[11]

Pavlova Cake, 1934[12]

Like many other organisations, the Wellington YWCA put out their fund-raising cookery book, the *Blue Triangle Cookery Book*, without a date. I obtained my copy from my Oamaru mentor, Noeline Thomson. Fortunately this copy, which had originally been given to Noeline's sister Eileen, included in the inscription on the cover the words 'from Mary Xmas 1934'. Mary Thomson was Noeline and Eileen's mother, and this book appeared about the same time as Aunt Daisy's second compilation. The YWCA Pavlova Cake recipe started with the whites of four eggs and was the first to stipulate caster sugar. Vanilla essence was included and one teaspoon of vinegar was added, but no cornflour. It was the first large pavlova not to be cooked in a tin. Instead the instructions were to 'Put on greased paper on scone tray ...'. Decoration was 'whipped cream, any fruits, chopped nuts or passion fruit'.[13] The *Blue Triangle Cookery Book* also provided a recipe for a three-egg white meringue cake, using ordinary sugar and half a teaspoon of vinegar. It was cooked as a single layer in a tin and, just like the pavlova cake, was topped with whipped cream and 'any such fruit as strawberries, pineapple, passion fruit etc.'[14] One other pavlova recipe, the Davis Gelatine type, appeared in this book, complete with a new coloured illustration forming part of their inserted advertisement.

Miss Isabella Finlay's Meringue Sponge Sandwich or Pavlova Cake, between 1934 and 1936[15]

Since serious research began into the origins and development of the pavlova cake, it has been accepted that the large pavlova began as a meringue cake.[16] The sequence of books produced by Miss Isabella Finlay, demonstrator of gas appliances for the Dunedin City Gas Department, provides a definitive example of the transformation. In the second edition of her book (named *The Osborne Cook Book* after a brand of gas stove), are two versions of a recipe for Meringue Sponge Sandwich.[17] In the third and subsequent editions of her book (renamed *Cookery*), Miss Finlay modified the recipe name to Meringue Sponge Sandwich or Pavlova Cake.[18] The third edition can be dated by the change of address of an advertiser to between 1934 and 1936. Were the recipes the same? In the second edition, the first version of the recipe required two egg-whites and eight ounces of sugar, and the second required three egg whites version and twelve ounces of sugar. Each was cooked in two tins and could be filled with cream and tart fruit such as loganberries or raspberries, with the same mixture piled on top. When she added the name Pavlova Cake in the third edition, Miss Finlay removed the ingredient list for the two-egg version and reduced the sugar for the three egg-white recipe to seven or eight ounces, introducing one teaspoon each of vinegar and vanilla essence.[19] The mixture could be cooked in two tins or as a single layer cake in a special 'Pavlova tin' – though what that looked like remains to be discovered. About 1937 or 1938, we see a reduction in the amount of sugar, vinegar, and vanilla; half an ounce of cornflour is listed as optional, along with the vinegar and vanilla.[20] In the eighth edition, readers were given the option of cooking the pavlova in a single tin or on greaseproof paper on an oven tray.[21] The tinkering with the recipe from 1934 to 1939 provides a fascinating insight into the rapid evolutionary changes of pavlova cakes during this decade. As a demonstrator, Miss Finlay had to keep up with the latest trends, and these were advancing rapidly.[22]

Of these five independent meringue cake recipes named pavlova and published between 1929 and 1934, only two were to be served layered, like the meringue cake. Only two included cornflour, the rest opting for vinegar as the added ingredient, and only two called for vanilla essence. The remarkable fact is that the five recipes were unrelated, their wording, units of measurement, and methods all indicating a separate origin. To my knowledge none of the recipes was reproduced verbatim in publications later than 1935 – recipes for this highly fashionable cake were spreading quickly and undergoing modification along the way. I have provided incontrovertible evidence of their emergence out of the class of dish known as meringue cakes.

As we might expect from the diversity in the earliest large pavlova cakes, meringue cakes themselves were highly variable. Two further questions arise: how long had New Zealand cooks been making meringue cakes before they started naming them pavlovas, and where did the concept of the meringue cake develop?

A brief history of meringue cakes in New Zealand and beyond

Before the 1920s, dishes called meringue cake are not commonly found anywhere in the English-speaking culinary world, and their origins are even more obscure than those of the pavlova cake. Dishes belonging to the category of large meringue used as a cake can, however, be traced back to nineteenth-century North America and Europe.

In New Zealand recipe books of the 1920s, I have located only seven dishes that are forms of meringue cake. One is 'Festival's' 1929 pavlova. The others have a variety of names. The second, Coffee Meringue, was contributed by Miss Joseph to the revised and enlarged edition of *The Manawatu Red Cookery Book* in 1926.[23] Four egg whites were beaten stiffly, then eight ounces of granulated sugar were added together with a tablespoon of coffee essence. The mixture was beaten till firm then cooked in two buttered sandwich tins. The two layers were sandwiched together with sweetened whipped cream flavoured with coffee essence. Then there is Meringue with Fruit Filling, published about 1926 in *Home Cookery for New Zealand*, by Australian author Emily Futter.[24] Her recipe combined four egg whites and ten ounces of sugar, but contained neither vinegar nor cornflour. It was cooked as a single cake on a sheet of paper (the traditional method for small meringues), then split and filled with cut-up fruit (she suggested pineapple, strawberries or passionfruit) mixed with stiffly whipped cream flavoured with any liqueur and sweetened to taste. The fourth variation, Meringue Cake, published in 1927 in *Terrace Tested Recipes*, was submitted by Mrs McRae, probably from

MERINGUE CAKE.

Mrs. McRae.

Whites of three eggs.
Eight ounces of sifted ~~flour~~. *sugar*.
One dessertspoonful of cornflour.

Method:

Beat whites of eggs until very stiff. Add sugar and beat again. Then add cornflour. Bake in two well greased sandwich tins.

Put in fairly hot oven on low shelf and leave until fire is almost out. Put filling of whipped cream and cherries, or strawberries, between or on top and serve as two cakes.

5.5 Mrs McRae's Meringue Cake in *Terrace Tested Recipes* (1927, p. 70) was a pavlova in all but name.

Wellington.[25] It used three egg whites and eight ounces of sugar, to which one dessertspoon of cornflour was added. It was cooked in greased sandwich tins then served either as a layered cake filled with cream and cherries or strawberries, or as two cakes with the same fruit and cream combination as toppings (Fig. 5.5). Another of the same name was published in 1929 in the first edition of *The Ideal Cookery Book*, contributed by Mrs C. Cooper of Sydney.[26] This large cake required six egg whites, two cups of sugar and one teaspoon of vinegar. It was cooked in two round tins then layered with whipped cream (or ice cream) and preserved fruit, and topped with whipped cream. The sixth is Coffee Meringue Cake, also in the first edition of *The Ideal Cookery Book*, which was sent in by Miss Mary Cornford of Napier.[27] This more modest meringue was made from three egg whites, six tablespoons of caster sugar, and a tablespoon of cornflour. It was flavoured with coffee essence and cooked in two sponge sandwich tins; no suggestions were made for filling. Finally, in the same book, is Strawberry Basket Meringue, contributed by Mrs W.H. Cameron of San Francisco.[28] The meringue was formed of four egg whites and one cup of sugar, to which one teaspoon of vinegar was added. This cake was cooked in a single sponge sandwich tin and was inverted when cool, forming a basket for strawberries and whipped cream.

Notable about these meringue cakes is their variation in ingredients and proportions. Two of the three New Zealand examples have cornflour but not vinegar, which is added to the recipes from the Sydney and San Francisco. All but one were cooked in round tins. However, there was much variation in suggested fillings or toppings. These cakes clearly do not represent a single line of recipe transmission from one primary source, but the diffusion of an idea and its separate interpretation in several different centres. In other words, the meringue cake represented a fashionable concept that reached New Zealand through a variety of means: from overseas recipe contributors to local cookbooks, from food writers with external connections, and from the great range of magazines imported and avidly read by New Zealand housewives.

The three New Zealand meringue cake recipes with overseas contributors show that in the 1920s the concept was known in Australia and North America. So where did the meringue cake develop? To answer this question requires a closer look at the history of meringues. As I have shown, over the course of the nineteenth century, meringues were usually made the size of half an egg, hollowed out, filled with cream and preserved fruits, and joined together to create an individual serving. The first example of a larger meringue that I have found is Meringue with Coffee Cream in Jules Gouffé's *Royal Cookery Book*,[29] published in London in 1869 and again in 1880: this was a construction of five five-and-a-half-inch (14 cm) meringue rings assembled on a base of 'Genoise paste' and filled with coffee cream. A later version of this ring cake, with seven-inch (18 cm) rings, appeared in a New York cookbook, *The Epicurean*, with the title Vacherin Cake with Cream.[30]

The concept at this stage seems closer to a confectionery construction than to our pavlova. In 1877 Mary N.F. Henderson informed readers of her *Practical Cooking and Dinner Giving* that the famous Delmonico's in New York made their Méringues à la Crême as two half balls, six inches (15 cm) in diameter. After the exterior had been cooked to form a crust a third of an inch (<1 cm) thick, the soft centres were removed and the balls were arranged like open clam shells on a plate, filled high with cream, and decorated with strawberries or raspberries.[31]

In 1886 the recipe for Cream Méringues in *Miss Corson's Practical American Cookery* offered the choice of making the usual small meringues or shaping the six egg-white meringue 'into two large mounds', which were presumably filled with the whipped cream or yolk and liqueur-enriched Italian cream mixture recommended for the small meringues.[32] The *Los Angeles Times Cookbook No. 2* offered the same choice of teaspoonful-size meringues or larger shells that 'may be made and filled with whipped cream flavored with sugar and vanilla'.[33] In 1903 one of these cream-filled shells was given the name Kiss Torte.[34] There was no suggestion that any of these enlarged meringues were cooked on anything other than paper-covered boards or, in the case of the Los Angeles recipe, on inverted tins.

As we approach the 1920s, the recipe names suggest that the large meringue was no longer viewed as an optional larger variant of small cream meringues or kisses, but was regarded as a separate dish. About 1914, Emma Conley, author of the American book *Principles of Cooking: A Textbook in Domestic Science* gave a recipe for Torte, a five egg-white meringue that included one tablespoon of vinegar, and was cooked very slowly for at least an hour in two shallow pans lined with greased paper. This cake was served with a filling of strawberries, pineapple or peaches between the layers, and whipped cream on top.[35] A similar cake named Foam Torte was included in Florence K. Greenbaum's *The International Jewish Cook Book*, first published in New York in 1918.[36] Like the earlier torte it contained one tablespoon of vinegar, but unlike it, it was cooked as a single layer in a spring-form tin. The topping consisted of sliced bananas and peaches with cream, or strawberries. The name Foam Torte is a translation of Schaum Torte, a famous European meringue cake brought to North America by German immigrants. Both names continued in use there after World War 1.[37]

Another name for a meringue cake, recorded from a 1925 Californian cookbook, harked back to its shared ancestry in America with the little meringues known as kisses. The *Spark Lid-top Gas Stove Cook Book* from Oakland provided recipes for both Kiss Cakes (the size of small saucers) and a much larger Kiss Cake. Made from six egg whites, the latter included vinegar and cream of tartar, and was cooked in a greased pan until the centre fell. When turned out and cooled, the depression was filled with whipped cream and decorated with either cut marshmallows together with fruit and nuts, or fresh berries.[38] In concept it looks

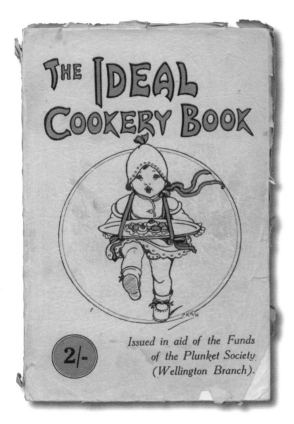

very similar to the Strawberry Basket Meringue contributed by a resident of San Francisco to Wellington's *The Ideal Cookery Book* in 1929 (Fig. 5.6). Both included vinegar and were cooked in a single tin.

American meringue cakes undoubtedly influenced those made in New Zealand in the 1920s, but we cannot rule out England as an additional source of prototypes. In early 1922 *The Times* of London published the recipe for a five-egg-white Gala Méringue in 'The Woman's View' column. It was described as 'the latest fashion in this sweet.' In method it followed the recipe for 'the usual small type meringues' cooked on a board, but instructed the cook to make 'two flat meringues about the size of a pudding or meat plate.' The filling consisted of fruit such as skinned, pipped white grapes and sliced bananas (or sliced canned apricots or peaches, or bottled maraschino cherries) stirred into whipped cream.[39] Though not identified in *The Times*, the author of this recipe was Lady Agnes Jekyll (sister-in-law of the famous garden writer Gertrude Jekyll), who later published the recipe in her collection *Kitchen Essays*.[40] Her comment about the fashionable status of the Gala Méringue may explain why meringue cake recipes are absent from middle class British cookery manuals and compendiums such as Mrs Beeton's and Cassells', for Lady Jekyll moved within high society where cooks and servants were still employed, and menus were written in French. How would such a recipe reach New Zealand?

5.6   Cover of *The Ideal Cookery Book*, published in 1929 to raise funds for the Wellington Branch of the Plunket Society.

New Zealanders not only read weekly newspapers such as *The Queen* but held subscriptions to American, British and Australian journals and magazines where the food and clothing fashions of the overseas élite were regularly reported.

Meringue cakes seem to have arisen as domestic versions of much more elaborate gâteaux and tortes that were made in professional kitchens during the nineteenth century. Home cooks found that the mixture they had been using for small meringues or kisses could be cooked as one or two larger meringues and then filled and topped with the same luxurious items as the tortes they encountered when dining out. In America by the start of the 1920s those tortes commonly had vinegar added to the meringue mixture. Cornflour was not a component of the European and North American meringue cakes, but was certainly present in two New Zealand meringue cakes in 1927 and 1929. The earliest meringue cake recorded with both vinegar and cornflour appeared in 'Aunt Daisy's Mailbag' in the *Auckland Weekly News* in December 1934.[41] Not surprisingly (given the close relationship of meringue cakes and pavlovas) both vinegar and cornflour found their way into the first generation of New Zealand pavlova cakes – at first either vinegar or the cornflour, but by 1937 some recipes called for both ingredients.

Pavlova cakes emerged from meringue cakes not, as most of us formerly supposed, by the addition of key ingredients (cornflour, vinegar) believed to have been absent from meringue cake recipes, but by a simple act of renaming. In New Zealand, meringue cakes continued to exist under their old name, side by side with pavlovas, for the next two decades, and their recipes are entirely comparable to those of pavlova cakes.

6

Pavlovas from 1935 to 1950

S O FAR, the early history of pavlovas in New Zealand has been reconstructed from the evidence of key recipes. I have described the first recorded recipes of the three main types, and outlined what we know about the people – or in the case of the Davis pavlova, the company – associated with them. I have listed the handful of meringue cake recipes circulating in New Zealand just before the practice of renaming them as pavlovas began. However, given the large number of pavlova recipes that followed these pioneers, it would be a mistake to continue this focus on particular recipes. It is too easy to pick out 'interesting' examples from the thousands of recipe books published in New Zealand, and miss the important trends in the evolution of pavlovas. We need to suspend the hunt for the first pavlova that included cornflour, or the first to be described as soft-centred, or the first to be decorated with kiwifruit – and not just because we can never be sure that the recipes we find were in fact the first. The most important reason to stop is that when we look for the earliest pavlova recipe with a particular characteristic, we have already decided, perhaps incorrectly, that having that feature is significant in the pavlova story. The only reliable way to find out which characteristics are significant is to examine a very large number of dated recipes, and then determine the trends in a more systematic fashion. Only then should we pick out the 'firsts' that are important markers of new developments.

Before I describe what happened to pavlova cakes from 1935 to 1950, I will introduce you to the exercise that occupied most of my evenings for several months in 2005: the creation of a large spreadsheet containing the details of every dated pavlova in my collection of New Zealand recipe books.

Number-crunching pavlovas

I have been collecting recipe books for over forty years. For me they combine enjoyment of food and cooking with a love of books and a professional interest (as an archaeologist) in past times. I am not a serious collector aspiring to have all editions or variants of a particular series, or all books by a particular author. In fact it matters little to me what sort of condition my cookbooks are in when I acquire them, as long as their content is legible. A photocopy will do just as well as an original. My interest lies in what these books reveal about our social history. The people who wrote and contributed to them were not consciously leaving a record of their times. Instead they were raising money for good causes, or promoting good health, new products or appliances. Unconsciously, however, they were conveying messages about the conditions and values of their times. The challenge for us is to interpret those messages correctly.

My first cookery book was a typewritten cyclostyled notebook of recipes taught in cooking classes at Macandrew Intermediate School in Dunedin in 1957. It did not include meringues of any sort. We were there to learn plain family cookery. By 1960, I had started writing out more fancy recipes in an exercise book and cutting out recipes from newspapers and magazines. Moving away from home and getting married initiated more serious cookbook collecting. I bought some international classics, influenced by the recommendations of my sister Mary who had studied Home Science at the University of Otago. But for the products of hunting and gathering which my husband and I sought out as impoverished graduate students, New Zealand-published recipe books were essential. It was in those books, often bought second-hand, that I found recipes for paua, pipis, and pavlovas. By the mid-1970s I had too many cookbooks to shelve in the kitchen, and too many to use as a working library. I started to ask questions about whether regional differences occurred within New Zealand cookery, and when we first became interested in Asian and other international cuisines. My cookbooks gradually became a reference collection, and were increasingly used for research. By the 1990s friends and family were handing on their old unwanted books in increasing numbers, and I reached the stage where I didn't know what books I had, let alone which editions. I decided to create a database, and to invest in stationery cabinets to house the more fragile cookbooks, so that they could lie flat. By 2005 there were nearly 1200 New Zealand-published books in the database, ready to use in some systematic research.

Analysis of the database revealed that only a quarter of the books in my collection have identified 'authors'.[1] The rest were the work of named compilers or editors, or of unnamed members of committees. Half of the books were published to raise funds for organisations such as churches, kindergartens, schools, and sports clubs, and in a large proportion of these (65 per cent), the recipe contributors' names are included. Writing the social history of cooking in New Zealand is made so much easier when we can identify the cooks, and where they lived. A quarter of the books could be described as commercial because they promoted products (e.g. Edmonds'), energy sources (e.g. electric stoves), retail chains (e.g. the Self Help groceries) or kitchen appliances (e.g. microwave ovens). Just under 60 per cent of the books include the date of printing. For the rest, internal clues have been relied on, such as addresses in advertisements that can be correlated with directories, to make a reasonable estimate of date of publication. But unless this could be tied down to a range of five years, I did not include their pavlova recipes in my analysis.

In the first stage of my analysis, pavlova recipes were extracted from a total of 273 sources, including thirteen newspaper and magazine issues. Even though only half the book collection consisted of fund-raising books, these made up 82 per cent of the sources supplying pavlova recipes, and though commercial promotional books made up a quarter of the collection, their contribution as pavlova sources was only 7 per cent. Similarly the educational recipe books comprised 4.3 per cent of the collection, but made up only 1.5 per cent of the pavlova sources. Teachers of cookery and home economics concentrated on family meals, leaving the fashionable items like pavlovas to the cookbooks produced out in the community. I quickly realised that the history of pavlovas in New Zealand lay predominantly within the covers, or what remained of them, of the sort of cookbook that lacks glossy illustrations, index, or any sign of professional editing. These fund-raising books were produced in their hundreds (perhaps even thousands), but are the least likely to be represented in libraries. No wonder so few studies of our culinary history have made use of them.

For the pavlova analysis, I set up a spreadsheet to record the details of the source book, magazine or newspaper, including location and date, the name of the recipe and contributor (if known), the quantities of each ingredient, the instructions for mixing and cooking, and recommendations for fillings or toppings. These were arranged in chronological order, with a cut-off date set at 1999. How did I decide which recipes to record? For inclusion a recipe had to have the word pavlova in its name, or if the recipe was called meringue cake, torte, or gateau, it had to have similar ingredients and methods to recipes named pavlova. The little pavlovas, first popularised by Rose Rutherford, had to contain coffee essence and walnuts, the ingredients which distinguished them from ordinary meringues, which continue to be made to the present day. I did not want to swamp the spreadsheet with common meringue recipes.

I began to analyse the data when the spreadsheet contained 572 recipes from 273 different sources. It has since grown to 667 recipes from over 300 sources. However, the trends were apparent as soon as I began to filter the data in search of patterns. The little pavlovas were prominent early on with their highly standardised recipe and distinctive instructions. Some rather unusual pavlova types showed up after 1950, such as the uncooked pavlova, and a 1980s cake occasionally referred to as the Snax pavlova. Another variety that stood out was the rolled pavlova that made its first appearance in 1980. The majority were, however, forms of pavlova that people identify as the 'real' pavlova: a large, crisp-shelled, soft-centred meringue, baked in an oven as a single layer and then topped with cream and fruit. Why bother to record the unusual or aberrant forms? They co-existed with 'real' pavlovas from the start, and often shared the name. Where they shared identical ingredients and method, but not the name, they sometimes represented the continuation of the recipe type from which renamed pavlovas emerged. To study the process of transformation, I needed the spreadsheet to include all recipes sharing the same recipe concept, regardless of name.

Even the 'real' pavlova was found to encompass several highly visible sub-types, one of which had six variants. Some pavlova recipes have mixing instructions that only work if an electric mixer is employed, while others include unexpected ingredients such as baking powder and cold or boiling water. One recipe type makes a large pavlova mimicking Rose Rutherford's little pavlovas with the addition of coffee and walnuts. Given such diversity, I found that great care was needed when making general statements about pavlovas, or calculating statistics for the data set as a whole, lest they created an 'average' pavlova which corresponded to no known type. Logically I had to examine the range of variation in the class of pavlovas first of all. Their variability came as a great surprise. I had been making just one recipe for the pavlova all my adult life, a very conservative three-egg-white sort, beaten with a rotary beater, with the sugar added progressively and the vinegar and cornflour folded in last. I had thought all pavlovas were made this way! In fact this recipe would not have been out of place in the 1930s.

Pavlovas of the late 1930s

My spreadsheet contains eighteen large meringues found in recipe books and columns between 1935 and 1939. Rose Rutherford's pavlovas were still common, so there was still some ambivalence about what to call these large meringue cakes. Seven were given the name Pavlova Cake or Pavlova, four had both names (including one helpfully named Pavlova Meringue), and six retained the name Meringue Cake. Though we can still detect a loose connection between concept and name as we move toward the tenth birthday of the pavlova cake, the trend towards a single layer cake was already well established – only four of the eighteen were cooked as two layers with a filling, the rest (78 per cent) having a single layer with cream and fruit on top. Pineapple and passionfruit were commonly recommended for this topping.

These post-Depression pavlovas were not small cakes, having between three and six egg whites (the average for the group was 3.5). All but one recipe included vinegar, and two-thirds recommended vanilla. Cornflour was added to just five of the eighteen cakes in amounts varying from half an ounce to four tablespoons. The cooking instructions for these pavlovas still show their close relationship to the meringue cakes of the previous decade: fourteen pavlovas were cooked in greased and lined tins, two recipes gave the option of a tin or a tray, while only one had fully embraced the modern method of cooking the pavlova on an oven tray. Apart from one recipe repeated in a later edition of the same book, the rest are like those for pre-1935 cakes – each one different in quantities and measurements. Cooks were still experimenting, and it was the concept that was spreading throughout New Zealand rather than individual recipes.

6.1 The table setting on the cover of *What's For Lunch?* (1938) suggested that it was aimed at hostesses who entertained friends at formal luncheon parties. The contributors' names read like a who's who of influential women.

To establish when or for what occasions these pavlovas and meringue cakes were served, I recorded the section of the cookbook where the recipe had been placed as I entered data on the spreadsheet. Of the thirteen recipes with such information, eleven were in the 'Cakes' section, along with the sponge cakes and fruitcakes. The other two, one called Meringue and the other Pavlova Meringue, were desserts to be served at the end of formal luncheons. The book they are found in is called *What's For Lunch?* which featured menus and recipes contributed in 1938 by well-known society hostesses raising money for the Waikouaiti Children's Health Camp Association (Fig. 6.1).[2] From this we can conclude that although pavlovas were still perceived as cakes to be brought out at afternoon tea, well-to-do women also served them as a luncheon dessert, as was being done with meringue cakes in North America.[3] This was an early indication of a shift of venue for the New Zealand pavlova – from drawing room to dining room, and from afternoon tea to dessert – which accelerated during the 1950s.

In the 1930s, however, the formal afternoon tea was an important social event, often reported in the social columns of the local newspaper. Home Science graduate Miss E. Neige Todhunter introduced *Creamoata Recipes* with the following remark: 'To plan something new, tasty, and tempting for the family table and the afternoon tea party is the aim of every efficient house-keeper'.[4] In 1939 the anonymous compiler of the '*Milkmade*' *Cook Book* remarked that

> Cake-making is probably the housewife's favourite department of the culinary art, and here milk is one of her most valuable allies. Cakes, scones, gems, biscuits, pikelets, and all the other delicacies which help to make the home happier can be varied and improved by the addition of milk.[5]

Afternoon tea parties were often very formal occasions, retaining the social rules of the Victorian period. In one of her letters written in 1998 (her ninetieth year), Noeline Thomson reminded me that it was still common for visiting cards to be presented as the guests arrived:

> Referring to NZ afternoon-teas ... my early memories of these included elegant visiting cards sometimes carried in a special card-case – copperplate style printing with 'curly' capitals. My mother had a special bowl on the hall stand where the cards were left. If the visitor was married she left 2 of her husband's cards (one paying his respects to the husband of the one being visited and one for the hostess herself) and one of the visitor's own cards for the hostess. If the hostess was unmarried there would be 2 cards, one from the visitor and one from her husband. I'm not sure what happened when unmarried ladies visited an unmarried lady but that would have been in the book of 'etiquette' on our bookshelf.[6]

Noeline went on to describe the items that were necessary for the proper afternoon tea:

> Mother had very elegant cake forks with initial T on the handle – a silver tea service, cream jug, sugar basin and silver tongs for the lump sugar, embroidered (and often lace edged) tablecloth and small serviettes, a three tiered silver cake stand (sandwiches on top layer, small cakes in centre and cream sponge or other large cake on bottom layer) and a silver hot water kettle on a silver stand which contained a little lamp (methylated spirits) to keep the water hot. She also had a silver hot water jug. I also remember an Oamaru friend in the 1930's who had a beautiful large silver tea urn (a family heirloom) which had a tap at the front bottom area. It stood on the tea wagon and it was quite a little ceremony as cups and saucers were held in turn under the tap! Another friend had a beautiful tea caddy (I think it was Japanned) which had compartments for different teas and had a lock and key; so it must have been pretty old. I have a feeling that for some reason the 3 tiered cake stand was called a 'curate'... [7]

The pavlova clearly had a lot of competition from other baked 'dainties' and especially from the sponge cake. Even during the height of the Depression, the Women's Division of the New Zealand Farmers' Union opened the second edition of their national cookbook with 'Cakes': in this section there were over thirty fruit cakes, thirteen cakes described as sponges, and thirty-three assorted cakes ranging from old favourites such as Seed Cake, Khaki Cake, Ladysmith Cake, Marble Cake and Madiera [sic] Cake to Pink Cocoanut Sandwich, Pineapple Cake, and Potato Caramel Cake. There were also six chocolate cakes from which the afternoon tea cook could make her choice.[8] What we need to remember was that during the Depression, the families of breadwinners whose salaries and wages were not reduced benefited from lower food prices. It was also still common for households to have a henhouse at the bottom of the garden, and though this cookbook offers recipes for an eggless gingerbread, a walnut and date cake without eggs, and three eggless fruit cakes, most of the cake recipes called for two to four eggs. The fruit cakes were generally very much larger and used from four to twelve eggs. The only pavlovas that appear in this book were Rose Rutherford's little meringues. It is probably safe to say that throughout the 1930s, both the little pavlovas and the large pavlova cakes jostled for space at the afternoon tea table.

New Zealand had five years of economic recovery from 1935; however, the last three years of the decade were marred by fears of war. During the 1930s the households of professional men and successful business owners had invested in refrigerators (Fig 6.2) and the latest electric stoves (Fig. 6.3). Some probably obtained electric food mixers from the United States, but electrical appliances were unevenly distributed and, by the outbreak of war, there were still many households where an electric 'rangette' or 'stovette' supplemented rather than replaced the coal range (Fig. 6.4).

6.2 The fund-raising *What's For Lunch?* (1938) included an advertisement for a New Zealand-made Frigidaire refrigerator (p. 36).

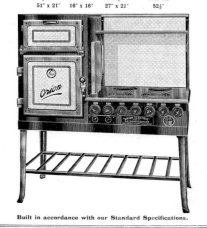

6.3 The 'Orion' Electric Range No. 75, manufactured in Dunedin by H.E. Shacklock, was the most expensive model in their 1929 catalogue, and included separate roasting and warming ovens.

6.4 This 1929 advertisement for a 'Stovette' was aimed at cooks without suitable wiring for a full-size electric stove (reproduced from *The Ideal Cookery Book*, p. 146).

In other households, the coal range had been replaced by a combination gas stove and 'destructor' which had a 'wet-back' designed to heat water in the hot water cylinder. Families who had not invested in new electrical appliances by 1940 faced nearly a decade of delay before they were once more available. The pavlova recipes from the late 1930s give little clue as to the type of stove they were cooked in, stipulating slow or very slow heat in all but four of the eighteen recipes. These four refer to a temperature (250 or 300 degrees Fahrenheit), which means that the stoves of the contributors had oven thermometers fitted to the doors. A few imported electric stoves had early forms of thermostat by the late 1920s, but locally made models did not.

The near extinction of the pavlova cake in the 1940s

Three ingredients could be described as essential to the composition and decoration of pavlova cakes: egg whites, sugar, and cream. Most people know that eggs and sugar were rationed during World War 2, but few are aware that rationing lasted several years after 1945, or that cream was officially unobtainable without a medical certificate. For the period 1940 to 1949, I entered only fourteen recipes into my spreadsheet: six were called Meringue Cake, seven Pavlova Cake, and one Pavlova. Considering the restrictions on the key ingredients, I was surprised to find any eligible recipes at all. I decided that I should take a closer look at the dates of publication, and the timing of the regulations that put rationing into place.

Four of the recipes were published in 1940 and 1941, before rationing began. One 1941 pavlova recipe from Auckland even called for six egg whites.[9] Seven recipes are post-war in date and some of them may reflect the progressive lifting of controls from 1948. Another three, all found in 1944 editions of books that first appeared before the war, can be described as survivals originating in peacetime conditions. In fact there is only one pavlova recipe from the period 1942 to 1948 that shows awareness of rationing. It was published in the *New Zealand 'Truth'* in 1947, in response to a reader's request. Made as two layers, it called for whipped mock cream as both filling and topping, and was decorated with raisins, crystallised cherries and blanched almonds.[10] The trouble with the pavlova is that it flaunts its ingredients – everyone knew that the meringue could not be produced without sugar or eggs, and a topping of real cream could hardly be passed off as mock cream. Other dishes could more readily conceal ingredients that had been acquired without coupons from the ration book.

There were several competing recipes for mock cream, some pre-dating the war. One published in 1940 instructed the cook to fold a whipped egg white into creamed butter and icing sugar.[11] Once egg rationing began, this recipe simply replaced one rationed product with another. Later, a mock cream recommended for use as the filling of a layer cake was made from milk thickened with cornflour, cooled, and then beaten into a creamed butter and sugar mixture. A variant on this method replaced the milk with condensed milk and water, and the cornflour with custard powder. Gelatine was added for extra body.[12] But the trouble with these two recipes was that they also called for ingredients that were rationed, such as butter and sugar.

Ration books were issued by post offices from the second week of April 1942. On 20 April people were told to register with their usual grocer in order to receive their sugar ration of twelve ounces per person per week. Sugar rationing started on Monday 27 April.[13] For those unfamiliar with imperial measures, twelve ounces is 340 g, which amounts to just over one and a half cups of granulated sugar. Per day each person was allocated just under fifty grams. If you took sugar in your tea there would be little left over to sprinkle on your porridge, let alone sweeten the stewed rhubarb. If a hostess served a pavlova cake for afternoon tea, her guests might suspect that the sugar had been obtained (unpatriotically) on the black market. There were minor fluctuations in the amount of sugar per head, with a low point of only ten ounces a week between 19 March and 30 September 1945. Special issues of three pounds of sugar at a time were provided for seasonal jam and marmalade making. Six such issues were made in 1942 and 1948, nine in 1945, 1946, and 1947, and twelve in 1943 and 1944.[14] What we don't know is how many cooks redirected their jam sugar allowance into their baking. Finally, on 27 August 1948, domestic sugar rationing ceased.[15]

The rationing of eggs was an even greater obstacle for pavlova makers than that of sugar. Shortages hit several urban centres from the middle of 1941, with Wellington and Auckland particularly affected. It was recognised that young children, pregnant women, and nursing mothers should have first claim on the scarce eggs, so a system of priority rationing was set up with the Plunket Society distributing the chits. Three eggs per week was considered the minimum requirement for children up to the age of five, and six for expectant and breast-feeding mothers. As the war dragged on, the government took control of the allocation of the remaining eggs, and by 20 March 1944 comprehensive egg rationing was extended over the whole country.[16] My mother found the shortage in Wellington particularly hard, for it involved queuing for the eggs to which she was entitled for her young children. She told me that on one occasion a woman pushing her way to the front of the queue lost her balance and fell into the basket containing the priority egg rations. There was a horrified silence, and such was their disappointment that not one of the onlookers was prepared to help her out! By 7 June 1950, egg production had picked up sufficiently for the government to leave any necessary sharing out to the retailers, at which point housewives in some parts of New Zealand had endured nine long years of cutting back on the eggs in their baking. Though many cookbooks offered eggless cake and pudding recipes, needless to say there could be no eggless pavlovas.

As for cream, the necessity for making as much butter as possible, to export to Britain, meant that after 28 October 1943, not only was butter was rationed to eight ounces (240 g) per person per week, but cream could not be sold for domestic or manufacturing purposes except to those with special permits. The permits required a doctor's certificate, and to qualify one needed to be diabetic, or have active tuberculosis, or be an underweight nursing mother, very aged or convalescing from a long illness. Backblocks farmers without access to dairy factories were supposed to turn all their cream into butter on the farm and cut coupons from those employees to whom they supplied it.[17]

Even during the war, there was considerable resistance to the cream and butter regulations. Miss Muriel May, the Principal of Southland Girls' High School from 1943 to 1955, described her brush with the authorities over the cream sponge served at a formal afternoon tea that followed the laying of a foundation stone:

> It was wartime and there were rationing restrictions, but a party is a party is a party, and so I told the country girls that any spare top milk would be acceptable. They responded generously and there was no doubt of the official enjoyment of afternoon tea. One guest hoed in (the expression is vulgar, but it fits) to cream sponge with particular avidity and with something sinister in his eyes.[18]

Top milk, the yellow, creamy milk that rose to the top of the billy or bottle, was also a euphemism for cream during the rationing period. Her pupils knew that Miss May wanted thick whipping cream. A few days later, the glutton returned in his official capacity to accuse Miss May of flouting the law. She pointed out 'the poor opinion National Party farmers had of coupons and food regulations' and reminded him of the 'sacred laws of hospitality,' but he left, angrily promising further action, which fortunately didn't eventuate.[19]

Other historical accounts speak of relatively free use of cream in other South Island communities during the period of regulation. As a locum minister at Kurow in 1945, Lloyd Geering frequently attended functions at the Memorial Hall to farewell departing soldiers. The occasion would close with a grand supper. He wrote:

> During my tenure in Kurow I must have consumed more cream-cake and pavlova than at any other period of life – and this at a time when cream was officially unavailable because of the war effort.[20]

Immediately after the war, Charles Brasch returned to New Zealand from Britain and had his first taste of pavlova at his aunt's home in North Canterbury:

> At Kate's in Amberley they seemed to live on eggs, butter and cream – I could hardly believe my eyes and palate; and I encountered for the first time that luxurious national dish the pavlova, a kind of quiche, a pasty meringue with fruit and whipped cream.[21]

It seems that by 1945 many New Zealand cooks were tired of rationing, especially when they were producing the butter, eggs, and cream from their own animals.

Officially the cream regulations were suspended on 22 February 1950, while butter rationing ceased on 4 June 1950.[22] However, the free booklet issued in December 1948 to customers of Grocers' United Stores, a South Island chain of independently owned shops, not only recommends whipped cream for topping a strawberry cake, and filling cream lilies, but includes a recipe for a four-egg-white pavlova cake with the cream 'piled high on top in a swirl' (Fig. 6.5).[23] Just how widespread was this open rejection of the regulations? Some contributors to *New*

Zealand 'Truth' recipe pages in 1947 and 1948 offered a choice of serving a dessert with 'custard or whipped cream',[24] or 'cream (if available)',[25] or with 'top milk'.[26] Other readers, like Mrs I.B. of Putaruru, had no qualms submitting a trifle de luxe recipe with the instruction 'pile with whipped cream'.[27] By 1947, it seems that no stigma was attached to the use of cream if you could get it.

I suspect that few pavlovas were made in the cities in 1942–5, and that even during the post-war rationing years, pavlovas were probably much more common in country towns than in urban centres. Of the few recipes that were published – and we should remember that paper too was in short supply at this time – there was little change from the pavlovas of the 1930s era. My statistics show a small increase in the number using cornflour (35 per cent), the average number of eggs was still the same (3.5), and most were still cooked in tins. The same proportion of the recipes were for single-layered cakes (79 per cent). The toppings included pineapple, passionfruit, and strawberries. Kiwifruit were also recommended, under their original name, Chinese gooseberries.[28] Cooking instructions reveal no marked advance in technology. One recipe provided a cooking temperature and another stipulated an electric oven. However, one recipe thought to be from the late 1940s departed from the progressive mixing required when making a pavlova by hand. Instead it instructed the cook to place five egg whites in a bowl with ten tablespoons of sugar and a teaspoon of vinegar, and beat the mixture stiffly. I think that this recipe was probably prepared with an electric mixer, the first of many in the post-war period. Most recipe books still classified them as cakes, but the one with the kiwifruit topping appeared as a 'cold sweet' and the option was given of cooking it in a tin or on an oven tray. It was a sign of pavlovas to come.

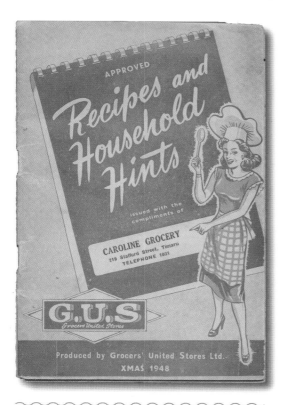

6.5 Approved Recipes and Household Hints was issued as a Christmas gift in 1948 to customers of the Grocers' United Stores Ltd, in the South Island.

7

Pavlovas come of age, 1950–59

THE YEAR 1950 marked the start of a new and much more prosperous half-century for New Zealanders. Rationing finally came to end, though egg prices rose steeply until 1957.[1] New appliances such as Neeco electric ranges and Kenwood foodmixers were in the shops. Pressure cookers were at the height of popularity, being both new and economical and therefore doubly justifiable. The first of the 'baby-boomers' started school. Afternoon teas were still held, but other more modern ways of entertaining were on the horizon. A few large pavlova cakes had already made their appearance as formal luncheon desserts in the 1940s, and during the 1950s were more frequently served as a dessert. Of the pavlova recipes I found in 1950s cookbooks, 20 per cent were placed in the pudding or cold sweet section, compared to 8 per cent in the 1930s.

Twenty-one years had passed since the first renaming of the meringue cake as a pavlova in 1929. Over those formative years there were nearly as many recipes as there were cookbooks. In my spreadsheet there are sixty-six large pavlova or meringue cake recipes from 1926 to 1949. Of these, four recipes can be paired with one other, each published one or two years later, and one recipe reappeared three times in 1934. Only two recipes became popular enough to show up four times over that period: one is a four-egg pavlova, into which one cup of caster sugar is beaten, followed by a teaspoon of vinegar – it was printed around 1935, then again in 1939, 1946 and 1948; the second recipe appeared under various names from 1929 to 1941, and contained six egg whites, two cups of sugar and one teaspoon of vinegar. These nineteen matches can be contrasted with forty-seven unique recipes. Although the matched recipes are evidence that some recipes were popular enough to be passed on unchanged, this cannot yet be called standardisation. But that was about to happen.

In the 1950s several recipes were published that have been faithfully reproduced in cookbooks (with only minor variations) for most of the second half of the twentieth century. They have become standard recipes that cooks are comfortable with, rely on, and see no reason to change. Was this process of standardisation happening simply because there were more cookbooks (and pavlovas) after 1950, or was there some other reason? With the pavlova becoming recognised as a national dish during the 1950s, was a new generation of cooks wanting a tried and true recipe for making it, in accordance with its growing status? To answer these questions I turned back to my early recollections of the 1950s, as one of those baby-boomers. Was I conscious of the significance of the pavlova? Was it taught at my school cooking classes?

I have a diary from 1956 in which I recorded the very first cake I ever made, a chocolate raisin cake. It was on a Friday in late September and I was home from school with a bad cold. That year I was in Form I at Macandrew Intermediate School in Dunedin. For all girls in New Zealand state schools, Form I (also known as Standard 5 and now Year 7) marked the first year of formal cookery lessons. I looked forward to one and a half hours of cooking every Tuesday morning at our purpose-built Manual Training Centre. Most Tuesdays I recorded in my diary the items we made. We started the year with stuffed tomatoes, custard mould, stewed apple, mince, chocolate raspberry steamed pudding, and crumbed sausages and chips. Then we moved on to hokey pokey biscuits, lemon buns, baked potatoes, apple charlotte, scones, cheese and bacon savories, cottage pie, apple dumplings, mince pies, and fruit jelly. After the August holidays our dishes became sweeter and sweeter. Straight after sausage rolls, we moved on to Oatina drop biscuits, coconut biscuits, Shrewsbury biscuits, Swiss jelly, hedgehogs, queen pudding, sponge cake, jam drops, queen cakes, kiwi crisps, and finished the year with butterscotch. No pavlova recipe was taught that year, nor does the recipe appear in my Form II recipe book which I saved from 1957. In fact the only home economics recipe book I have that includes a pavlova recipe was published much later, in 1976.[2]

This does not mean that schools disapproved of pavlovas. During the 1950s, at least four school parents' and old girls' associations issued highly successful fund-raising cookbooks containing multiple pavlova recipes: in 1956, the cookbook from St Mary's School in Stratford provided recipes for six different pavlovas, Taieri High School had two in its 1958 book, and Queen Margaret College had three, and South Otago High School four recipes in their cookbooks, both issued in 1959.[3] Pavlovas were highly popular and recipe book compilers found it easier to include all the contributed versions than to decide whose recipes should be excluded. Perhaps pavlovas were considered too extravagant to be added to our school's plain family cookery curriculum. As well, they take a long time to cook and our cookery classes only lasted one and a half hours, raising timetabling difficulties for the teachers. However, pavlovas were on the menu at home, and in my friend's homes, on special occasions. I can recall arguing with my sisters as to who would lick the cream bowl, and who the beaters.

Standardised pavlovas of the 1950s

During the 1950s the first standardised pavlova recipes emerged, though it took a decade or more of repetition for some of these recipes to be recognizable as standard forms. Even today most cooks are unaware that standard recipes exist, and blithely make the recipe that has been successful for them in the past. The standardised forms of the 1950s introduced some new methods and ingredients which distinguished them from the pre-war pavlovas – like adding cold or boiling water to the whites, or beating the mixture over hot water, or, most drastically, not cooking the pavlova at all. One standardised recipe originated just before World War 2 – the Edmonds' pavlova (Fig. 7.1) – but its repetition in fund-raising cookbooks is not obvious until the mid-1950s.

PAVLOVA

3 Egg Whites
9 oz. Castor Sugar
Pinch of Salt

1 teaspoon Essence of Vanilla
1 teaspoon Vinegar

Beat egg whites until quite stiff, fold in sugar, add vanilla and vinegar. Place on greased paper on greased tray and bake very slowly about 1 to 1½ hours. (Very slow oven, 250° F.). Pile whipped cream and chopped fruit on top and decorate with **Edmonds Jelly** (chopped).

7.1   This pavlova recipe in the seventh edition of *Edmonds 'Sure to Rise' Cookery Book* (p. 25), published in 1939, was their first for the large pavlova cake. The sixth edition provided only the recipe for Rose Rutherford's little pavlovas and a meringue cake.

The first Edmonds' pavlova recipe 1939–78

Edmonds' series of recipe books began with a modest booklet advertising the company's products in 1908 and became New Zealand's best-selling book of the twentieth century. Despite its popularity, it was slower to include a pavlova recipe in the 1930s than the majority of fund-raising cookbooks. There were no pavlovas at all in the first five editions. Then, in the sixth edition of 1936, we find Rose Rutherford's little pavlovas and a recipe for a meringue cake.[4] Edmonds' first large pavlova was printed in the seventh edition from about 1939, replacing the meringue cake; the same recipe was repeated until 1978.[5] This three-egg-white pavlova with nine ounces of caster sugar and one teaspoon of vinegar was copied and contributed to three school recipe books, a church and an arts centre cookbook from 1956 to 1974, so to a limited extent it can be considered a standard. It disappeared from circulation when Edmonds replaced it with an already widely made three-egg-white pavlova which contained vinegar, cornflour, and water (see the 'three-plus-three' pavlovas described below).[6] First printed in the 1978

How to make Edmonds' First Large Pavlova *(c. 1939)*

Serves 6–8

This colourful pavlova is a popular choice for a children's party or Christmas celebration. For the topping, glacé cherries are combined with cubes of raspberry and lime jelly. Alternatively, for a tangier balance to the sweetness of the pavlova and jelly, choose fresh fruit (for example, strawberries or blackberries). The mixing method is ideal for hand beating with a rotary beater. (If you plan to use an electric mixer, see Hint 5, p. 146.)

- **2 half packets of jelly crystals (choose flavours and colours to complement chosen fresh fruit)**
- **3 egg whites**
- **pinch salt**
- **250 g caster sugar**
- **1 teaspoon vanilla**
- **1 teaspoon malt vinegar**

Topping

- **200 ml cream**
- **fresh fruit (e.g. strawberries)**

Make the jellies according to their packet instructions but using only half of the crystals and a third of the recommended quantity of boiling water. Pour into shallow containers and allow to set until very firm in a fridge.

Cover a tray with non-stick baking paper and draw a circle 20 cm in diameter in the middle. Preheat oven to 120°C with a rack in the centre position.

Beat the egg whites until very stiff (12–15 minutes). Using a spatula, gradually fold in the sugar and lastly the vanilla and vinegar. Spoon the mixture into the circle on the baking paper and carefully spread to just fill the outline.

Bake for 1½ hours. Remove to a wire rack and when cool invert and carefully lift off the paper. Store in an airtight container until required.

Beat the cream until stiff and spread on the pavlova. Cut the firm jelly into small cubes and arrange on the top. Add chosen fresh fruit, cut into similar sizes to the jelly cubes.

centennial edition, this pavlova was briefly replaced in the 'new revised edition' of 1992 by a four-egg-white pavlova, containing vinegar and cornflour, but no water.[7] Some later editions returned to the 1978 recipe. Surprisingly, it was the 1992 four-egg-white version that Edmonds published in their recent collection of New Zealand classics, instead of the 1939 recipe with a pedigree of nearly forty years.[8]

The one-egg pavlova, from about 1952

The one-egg pavlova was surely a product of post-war egg-rationing, for not only does it cut down on eggs, but it bulks up the single white by the addition of water. Not one pavlova recipe prior to the 1950s made do with a single egg. In fact, most used three or four. The earliest one-egg pavlova that I have found is Mrs P.L. Kime's one-egg Pavlova and Cream, contributed to the Springs-Ellesmere Plunket Society's *Recommended Cooking* around 1952 (Fig 7.2).[9]

7.2 *Recommended Cooking* was a fund-raising project of the Springs-Ellesmere Branch of the Plunket Society about 1952.

Mrs Kime's recipe adapts a technique of meringue mixing that had been used commercially from the early twentieth century: standing the mixing bowl over hot or boiling water. This was described in the recipe for *Rochers à l'Italienne* [Italian Rocks] in a professional manual published in London in 1908[10] and was also the method that the American domestic scientist Ida C. Bailey Allen used for her French Meringue in 1924.[11] The instructions given by the widely read English writer Elizabeth Craig in her recipe for American Meringues may also have influenced Mrs Kime. In Craig's recipe the whites and sugar were beaten in the top half of a double boiler while water in the lower half was brought to simmering point.[12] It is possible that Mrs Kime, who also contributed German Cream Biscuits to *Recommended Cooking*, had picked up this tip from one of these overseas sources. However, closer at hand was a New Zealand book that described the method in 1947: *A Practical Recipe Book for Bakers, Pastrycooks and Caterers*, written by British-trained baker George Woolley. In his instructions for Meringue Rocks, we see a modified *Rochers à l'Italienne*.[13] All the ingredients are assembled in the mixing bowl, which is then placed over a saucepan of boiling water, but not in contact with the water. The mixture is beaten until it is comfortably warm to touch then transferred to a commercial mixer where it is beaten at medium speed till smooth and shiny. Many New Zealand bakers and cake kitchens would have had Woolley's comprehensive manual on hand.

Mrs Kime also added two tablespoons of *boiling* water to the egg white and sugar (Fig. 7.3). This increased the volume, but why didn't she just use cold water? So far, I have not found direct precedents for this in overseas' cookbooks. Water was of course used in the Italian meringue, as taught to chefs, but in this commercial method it was a component of the sugar syrup that was heated to soft-ball stage before being poured into the beaten whites. *Cold* water was, however, recommended as an egg-white extender in the 1940s. In 1947 another of Elizabeth Craig's books, *1000 Household Hints*, stated that to 'eke out egg white, add 3 or 4 teaspoons of cold water to it, very gradually, while beating'.[14] As we will see, this practice was incorporated into two other standardised pavlovas that emerged in the 1950s, but the boiling water in Mrs Kime's recipe was more than just an egg-white extender. It dissolved the sugar before beating commenced.

PAVLOVA AND CREAM (Mrs P. L. Kime)

1 egg white	1 teacup sugar
2 tablespoons boiling water	pinch salt

Stand basin in boiling water and beat till stiff. Wet greaseproof paper and pile mixture on it. Cool oven.

7.3 The earliest known recipe for a one-egg pavlova, contributed by Mrs Kime to *Recommended Cooking*, was modified from a popular and economical recipe for making meringues, circulating in the late 1940s.

A search through New Zealand recipe books published just prior to 1952 has provided a clue to the origin of Mrs Kime's recipe. Two fund-raising cookbooks published in Wellington in 1950 each contain a meringue recipe in which two tablespoons of boiling water are added to a single egg white and a cup of sugar, the mixture beaten over hot water, and vinegar and a little baking powder folded in at the end. One of these recipes, contributed by Beverley Keys, was named Infallible Meringues; the other, by Mrs A.D. Grocott, was simply Meringues.[15] A similar recipe from a 1952 book was accompanied by this comment from the contributor, Mrs Lukeman: 'Worth the extra beating for the number [of meringues] and firmness of texture'.[16] Mrs Lukeman's recipe for meringues was identical to Mrs Kime's recipe for pavlova, except in name. Other contributors offered the recipe as an all-purpose meringue. In the Hora Hora Kindergarten's recipe book published about 1955, Mrs D.M. Bevington's recipe is called Meringues (or Pavlova), and in the Maungaturoto branch of the Women's Division of Federated Farmers' 1960 recipe book, Vera Cullen's recipe title is One Egg Pavlova or Meringues.[17] We can now see that Mrs Kime was one of probably many New Zealand women who tried the one-egg meringue recipe and liked the result. So far as I can tell from my cookbook collection, she was the first to convert the recipe into a pavlova. However, I still don't know the original source of the idea of adding boiling water to dissolve the sugar. It appeared suddenly in Wellington and within the space of just five years was known from Northland to Otago. No international precedent has yet been found.

Fifteen one-egg pavlovas have been recorded in New Zealand recipe books, and two have been noted in a single Australian book.[18] Of the New Zealand examples, five were published in the 1950s, four in the 1960s, and six in the 1980s. Ten contain baking powder and one cream of tartar. As a product of wartime egg shortages and post-war price rises, it is perhaps surprising that the one-egg pavlova lasted nearly three decades. However, the recipe was obviously successful as well as economical, and it is likely that the use of hot or boiling water in the recipe, and sometimes under the mixing bowl as well, would have contributed to the stability and lasting quality of the meringue.

In 1951 two other standard pavlova recipes containing water made their first appearance side by side in the Roslyn Presbyterian Church's fiftieth anniversary *Jubilee Cookbook* from Dunedin (Fig. 7.4). One was a three-egg-white pavlova, with three tablespoons of cold water added to the whites before beating; the other was a four-egg-white

Roslyn Presbyterian Church

JUBILEE COOKERY BOOK

SECOND EDITION

Proceeds in aid of Furnishings for
Jubilee Building

7.4 The Roslyn Presbyterian Church's fiftieth anniversary *Jubilee Cookbook*, published in Dunedin in 1951, proved so popular that a revised edition was issued in 1952.

pavlova with one tablespoon of water added at the end of the mixing.[19] For the sake of convenience, I have called the first type the 'three-plus-three' for the number of whites and tablespoons of water, and the second the 'four-plus-four' because it has a distinctive instruction for adding the sugar, in two lots of four ounces (Fig. 7.5).

PAVLOVA CAKE   *Mrs. Knight*
    3 Egg whites, 3 tablespoons cold water, beaten together, add 3 teaspoons cornflour and 1½ cups sugar, beat again, add 1 teaspoon vanilla and 1 teaspoon vinegar, place on greased plate lined with wet greaseproof paper. Oven at 350 degrees and turned off.

PAVLOVA CAKE (2)   *Miss E. Patterson*
    Whip 4 egg whites with a pinch of cream of tartar until stiff. Add 4 ozs. castor sugar gradually, and then add another 4 ozs. Add 1 teaspoon of vanila essence, 2 teaspoons vinegar, 1 dessertspoon of cornflour, and 1 tablespoon water. Put on greased wet paper and bake 1½ to 2 hours. No. 3. (Will serve 8 or 10 people.)

7.5 The Roslyn Presbyterian Church's fiftieth anniversary *Jubilee Cookbook* (1951) contained two pavlova recipes that went on to become standards.

The three-plus-three pavlova, from 1951

Of all the standardised pavlovas, the three-plus-three is the best represented, with forty-six examples in the spreadsheet, ranging in time from 1951 to the present day. The recipe did not remain precisely the same over the five decades, but branched into four main versions. What they have in common are three egg whites, three tablespoons of cold water, and one teaspoon of vinegar (in all but one recipe). All display what can be described as progressive mixing, with the whites whipped first, sometimes with the water, and the sugar added gradually. The remaining ingredients are folded in at the end. The recipes sometimes mention the use of an electric beater, but the three-plus-three can be made by hand just as well. Where the versions show systematic variability is in the quantities of sugar and cornflour.

The earliest version in the Roslyn Jubilee Cookery Book had one and a half cups of sugar and three teaspoons of cornflour; seven examples occur in South Island recipe books from 1951 to 1993. Apart from one called Pavlova Supreme, and another Never Fail Pavlova, the rest were called Pavlova Cake or simply Pavlova. In 1961 a version with one and a quarter cups of sugar and three teaspoons of cornflour was published in the nationally distributed GHB Cookery Book, compiled by Mrs S.D. Sherriff, who had gained qualifications from both the Home Science

How to make a Three-plus-Three Pavlova (1951–)

Serves 6 generously

Mary made this version of the three-plus-three pavlova as a contribution towards a shared lunch at a Rural Women's Branch meeting. Several members still use this reliable recipe to produce the classic structured pavlova – a crisp, but often fragile, outer shell with the softest and smoothest marshmallow centre. The general consensus on the fragile shell was that any breaks were easy to cover with whipped cream. The use of a pan with a loose base will make it easier to remove the pavlova. Transfer complete with its metal base and circle of baking paper to a serving platter. Use a spatula to slip cut slices onto individual plates, leaving the baking paper behind.

- **3 egg whites**
- **3 tablespoons cold water**
- **1¼ cups caster sugar**
- **1 tablespoon cornflour**
- **½ teaspoon vanilla**
- **1 teaspoon malt vinegar**

Topping

- **200 ml cream, beaten until stiff**
- **fresh fruit (make a selection from the following – kiwifruit, peeled and cut into wedges or slices; passion fruit pulp; sliced bananas dipped in lemon juice; pineapple cubes)**

Line base and sides of a 20 cm diameter cake pan with non-stick baking paper (see Hint 7, p. 146). Preheat oven to 180°C.

Beat the egg whites until stiff, add the water and beat a further minute. Gradually add the sugar, a quarter cup at a time, beating well between additions until the mixture is glossy and very stiff. Lastly beat in the cornflour, vanilla, and vinegar. Pile the mixture into the pan and spread evenly.

Bake for 15 minutes at 180°C, then switch oven off and leave pavlova to cook for a further hour. Cool on a rack for few minutes. Invert onto a flat plate and remove the paper. Allow to cool completely before filling. Spread with cream and top with a selection of fruit. Serve immediately, or store in a covered container in the fridge for up to 24 hours.

School at the University of Otago and the City and Guilds of London before she became an active member of the Women's Division of Federated Farmers in Central Otago. Her recipe was called Pavlova (Soft Centre)[20] and it reappeared in fund-raising books under that name in 1966, 1972 and 1981; other names were Pavlova (1971, 1981, 1995), 3 Egg Pavlova (1982), and Never Fail Pavlova (twice in 1983). A chocolate variant of the recipe developed by Mrs J.E. Landsborough of Wanaka was published by television chef Des Britten,[21] and it subsequently found its way into fund-raising books in 1984 and 1997. Given the wide distribution of both Mrs Sherriff's and Des Britten's books, it is not surprising that this version became the most popular of the three-egg-white pavlovas, with examples recorded from both North and South Island community cookbooks.

In contrast, the version with one and a half cups of sugar and only one teaspoon of cornflour was localised to Otago and Southland.[22] Only six examples have been recorded in my spreadsheet, four named Pavlova (1966–83), one Simple Pavlova (1981), and the latest is Winkys Pavlova (1992). Apart from Winkys, which appeared in the *Otago Daily Times*,[23] the rest were published in fund-raising books. The fourth version has the least amount of sugar – just one cup – but retains the original three teaspoons of cornflour. My first recorded example is from a 1967 fund-raising book published in Gore.[24] Its next appearance, in the *New Zealand Woman's Weekly Cookbook* edited by Tui Flower, ensured its subsequent popularity.[25] Apart from eight examples found in community cookbooks dated between 1975 and 1990, this sugar-reduced version was published in the centennial edition of *Edmonds Cookery Book*, and by Tony Simpson in his historical study *An Innocent Delight*.[26] It was called Never Fail Pavlova in a 1981 cookbook and was embellished as a Cinnamon Chocolate Pavlova in 1990.[27] Otherwise it is simply Pavlova, and along with Mrs Sherriff's version became one of the most familiar three-egg-white pavlovas known in New Zealand.

The four-plus-four pavlova, from 1951

Making its earliest appearance in 1951, in the Roslyn Presbyterian Church of Dunedin's *Jubilee Cookery Book*, the four-plus-four pavlova at first had the nondescript names Pavlova Cake (1951–83) and Pavlova (1966–85), but went on to more memorable titles, such as Pavlova Soft Centre (1963, 1986), Perfect Pavlova (from 1974), Pavlova with Marshmallow Centre (1975, 1983), Timeless Pavlova (1981), and Never Fail Pavlova (from 1984). With four egg whites, it was not as economical as the one-egg pavlova, but with the help of a tablespoon of cold water, two teaspoons of vinegar, one dessertspoon of cornflour and a pinch of cream of tartar, it produced a cake that its first contributor, Miss E. Patterson, insisted 'Will serve 8 or 10 people'.[28] Besides this standard type, of which nineteen examples have been recorded so far, three otherwise similar recipes use only a dessertspoon of water and two reduce the quantity of water to one teaspoon. The four-plus-four method was also applied to a further five pavlovas made with four egg whites but which did not include water.

The distinctive instruction from which the four-plus-four pavlova gets its name applied to the process of mixing the eight ounces of caster or ordinary sugar into the whites. After the whites and cream of tartar were whipped till stiff, the first four ounces of sugar were *beaten* in gradually, with the remaining four ounces then *folded* in, followed by the vinegar, vanilla, cornflour, and water. The instructions are based on the progressive mixing of the pre-war pavlovas, but in stopping the hard beating before all the sugar has been added, they recognise that if the beating was thorough, the mixture would be very stiff by the time half the sugar had been added. Folding in the rest made it much easier on the arm. There is no indication in the instructions for this pavlova that an electric mixer was to be used.

With very little variation, the original four-plus-four recipe continued to appear in fund-raising books from Invercargill to Stratford (Taranaki) until 1983. Of its six recorded occurrences, the one that might have cemented its popularity, in the 1965 edition of the nationally distributed *Cookery Book* of the Women's Division of Federated Farmers of New Zealand, was its second to last appearance.[29]

In 1961 a version of the four-plus-four recipe was published in *S. Hilda's Recipe Book*, Dunedin, with a slight change in proportions, the two teaspoons of vinegar reduced to one. As well, a warning appeared in the instructions: 'Oven door must NOT be opened during baking'.[30] It was this version (with its threat of calamity) that went on to achieve greater popularity and grander titles than the original. The warning reappeared about 1967 in a fund-raising book from Gore, and in another originating from Hamilton about 1974.[31] These two recipes, however, contained a further innovation concerning the cooking instructions. Whereas the earlier recipes for this version suggested a wide range of temperatures for the one-and-a-half to two-hour cooking time, the newer version specified preheating the oven to 400 degrees F, then turning the oven off completely when the pavlova was placed inside. Eleven recipes have been recorded with this instruction from 1967 to 1998. In the 1980s this recipe acquired yet another distinctive instruction: the second measure of sugar was to be folded in with the blade of a knife. Five examples exist: from Wanganui (1983 and 1987), Christchurch (1984 and 1985), and East Otago (1998).[32]

Another offshoot of the original four-plus-four recipe replaced the tablespoon of water with a dessertspoon of water. First recorded from Masterton in 1963 in the Solway Old Girls' Association's *Silver and Green Jubilee Cookery Book*, it reappeared in the recipe book of Martinborough's First Church Women's Fellowship in 1972 and then in the Puketapu (Hawke's Bay) Women's Fellowship *Good Harvest Cook Book*.[33] In twenty-three years it seems not to have travelled beyond the Wairarapa–Hawke's Bay region.

How to make a Four-plus-Four Pavlova *(1951–)*

Serves 8–10

The classic large pavlova! This recipe has been popular for over half a century because it can be made by hand or with an electric mixer, and delivers excellent volume for the number of egg whites. Mary cooked this pavlova in a rectangular pan as the shape is easier to cut for a crowd than the more traditional circular form.

- **4 egg whites**
- **¹/₈ teaspoon cream of tartar**
- **230 g caster sugar, divided into 2 portions**
- **2 teaspoons cornflour**
- **1 teaspoon vanilla**
- **2 teaspoons malt vinegar**
- **1 tablespoon cold water**

Topping

- **300 ml cream**
- **selection of seasonal fresh fruit (or see page 113 for information on the traditional toppings)**

Line the base of a rectangular or square cake pan (18 x 28cm or 23 cm square, approximately). Spray the sides with non-stick cooking oil (see Hint 7, p. 146). Preheat the oven to 150°C and position a rack in the centre.

Beat the egg whites and cream of tartar until stiff. Gradually beat in the first portion of caster sugar (8–10 minutes with an electric beater or longer by hand). Fold in the second measure of caster sugar and the remaining ingredients, thoroughly but gently. Spoon into the prepared pan and spread evenly right out to the sides. Bake for 1½ hours. Remove from the oven and use a knife to cut round the sides to loosen from the pan. Turn out on to a rack and peel off the paper. Invert onto a flat serving plate.

Whip the cream until stiff. Spread evenly over the pavlova. Decorate with fresh fruit. Store in a fridge until serving time (up to 24 hours).

Overall, thirty-one examples of the four-plus-four pavlova have been recorded, spanning the period from 1951 to 1998 and geographically most of New Zealand. With just two exceptions, it shows up in highly localised community cookbooks, and I have found no evidence that it reached them via magazines or newspapers. The mechanism by which this recipe and its offshoots travelled appears to have involved the dispersal of the original fund-raising book to other communities, the resultant increase in the number of cooks making the recipe, and then its inclusion in further community cookbooks. In the Wairarapa–Hawke's Bay version, boarding school alumnae appear to have transferred the recipe to their home areas, or to new locations after marriage, and subsequently exchanged recipes and books as members of church fellowship groups. In other words, this standard form originated out in the community, and for over fifty years has been passed from household to household, its popularity boosted from time to time by inclusion in fund-raising cookbooks.

The coffee-walnut pavlova cake, from 1959

In New Zealand, as we have seen, coffee has been intermittently used as a flavouring for meringue cakes and pavlovas since the late 1920s. Five recipes for two-layered coffee-flavoured meringue cakes and two for single-layered examples have been recorded up to 1956, but only the latter two of these, a Coffee Meringue Cake from the late 1940s and a Meringue Cake from about 1950, shared the same recipe. Then in 1959 a Coffee Pavlova recipe[34] was published that was repeated with very few changes in twenty other recipe books, most recently in 1996. It used three egg whites, one and a half cups of sugar, two to four tablespoons of boiling water, and one teaspoon of instant coffee. Neither vinegar (except in one book) nor cornflour were included; some recipes stipulated a pinch of salt, while others left it out. Twelve of the recipes made a two-layer cake with a very distinctive filling composed of walnuts pre-cooked in sweetened, coffee-flavoured milk folded into the whipped cream. In four of the nine single-layer examples, the same walnut and cream recipe was given as a topping. Was the recipe influenced by Rose Rutherford's little pavlovas? These were still made in the 1950s; but, with their final appearance in 1966, were clearly not widely known. I like to think that the flavour and texture combination that Rose pioneered was somehow rejuvenated in the large coffee-walnut pavlova.

The first example of this standardised coffee-walnut pavlova was published in the widely distributed *Triple Tested Recipe Book* compiled by Thelma Christie for the Lower Hutt Plunket Society in 1959 (Fig. 7.6). She explained that the whites had to be covered with sugar before the boiling water was poured over them. The bowl was placed over a pan of boiling water, just as in Mrs Kime's method, beaten till the sugar dissolved, then transferred to the electric mixer stand and whipped till stiff (Fig. 7.7). It was not long before this preliminary beating over hot water was

7.6 Thelma Christie compiled *Triple Tested Recipes* for the Lower Hutt Plunket Society in 1959, but it was sold nationally and reprinted several times until the 1980s (with the permission of the Lower Hutt Plunket Society).

COFFEE PAVLOVA

3 egg whites
1½ cups sugar
1 teaspoon instant coffee
2 tablespoons boiling water

FILLING

Walnuts
1 teaspoon sugar
½ teaspoon instant coffee
2 tablespoons milk

½ pint cream whipped

1. Place all ingredients in bowl, covering whites with sugar before adding boiling water.
2. Beat over pan of boiling water till sugar is dissolved.
3. Put in mixer and beat till stiff.
4. Divide mixture into two and put on grease-proof paper.
5. Place in centre of oven and bake for 40 minutes at 325°.

6. Break walnuts into saucepan. Add other ingredients and boil for a few minutes.
7. Strain liquid away and cool nuts.
8. When nuts are cool, add to cream.
9. Fill pavlova the night before using.

7.7 The original recipe for the Coffee Pavlova (reproduced from *Triple Tested Recipes*, 1959, p. 111, with the permission of the Lower Hutt Plunket Society).

How to make a Coffee Pavlova *(1959–)*

Serves 8–10

The excellent flavour combination of coffee, walnuts, and a coffee-flavoured liqueur in a double-layered pavlova results in a star-quality dessert for a special occasion. Use freshly roasted espresso ground coffee beans for maximum flavour, or substitute fresh instant coffee ground to fine powder with a mortar and pestle. For best flavour and texture, fill the pavlova 12–24 hours before serving.

- **3 egg whites**
- **1½ cups caster sugar**
- **1 teaspoon finely ground coffee (plus ½ teaspoon for filling)**
- **2 tablespoons boiling water**

Filling

- **70 g freshly shelled walnuts**
- **1 teaspoon brown sugar**
- **½ teaspoon finely ground coffee**
- **2 tablespoons milk**
- **300 ml cream**
- **1 tablespoon Tia Maria or Kahlúa**

Cut two 20 cm circles from non-stick baking paper. Position circles on a baking tray, greasing lightly underneath to prevent slippage when spreading the meringue mixture. Preheat the oven to 160°C with a rack in the centre position.

Pour the egg whites into a mixer bowl, cover with the sugar and sprinkle over the coffee. Pour in the boiling water and beat with an electric mixer for 10–12 minutes, or longer by hand. Divide the mixture evenly and spoon onto the circles, spreading to within 2 cm of the edges. Bake for 45 minutes.

Allow to cool on a rack. Carefully peel off the papers.

Prepare the filling while the meringues are cooking. Break the walnuts into small pieces and place in a small saucepan. Add the sugar, coffee and milk. Bring to the boil and simmer for a few minutes. Drain off any remaining liquid and cool nuts. Whip the cream until stiff. Fold in the nuts and liqueur.

Place one meringue on a serving platter. Cover with half the cream mixture. Position the other meringue on top and spread it with the remaining cream.

Cover the pavlova and store in a refrigerator.

abandoned and the mixture was put under the electric beater from the start, as in the coffee-flavoured Jolly Good Pavlova from Masterton's Solway Old Girls *Silver and Green Jubilee Cookery Book*.[35] This recipe was the only repeat of Thelma Christie's Coffee Pavlova recorded from the 1960s. Nevertheless the recipe was obviously in use in various communities, for in the 1970s it was submitted to fund-raising books from Dunedin (1971), Wanaka (1972), Timaru (1974), and Lee Stream, near Dunedin (1979). It gained greater momentum in the 1980s, appearing in ten community cookbooks between Dunedin and Palmerston North. By 1993 it had been submitted to a fund-raising book in Tauranga, but was becoming generally less common.

Over the four decades in which the *Triple Tested Recipe Book* coffee pavlova was in circulation, several other versions co-existed. Some had retained the walnut filling or topping, but had increased the egg whites to four, or substituted cold water for boiling, or added some vinegar or cornflour. Others appear to be independent recipes, for example Tui Flower's Coffee Pavlova from *The New Zealand Woman's Weekly Cookbook*.[36] Apart from two recipes contributed to Oamaru and Waimate fund-raising books in 1985, none of these other versions were repeated.

The uncooked pavlova, from 1959

One other standardised pavlova, of rather mysterious origins, emerged in the 1950s: the uncooked pavlova. Although it gains strength from the setting powers of gelatine, it has no direct connection to the Davis Gelatine Pavlova described in Chapter Two, though its ancestors may well have appeared in *Davis Dainty Dishes*. It emerged out of a suite of older gelatine desserts called snows, foams, or marshmallow puddings, as cooks celebrated the end of rationing and economical menu planning with excursions into airy desserts and cakes, aided by the spread of electric food mixers.

Three types of this uncooked dessert existed under the name uncooked or unbaked pavlova. The most common and economical version of these, first known from two 1959 fund-raising books, had a single egg white, and most examples had a teaspoon of baking powder. A three-egg-white version first recorded in 1960 included half a cup of lemon juice but no raising agent. A two-egg-white version appeared first as a meringue cake in 1956 and then as a pavlova in 1961; it contained a quarter teaspoon of cream of tartar. This version was published under the title Meringue Cake or Sweet (No Baking) in 1956,[37] and Quick Substitute for Pavlova (No Baking) in 1961.[38] The three egg-white-version was named Uncooked Pavlova, and was introduced about 1960 in *New Zealand Dishes and Menus* produced by the Home Science Alumnae.[39] It was duplicated twice in 1984 and again in 1991, and in a modified version in 1982.[40]

Twenty-six recipes for the economical one-egg-white and baking powder version have been recorded. Its appeal lay in the simpler mixing instructions: once the gelatine had been dissolved in half a cup of boiling water, all the ingredients except for the baking powder were beaten together on fast speed in the bowl of an electric mixer for fifteen minutes. The baking powder was folded in last. The first two recipes that I have found calling for baking powder were printed in the *South Otago High School Recipe Book* and Queen Margaret's College's *40th Birthday Recipe Book* in 1959, just three years after the cream of tartar version.[41] These two recipes are very similar in wording and I suspect they may both have been extracted from another source, perhaps a magazine or newspaper column. The one-egg-white uncooked pavlova persisted into the 1990s, and was converted into a Pavlova for Diabetics about 1997, arguably the only type of pavlova that could succeed without sugar.[42]

The use of baking powder is unusual in an unbaked dessert cake. One contributor commented in 1974 that it was not necessary, and three others omitted it. The tenth edition of *The Schauer Australian Cookery Book* (1952) recommended the addition of a pinch of baking powder for every two whites in a meringue, noting that 'If baked slowly, the meringue will be firm and will keep its shape'.[43] It is possible that initially the baking powder was added for its acidic cream of tartar, which stabilises egg-white foams,[44] and was found to lighten the mixture as well as prevent collapse, an explanation supported by the use of cream of tartar in the 1939 prototype of one type of uncooked pavlova. But not all baking powders contain cream of tartar, so which sort was intended for use in the 1959 and subsequent recipes?

The function of baking powder – to release carbon dioxide gas and lighten the product – is delayed in modern formulations until the mixture is placed in the oven. The components are selected so that the acid salts (e.g. sodium acid pyrophosphate and sodium aluminium phosphate)[45] only start reacting with the baking soda (sodium bicarbonate) when they are dissolved and heated.[46] Older baking powders such as Edmonds' original Sure to Rise formulation, were a mixture of baking soda, cream of tartar, and tartaric acid. The tartaric acid worked rapidly from the moment that liquid was added, while the cream of tartar was slower to dissolve.[47] Both products can initiate the production of carbon dioxide gas without heating. In the unbaked pavlova, the gas cells formed by the initial reaction would be sealed by the setting of the gelatine, and would add to the spongy texture. Although Edmonds no longer uses tartaric acid,[48] their packets still list cream of tartar alongside the heat-activated acid phosphates mentioned above; however, modern baking powders are clearly not designed for aerating unbaked products. During World War 2, when cream of tartar was temporarily unavailable, acid phosphate baking powders took over by default. Edmonds called their acid phosphate product 'Acto' and it remained on sale during the 1950s, even after the Sure to Rise powder reappeared with cream of tartar as one of the

How to make an Uncooked Pavlova *(1959–)*

Serves 6–8

〰〰〰〰〰〰〰〰〰〰〰〰〰

'This is not a pavlova!' was the reactionary cry from the family. Even so the dessert was enjoyed. Was it worth making? Yes – the texture was velvety and the tangy lemon flavour complemented the fruit.

〰〰〰〰〰〰〰〰〰〰〰〰〰

- ½ cup boiling water
- 2 tablespoons gelatine or two 10 g sachets
- ½ cup freshly squeezed lemon juice
- ½ cup caster sugar
- 3 egg whites

Filling

- fruit (e.g. seeded grapes, canned and drained pineapple pieces or lychees, peeled and chopped kiwifruit, berries, etc.)

Sprinkle the dry gelatine onto the hot water in a measuring cup and stir briskly with a small wire whisk or fork until dissolved. Stir in the lemon juice and sugar and allow to cool but not set. Beat the egg whites until stiff. Pour in the gelatine mixture and beat together. Pour and spoon into a ring mould and leave to set in a fridge until firm.

To unmould, dip a knife in warm water. Dry well. Run the tip of the knife around edge of mould. Dip the mould into a bowl of warm water for about 10–12 seconds (a china or plastic mould may need longer than a metal mould). Lift from the water and shake gently to loosen. Moisten a chilled plate – this will allow an off-centre pavlova to be moved if required. Place the plate over the mould and invert and shake gently. Lift off the mould. Repeat the procedure if necessary. Store in the fridge until serving time. Fill the centre with a selection of seasonal fruit.

〰〰〰〰〰〰〰〰〰〰〰〰〰

ingredients. Acto would have been totally unsuitable in an unbaked pavlova. I don't think that any baking powder containing acid phosphates should be used in an unbaked dessert, so I replaced the baking powder with one half teaspoon of cream of tartar and a quarter teaspoon of baking soda when trying the old recipes.

Was the unbaked pavlova an inspired departure from a cooked pavlova, or did it have a prior history and simply acquire the name pavlova by attraction? A type of cold dessert, often termed a 'snow', contains nearly all the ingredients of the uncooked pavlova, and has a very long history in its own right. Snows set with gelatine are usually made by dissolving the gelatine in water, sweetening and flavouring the mixture, beating it as it cools, and then folding in stiffly beaten egg whites.[49] American community cookbooks commonly include recipes with this name as far back as the 1870s, when packaged gelatine first became available. These recipes were usually flavoured with lemon juice. However, the popular New Zealand dessert named 'lemon snow' is normally thickened with cornflour instead of gelatine. Neither type of snow contains baking powder or cream of tartar.

Another possible forerunner is Nan Kent-Johnston's Marshmallow Pudding, published in two Christchurch cookery books, the first about 1938 and the second late in 1939.[50] Like the two-egg-white unbaked pavlova, it contains two egg whites and a small quantity of cream of tartar, but twice as much water. A possible ancestor of the three-egg-white unbaked pavlova with lemon juice is *Davis Dainty Dishes*' Orange Snow which calls for the juice of a lemon and a cup of orange juice.[51] In both recipes the egg whites are whipped separately then combined with the whisked gelatine mixture.

As for the one-egg unbaked pavlova, Deaconess Jean Henderson's Marshmallow Pudding contributed to a 1947 fund-raising book from Papanui (Christchurch) matched the pavlova in both method (whipping all together) and ingredients, but included no baking powder.[52] A 1952 recipe called Marshmallow Cake, from the *Nelson Intermediate School Cookery Book*, is similar.[53] Even though it does not include cream of tartar or baking powder, all the ingredients are beaten together, giving this recipe a place in the line leading to the uncooked one-egg-white pavlova.

The story of the unbaked pavlova is not one of a single innovation or renaming, followed by proliferation of varieties, but the transformation during the 1950s of three related forms of gelatine dessert into three distinctive types of unbaked pavlova. At the heart of this mutation was an increasingly powerful concept, that of the New Zealand pavlova. Like a magnet it began to attract recipes that had existed earlier as snows, foam, and marshmallow puddings, its drawing power perhaps linked to the iconic status that the pavlova acquired during the 1950s. This dynamic renaming gave new life to these types of desserts and ensured their survival (as both pavlovas and marshmallow puddings) through to the end of the twentieth century.

Non-standardised pavlovas

The many unique pavlovas that existed before World War 2 did not vanish when standardised forms began to develop after 1950. Of the fifty-two large pavlova or meringue cake recipes in my 1950s data set, thirty-four do not fit comfortably into any of the standardised forms described above. Their continued existence after standardisation began confirms that pavlovas were not simply developed by food-writers and copied by home cooks, but were 'owned' and interpreted by many individuals. The recipes that constitute this variable group use from two to six egg whites and normally two tablespoons of sugar per white, have from a half to two teaspoons of vinegar, may or may not include cornflour (from one teaspoon to one tablespoon) and a pinch of salt, and are usually flavoured with vanilla. Most say beat the whites first, then beat or fold in the sugar before adding the other ingredients. All appear to be mixable with hand-operated beaters or electric ones, unlike some of the variants that stipulate electric beaters. It is easy to ignore these non-standard pavlovas and concentrate on the oft-repeated standard forms, but the unique recipes actually outnumber the standardised.

Toppings and fillings

For the formative years of the 1930s and 1940s, when the concept of the large pavlova or meringue cake was still comparatively new to New Zealand cooks, over 80 per cent of the recipes in my spreadsheet provided suggestions for the toppings (and fillings if there was more than one layer). In the 1950s that figure fell to 46 per cent, and continued to decline to 28 per cent in the 1980s. By then everyone knew that you put whipped cream on top of a pavlova and decorated it with something sweet and fruity that contrasted with the cream. Fortunately there are enough recipes where the toppings were spelt out for us to determine what was popular. Whereas pineapple had been prominent between the layers and on top of 1930s pavlovas, with passionfruit and strawberries in second and third place, passionfruit became more popular than the other two in the 1940s. All three were equally popular in the 1950s, sharing first place with chopped brightly coloured jelly. In this respect we can see the influence of the Edmonds' cookbooks, for their long-running pavlova (first published in 1939) recommended chopped Edmonds' jelly as an attractive topping. No particular flavour was suggested, though later versions submitted to newspaper columns and community cookbooks of the 1950s and 1960s chose raspberry and orange.

The first specially prepared pavlova topping appeared in the early 1950s. Promoted in Helen Cox's popular *Hostess Cook Book* in 1952 (Fig. 7.8), it was a cooked lemon cream made from the left-over egg yolks from the meringue, sweetened, and flavoured with the rind and juice of a lemon.[54] The recipe can be found in North American cookbooks in the 1940s, in particular in the 1949 edition of the highly influential *The Boston Cooking-School Cook Book*.[55] There it is listed as a topping for

7.8 The dust jacket of Helen Cox's *The Hostess Cook Book* (1952).

7.9 Helen Cox adapted an American topping for Angel Pie for its New Zealand equivalent, the pavlova (reproduced from *The Hostess Cook Book*, 1952, p. 145).

297. LEMON CREAM PAVLOVA   *Serves 6*

INGREDIENTS: *Eggs; sugar; vinegar; lemon; cream.*

Step (1) Brush a piece of greaseproof paper with butter then pop quickly under the cold tap. Shake off the surplus liquid and place on an oven slide or in an 8- or 9-inch cake tin.

(2) Separate 4 egg whites from the yolks. Place the whites in a large basin. Beat until they will stand stiffly in peaks.

(3) Add gradually 1¼ cups sugar, beating vigorously so that the meringue will become very stiff. Add a pinch of salt and 1 teasp. vinegar. Pile onto the paper, making a round pavlova, or spread into the tin.

(4) Bake in a slow oven for 1¼ hours.

Temperatures: Electric ovens, 225–300 deg. F. for ¾ hour, then switch off and leave the pavlova in; gas ovens, Regulo 1 for ¾ hour, then down to ½ for the rest of the time. The pavlova is cooked when it will lift dry from the paper. Too long cooking will make it sticky underneath.

(5) Cool before removing from tin.

(6) Beat the 4 egg yolks until thick and light, adding ⅓ cup sugar, 4 tablesp. lemon juice, and the grated rind of 1 lemon. Cook, preferably in a double boiler, until the mixture is thick. Do not allow to boil. Cool.

(7) Place the pavlova on a flat serving dish and spread with the cooled lemon filling. Cover thickly with whipped cream.

a lemon or orange variant of the Angel or Meringue Pie, the American equivalent of the New Zealand pavlova. But while the American recipe instructs readers to 'cover with thin layer of unsweetened whipped cream', Helen Cox wrote, 'Cover thickly with whipped cream' (Fig. 7.9). Using up leftovers was very important in the price-conscious 1950s, and particularly so with eggs which doubled in price between 1945 and 1957. Later this lemon cream sometimes incorporated whipped cream and orange juice, or was given more body with gelatine. Lemon cream peaked in popularity in the 1960s.

The second specially prepared topping or filling was included in the recipe for the Coffee-Walnut Pavlova in *Triple Tested Recipes* (1959). Whereas the lemon cream formed a separate layer underneath the whipped cream, the cooked coffee-flavoured walnuts were folded into the cream to make the filling for this two-layer pavlova. Later in the 1970s, the same walnut mixture was used to garnish the cream topping of a single layer pavlova.[56]

The 1950s was a critical decade in the development of New Zealand pavlovas. As a single concept with a growing range of recipe types, the pavlova come to be regarded as a national dish during this decade. Though not taught in our cooking classes, popular versions of pavlova recipes spread rapidly. We will never know how many were jotted down on a scrap of paper or on the back of an envelope and handed on, but there is plenty of evidence of the role played by fund-raising cookbooks, magazines, and newspapers in disseminating these recipes. The pavlova name itself had such potency that it appropriated some desserts that had existed for decades with quite unrelated names. The standard forms that emerged from home kitchens during this decade nearly all added water to the mixture, a modification that marks them out as distinctively New Zealand – very few Australian pavlovas adopted this practice. Though still served for formal afternoon teas, they were proving versatile enough to grace a dinner table or supper buffet, a shift in job description that would have been impossible for the little pavlovas (Fig. 7.10). Their future looked as rich as the cream we piled thickly on top of them.

7.10 Helen Cox recommended serving her Lemon Cream Pavlova at a sit-down wedding breakfast, comically illustrated by New Zealand artist Russell Clark (reproduced from *The Hostess Cook Book*, 1952, p. 47).

Pavlovas consolidate, 1960–79

IN THE 1950s three-quarters of the pavlova recipes in New Zealand cookbooks were classified as cakes and were inserted between the madeira cakes and the sponges, just as they had been in earlier decades. In the next decade, however, 30 per cent of the pavlovas were placed in the desserts or cold sweets section, and in the 1970s the balance had tipped dramatically to the point where 60 per cent of pavlova recipes were classified as desserts. By the 1980s, 90 per cent were desserts. These figures from my database, confirm the major switch that occurred in our patterns of entertaining in the 1960s and 1970s. Formal afternoon teas, with all their silverware, fine china and white linen, were on the way out, and dinner parties and buffet suppers became the modern way to entertain.

Tui Flower's Modern Hostess Cook Book, published in 1972, opens to view this exciting and sociable era (Fig. 8.1). She provided recipes for many different sorts of parties: lunch, dinner, breakfast and brunch, birthday, cake and dessert, and buffet parties, along with ideas for picnic, barbecue, after-theatre and even impromptu entertaining. Where did she position the by now iconic pavlova? In the dinner party for foreign guests, of course. Her recipe, Pavlova With Chinese Gooseberries, was a classic three-plus-three (Fig. 8.2).[1] It was cooked in a loose-bottomed tin, perhaps to ensure height and a regular edge – because pavlovas containing water sometimes spread when cooked on a tray. In the 1960s, however, only 32 per cent of pavlovas were still cooked in tins, and that percentage dropped further to 23 per cent in the 1970s.

The number of recipe books in my collection published in the 1960s was 50 per cent over and above those from the previous decade, and climbed steadily in the 1970s. Just over half the recipe books of the 1960s were fund-raisers, most frequently put together by church groups. In the 1970s these community cookbooks make up two-thirds, but in this decade school projects over-shadowed the church efforts. No other decade produced so many fund-raising recipe books,

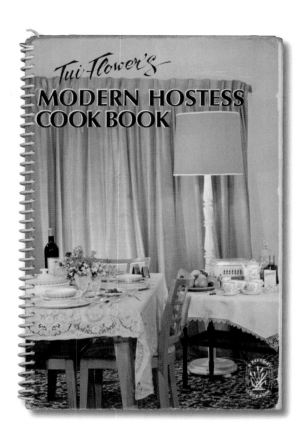

8.1 The cover of *Tui Flower's Modern Hostess Cook Book*, published in 1972, invited readers to modernise their mode of entertaining.

Reproduced with permission from Tui Flower and Penguin Books.

8.2 The recipe for Pavlova With Chinese Gooseberries in *Tui Flower's Modern Hostess Cook Book* (1972, p. 19) added to the popularity of the standard three-plus-three pavlova.

Reproduced with permission from Tui Flower and Penguin Books.

PAVLOVA WITH CHINESE GOOSEBERRIES

3 egg whites	1 teaspoon vanilla
3 tablespoons cold water	1 teaspoon vinegar
1 cup castor sugar	Icing sugar
$\frac{1}{4}$ teaspoon salt	About 1 cup cream, whipped
1 tablespoon cornflour	3 to 4 ripe chinese gooseberries

Have an 8 inch loose-bottomed cake tin lined bottom and sides with buttered paper.
Beat egg whites until very stiff.
Add water and beat again.
Add sugar 1 tablespoon at a time beating well after each addition.
Fold in salt and cornflour mixed together then the vanilla and vinegar mixed together.
Run cold water into lined tin and tip out water so a little clings to paper.
Spread mixture into tin.
Bake at 350 degrees for 10—15 minutes then, in an electric stove, turn the oven off, and leave the pavlova in it for 1 hour. In a gas stove turn to lowest setting and cook about 1 hour.
Take pavlova from tin and turn on to plate dusted with icing sugar.*
When cold decorate with whipped cream and peeled and sliced fruit.

and pavlova recipes are in nearly all of them. By now there were so many different sorts of pavlova that these books have an average of 2.35 recipes per book. Some, such as the Wanaka Improvement Society's 1972 *Souvenir Recipe Book*, provided up to six different recipes.[2]

In the 1960s single-layer pavlovas had the field largely to themselves, making up nearly 90 per cent of the recipes for all large meringue cakes. However, the 1970s saw some competition from multi-layer meringue cakes, sometimes described as tortes or gateaux. These were not a resurgence of the old multi-layer meringue cake from which the pavlova itself emerged, but a new food fashion, promoted by food-writers who watched overseas trends and introduced them to New Zealand readers. Rosemary Dempsey, who wrote for the *New Zealand Herald*, published her Meringue Torte late in the 1960s.[3] A very similar recipe containing six egg whites and twelve ounces (or twelve large tablespoons) of caster sugar showed up as Sylvia Morris's Party Pavlova Cake in Wanaka in 1972, and as Helen Kinaston's Meringue Gateaux in Roxburgh in 1976.[4] While it is likely that some of these multi-layered meringues were assimilated into New Zealand cuisine by having their name changed to pavlova, in subsequent decades the name torte came to co-exist with pavlova, and to resist its magnetic attraction.

Before the tortes arrived, the 1960s saw a consolidation of the new versions of pavlovas introduced in the 1950s. With egg prices falling relative to income, the economical one-egg-white pavlova lost ground to the popular three-plus-three and four-plus-four and then disappeared from the cookbooks in the 1970s. Uncooked pavlovas developed a loyal following, however, and remained popular into the 1970s. Non-standardised recipes made up 70 per cent of the pavlovas in both decades, once again

HOME FREEZE, the American Housewife's greatest boon . . .

NOW AVAILABLE
TO YOU!

Garden fresh vegetables and fruit out of season, game and meats right on hand whenever you want them. Bread in particular is ideal for freezing — no stale bread on week-ends or holidays. Freezing of foods is fun — no more drudgery of preserving.

CHAMBERSON

HOME FREEZER

JOHN CHAMBERS & SON LTD.
CHRISTCHURCH :: ASHBURTON

10

8.3 Home freezers had particular appeal to rural families and were first advertised in the 1950s (reproduced from *Recommended Cooking*, 1952, p. 10). Fund-raising cookbooks began to mention them from 1960.

demonstrating that contributors to fund-raising cookbooks were more likely to submit their own customised recipe than replicate a standard form.

Kitchen appliances began to proliferate in the 1960s (Fig. 8.3). Soon after I married in late 1966, my kitchen acquired its first food mixer, a Kenwood (which I have only just replaced). We also had to find space for a Sunbeam electric frypan, with its high domed lid. I was not one of those New Zealand cooks who pondered the prospects of cooking their pavlovas in a frypan, but there were some out there who left evidence of their experimentation in several cookbooks.

Standardised Pavlovas 1960–79

Electric frypan pavlovas, from 1964

Electric 'frypans' (as they were known) became popular items of kitchen equipment in North America in 1953,[5] and reached New Zealand in the early 1960s. It was inevitable that demonstrators and food-writers promoting them should make the most of their versatility, even to the extent of devising a frypan pavlova. But pavlovas had never before been cooked in conventional frying pans; so what stimulated this adaptation? It was the fact that electric frypans were being sold as substitutes for ovens as well as for griddles and frying pans. Four recipes have been recorded for pavlovas cooked in the electric frypan. The first, a standard one-egg pavlova, was printed in Sunbeam's electric frypan cookbook in 1964, and was repeated in Kevin Mills' radio cookbook about 1987.[6]

Although the Sunbeam recipe was a standard one-egg pavlova in its ingredients and mixing, its cooking instructions required that the mixture be piped onto the papered underside of an eight-inch sponge tin, which kept the pavlova from over-cooking on the frypan surface. The inverted tin had been used before in pavlova cooking in conventional ovens,[7] and there is an earlier Australian example,[8] so we cannot argue that the inverted tin was an invention in response to new cooking technology – it was merely an adaptation to yet another instance of excessive bottom heat. Kevin Mills provided two recipes for electric frypan pavlovas, and his larger four-egg-white version was cooked on a foil plate. The only difference between his 1987 recipe and the 1995 example was in the use of an imperial measurement in the former and its conversion to metric in the latter.[9]

Frypan-cooked pavlovas were not popular, judging from their rarity in community cookbooks. Instructions to open the vent after the first one and a half hours' cooking suggest that steam may have built up in the confined space between pavlova and lid. Despite this, there must have been enough interest among cooks who had unsuitable ovens, or no oven at all, to keep the recipes in circulation for four decades.

The all-in-one pavlova (from 1959), standardised from 1970

The name 'all-in-one' was first given to this standardised pavlova in 1972, and I have applied it to the whole group, since it sums up their revolutionary character. Instead of beating the whites and slowly adding the sugar, then the remaining ingredients, this recipe told cooks to put all the ingredients into the bowl and beat them hard and long! No, you didn't have to work out with weights to succeed with this recipe – just invest in a heavy-duty food mixer!

From 1970 the majority of the recipes for this type were based on two egg whites, one and a half cups of sugar, four tablespoons of boiling water, one teaspoon of vinegar, one teaspoon of cornflour, and varying amounts of vanilla. Others increased the number of whites to three while retaining the same quantities of the other ingredients. Another group used three egg whites to one cup of sugar, three dessertspoons of water, and one teaspoon of vinegar, but omitted cornflour. These differences may prompt the question of why the three groups are clustered as a standard form. The answer is that they share the mixing instructions: beat all together.

The all-in-one pavlovas were clearly influenced by earlier recipes in which the sugar was dissolved with boiling water and then all the ingredients were beaten together. This distinctive method was first applied (about 1952) to one-egg-white pavlovas such as Mrs Kime's, and then in 1959 to Thelma Christie's three-egg-white coffee-flavoured pavlova recipe. This 1959 pavlova recipe was the first to refer to an electric beater in its instructions, but before turning on the electric mixer, cooks were advised to beat the whites over boiling water. Soon, however, they realised that this step could be omitted and the mixing could start under the electric beater.

So far the earliest two-egg-white all-in-one pavlova recipe is from the 40th *Birthday Recipe Book 1919–1959* issued by the Queen Margaret College Old Girls' Association in Wellington. Contributed by Venie Whale (née Coleman), it called for one and a half cups of sugar, four tablespoons of boiling water and one teaspoon of vinegar, and the instructions simply stated 'Beat all ingredients until very stiff'.[10] By about 1967, a contributor to the League of Mothers' *Calling All Cooks* had increased the sugar to two cups (Fig. 8.4).[11] This recipe was soon adjusted to become the most common of the standardised all-in-one form, with a reduction in the sugar back to one and a half cups and the addition of some cornflour. My earliest example was contributed by Richard Prattley to the Newlands' School recipe book in 1970.[12] His recipe simply stated: 'Put all ingredients into a bowl and beat until thick.' Other versions were more fussy about the order, recommending that the egg whites should be covered by the sugar before the boiling water was added to the mixing bowl.

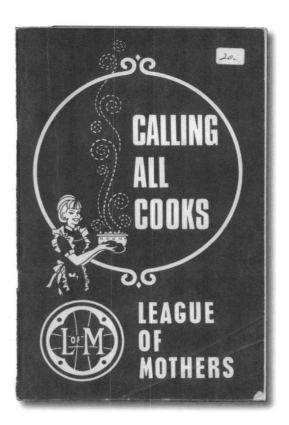

8.4 The League of Mothers'
Calling All Cooks recipe book
was published about 1967, and
reproduced recipes previously
contributed to their magazine.

Sixty examples of all-in-one recipes have been recorded from all over New
Zealand, ranging in time from 1959 to the present. Only six specifically refer to
an electric mixer, but others imply its use in comments such as beat 'all together
15 minutes at full speed' or 'on fast for 15 minutes'. Recommended beating times
range from eight to fifteen minutes, with most recipes advising the longer time.
While most of the published examples have been found in community cookbooks,
the all-in-one was included by Jan Bilton in her 1981 *New Zealand Kiwifruit Cook
Book*, and can be found in Gordon Dryden's 1984 book *The All-Colour Guide to New
Zealand Entertaining* and the first edition of the *Farmers Cookbook* in 1996.[13]

For nearly fifty years, recipes of this type have been called Pavlova (1959–91), All in
One Pavlova (1972–85), Two-Egg Pavlova (1982, 1984), Can't Fail Pavlova (1983),
Economical Pavlova (1985), Soft Centre Pavlova (1990), Never Fail Pavlova (1991),
Quick and Easy Pavlova (1992), Quick Pavlova (1992) and Easy Pavlova (1996).
While some other varieties of pavlova have been named for their soft centres,
or their reliability, the all-in-one type was the first to be identified as simple and
quick to make.

How to make an All-in-One Pavlova *(1959–)*

Serves 6–8

The use of an electric mixer ensures a 'never fail' pavlova with the classic crisp outer meringue shell and soft marshmallow centre.

- 2 egg whites from large eggs
- 1½ cups caster sugar
- ½ teaspoon vanilla
- 1 teaspoon white vinegar
- 1 teaspoon cornflour
- 4 tablespoons boiling water

Topping
- 200 ml cream
- sliced kiwifruit, strawberries, or other fruit

Place a piece of non-stick baking paper on an oven tray and draw a 23 cm circle in the centre (see Hint 7, p. 146). Preheat the oven to 180°C with a rack in the centre position.

Place all the ingredients (except those for the topping) into the bowl and beat on high speed for 10–12 minutes until the mixture is shiny and stiff. Spoon into the marked circle and use a spatula to spread evenly. Bake for 10 minutes and then lower the heat to 150°C and bake a further 45 minutes. Allow to cool in the oven for at least an hour.

Carefully transfer to a flat serving platter. Whip the cream until stiff and spread on the pavlova. Decorate with fruit.

This type of pavlova might equally have been called the 'electric beater pavlova', since its success is probably dependent on the power of mechanical mixing. However, the standard recipe does not occur in the cookbooks supplied with three of the most popular brands of food mixers sold in New Zealand: Sunbeam, Westinghouse, and Kenwood. The first two mixers were made in Australia, but only the Sunbeam series of books included a recipe for a pavlova. Making its first appearance in the early 1950s, it was based on six egg whites, six (Australian 20 ml) tablespoons of caster sugar mixed in progressively – an unusually low quantity of sugar given the number of egg whites – and two teaspoons of vinegar.[14] Sometime after 1961 the amount of sugar was increased to one and a half cups. The Kenwood book was produced in Britain, and contained a recipe for small conventional meringues only.

Domestic food mixers went on sale in North America in the early twentieth century, and it is likely that some New Zealand households had them by the 1930s. Mrs L. Walker's pavlova recipe, published in the *Christchurch Boys' High School Cookery Book* in the late 1930s, instructed readers to beat the mixture for twenty minutes, an instruction that implies either very strong arms or access to an electric mixer.[15] The recipe book from about 1952 that included Mrs Kime's one-egg pavlova had advertisements for several brands of food mixer: the Mixmaid, sold for £6 1s 0d, the Gremlin £21 10s 0d, and the powerful Kenwood £39 15s 0d (Fig. 8.5).[16] The versatile Hamilton Beach food mixer was advertised in a Christchurch cookbook in the late 1930s.[17] Home cooks probably switched from their hand-operated rotary beaters over an extended period until electric mixers were common enough for recipe writers to refer to them explicitly. Both the one-egg-pavlova and the three-plus-three would have benefited from high-powered mixing, along with another 1950s type, the uncooked pavlova. In my data set there are twenty-eight recipes for pavlovas of all types that specifically mention electric mixing, and 79 per cent are for standardised types that include water. However, the persistence in the recipe books of larger numbers of non-standardised pavlovas, in which ingredients are added progressively, suggests that hand-mixing has continued to be a common practice, even in the gadget-rich 1990s. Until I bought myself a new food mixer, I often preferred the effort of using my rotary hand-beater to the noise of the old machine!

8.5 Advertisement for electric food mixers increased markedly from the 1950s (reproduced from *Recommended Cooking*, 1952, p. 80).

FOOD MIXERS

MIXMAID. £6/1/- KENWOOD
GREMLIN £21/10/- £39/15/-
PULVERISERS
CHEETO £10/4/9
A. I. Vasta, Leeston

The jelly-crystal pavlova, from 1970

A pavlova which included a half packet of jelly crystals, added after the whites were beaten, was contributed to the Lovell's Flat Country Women's Institute's recipe book in 1970 and repeated in a Dunedin fund-raising book in 1991.[18] A smaller version, using four instead of the original six egg whites, was found in another Dunedin recipe book in 1981.[19] It was repeated with the same name, Jelly Pavlova, in a 1985 book published in Waimate.[20] This unexpected variation must have been a 'good idea' that was passed on through several South Island kitchens and had enough novelty value to appear in print four times in twenty-one years.

Toppings and Fillings

The cooked lemon cream that used up the spare egg yolks peaked in popularity in the 1970s then slowly declined through the 1980s as another prepared topping mixture displaced it: a chocolate equivalent of lemon cream. The idea of combining melted chocolate with the egg yolks first shows up in 1959 in the Chocolate Torte in Thelma Christie's *Triple Tested Recipe Book*.[21] The cook started by spreading a thin layer of melted chocolate over the meringue, then mixed the egg yolks and some water into the remaining chocolate. When this was cold, half a cup of cream was spread over the cake, followed by whipped cream combined with the chocolate and egg yolk mixture. As if this wasn't enough, the torte was decorated with more whipped cream and walnuts. The topping for the Chocolate Pavlova Cake in the 1967 edition of *Cadbury's Chocolate Cookery* was much simpler: the egg yolks were pre-cooked with water, chocolate, sugar and butter.[22] Whipped cream was spread on top. The topping of Mrs Landsborough's prize-winning Choc-o-Pav of 1977 included sherry, brandy or rum as well as whipped egg whites.[23] The chocolate mixture was poured into the centre of the pavlova, which was then decorated with whipped cream and chopped walnuts. Liqueurs such as Cointreau and Tia Maria flavoured later versions of this topping. The simplest of the chocolate toppings was chocolate melted with water, first recorded in 1969.[24] It formed a foundation layer for cream whipped with orange jelly. Since 1976, chocolate has played an increasing role in the fillings of layered pavlovas, tortes, gateaux, and meringue cakes, often echoed by chocolate grated over a cream topping.

Recipes that included advice on pavlova toppings in the 1960s continued the tradition of a layer of whipped cream, covered with fruit. Three fruits dominated: pineapple, passionfruit, and strawberries, but kiwifruit was close behind. In the 1970s strawberries were the most popular fruit, followed by kiwifruit and orange or mandarin segments. However, two-thirds of the 1960s recipes for single layer pavlovas made no suggestion at all for toppings. In the 1970s, that proportion fell to half. If you added the recipes that simply said 'cover with whipped cream and any fruit or nuts', it would soon become obvious that most recipe contributors and their readers followed the well-established principle that a pavlova was a platform for cream and a contrasting garnish, with the details left to the discretion of the cook.

When did pavlovas go metric?

In 1974, every household in New Zealand received a booklet from the Ministry of Trade and Industry entitled *At Home With Metrics* (Fig. 8.6). The Minister, Warren Freer, made the following statement in his introduction:

> With more than 90 per cent of the world's population already using the metric system, and virtually every other part of the British Commonwealth planning the change, New Zealand could not but follow.[25]

He went on to declare that metrication made calculations easier, and would take us one step closer to 'that greatest goal of all – a universal language'. What he did not mention was that metrication would put an end to the confusing array of measuring devices used by New Zealand cooks. Sugar, for example, was measured in pounds and ounces, tablespoons, large tablespoons, rounded tablespoons, 'fairly heaped tablespoons', cups, breakfast cups, teacups, small cups, scant cups, medium-sized cups, 'a good cup', and large cups. As the changeover approached, food-writers became very conscious of these informal volume measures, and began to give imperial equivalents (e.g. a scant cup of caster sugar weighs six ounces). They probably recognised that when dealing with dry ingredients, there would be fewer errors in a conversion from imperial to metric weights than from imperial volume measures. In the process, however, it was revealed that many of the tablespoons in New Zealand kitchen

8.6 In 1974 the booklet *At Home With Metrics* was delivered to every New Zealand household. The change to metric measurements affected many domestic activities, from dressmaking to cookery, but most cooks adopted metrics only when absolutely necessary.

drawers hold rather more than three standard imperial or metric teaspoons – remember that three 5 ml teaspoons today are equivalent to one 15 ml metric tablespoon. In fact the old tablespoons often hold four metric teaspoons of water. When measuring caster sugar, this old-style tablespoon (rounded) contains an ounce, and that is the figure given by a contributor of a 1967 pavlova recipe (six tablespoons equal six ounces).[26] The rule of thumb for pavlovas or meringue cakes was either two ounces or two tablespoons of sugar per egg white, and it is clear that they meant the same amount.

Although metrication offered cooks a chance to escape from a world of non-standard tablespoons and cups, there was some resistance in community cookbooks. From 1975 to 1979, only two pavlova recipes gave their sugar measurement in grams alone, and only three gave the quantity in both grams and ounces. Seven recipes continued to use teacups or breakfast cups, while the rest measured the sugar by unspecified cups that may or may not have been metric measuring cups. In the 1980s, forty-four recipes gave the weight of sugar in ounces, twelve in grams, and only four offered equivalents. Eleven recipe contributors assumed that their readers still had breakfast cups and teacups, as did three in the 1990s. Similarly eleven recipes contributed in the 1990s still used ounces. Considering the total number of recipes in each decade, these non-metric recipes are a small proportion. However, we do not know how many cooks who used cups had followed the official advice of the 1974 booklet: 'To get the best results, buy metric measuring spoons and cups.'[27] I know from experience how easy it is to keep an old favourite cup from the pre-metric era in the sugar bag or flour bin.

Though it was inexpensive to re-equip the kitchen with metric measuring containers, at the time of the metric changeover most cooks had stoves that measured temperature in degrees Fahrenheit. This should not have deterred the editors and compilers of cookbooks from also giving the Celsius equivalent, but a surprising number did not bother. In view of the local manufacturers' willingness to equip the oven thermostat dials with both Fahrenheit and Celsius scales leading up to the 1974 changeover, it might be expected that by the 1980s most cooks would have become familiar with Celsius temperatures as old stoves were replaced or when kitchens were refitted, but this is not evident in many of their contributions to cookbooks. For ninety-four pavlova recipes published in the 1980s, the cooking temperature was given only in degrees Fahrenheit. Thirty-three recipes included the Celsius equivalent, and fifty-six assumed readers were fully familiar with metrics. In the 1990s Celsius-only recipes became more common (forty-six) than Fahrenheit-only (thirty-one), and only seven contributors offered both. Intriguingly the four recipes where what were clearly Fahrenheit temperatures were incorrectly given the Celsius abbreviation (e.g. preheat oven to 400 deg. C), occurred between 1985 and 1990, over ten years after metrication.

The contributors knew that their oven dial should be turned to 400 – the scale of measurement was of no relevance to them. Whether they or the editors added the incorrect 'C' is not known.

Though it is tempting to cite the slow adoption of the Celsius scale, and the continued use of imperial measures into the 1990s, as examples of resistance to a state-imposed change, this would imply a conscious and deliberate rejection of the new systems of measurement. There is little evidence of this. Instead, we see a pragmatic and economic response: there was no need to convert a pre-metric recipe while kitchens still contained balances that weigh in pounds and ounces, imperial cups and spoons, and ovens with Fahrenheit scales. In their own homes, cooks allowed themselves the liberty of compliance or non-compliance with metrication, in the same spirit as they modified previously published recipes to suit their own tastes and culinary style. It was the compilers' job to make the conversions, and not all compilers were prepared to do so. Doing tidy imperial-to-metric conversions that suit simple metric measuring equipment is actually very difficult, and because of the rounding that is required – for example one ounce (28.35 g) can be rounded to either 30 g or 25 g – recipes should ideally be tested. How many fund-raising recipe book committees have the time?

Pavlovas paramount, 1980–99

I<small>N THE</small> 1980s more recipe books than ever before included pavlovas, with the average number of pavlova recipes per book peaking at 2.6. For the 1990s, the corresponding average is 2.2. What does this recent decline mean? Should pavlova lovers be perturbed by it, and is there now more competition for a place on the dessert menu? At first I wondered whether it was the result of a change in the mix of cookbooks in my study collection. If the 1990s were represented by more books by prominent food-writers rather than community fund-raiser books, that might account for the decline, since single-authored books rarely contain pavlova recipes and never more than one. However, the difference between the decades is neither large nor significant: 85 per cent of the books were fund-raisers in the 1980s, compared to 80 per cent in the 1990s. So the decline is real and needs further investigation.

Judging by the content of the cookery pages of newspapers and magazines, the most fashionable desserts in the 1980s and 1990s did not include pavlovas. Instead we embraced tiramisu, black forest cake, cassata, syrup cakes, many different cheesecakes and mousses, clafouti, crepes, pecan pie, baklava, zabaglione, strudels, sticky date pudding, and banoffie pie. Pavlovas made the occasional patriotic appearance on these pages, as befits a national icon. Over the same period they became rare on café and restaurant menus, reinforcing my feeling that they no longer belonged in the category of fashionable dessert. Before we blame the fashion game for threatening the pavlova's future, we need to remember that some iconic dishes such as Christmas puddings have not been trendy for several centuries yet no one is suggesting that they are in danger of extinction! Rules for symbolically important dishes are different from those for the fashionable 'creations' in magazines for gourmets and practitioners of haute cuisine.

The decline in number of pavlova recipes might suggest that the dish has become a victim of the healthy-eating campaign. Over the past two weight-watching decades we have been encouraged to view cream as white fat, just as butter is portrayed as yellow fat; but that shouldn't stop us eating pavlovas, provided we substitute another topping for the cream – after all the meringue part is not excessively rich in calories compared to some of the popular desserts mentioned above. Another possible reason for the decline is the fact that we have been making and eating fewer desserts over the last decade or two, but we should remember that many dishes in our dessert repertoire have only ever been served on special occasions. From the 1950s to the 1980s we made pavlovas when entertaining guests, not for weekday family meals. A decline in the consumption of everyday desserts need not affect those we make just for special occasions. After rejecting these reasons, I decided that what my pavlova statistics suggest is that since the 1990s we have been increasingly tempted to try other dishes at our dinner parties, saving the pavlova for overseas visitors.

In the same decade as pavlovas peaked in popularity, we saw the first appearance in New Zealand of two dishes that were related to the pavlova, but were by no means the conventional variety. Both have reasonably consistent ingredient lists and proportions, and can be treated as standardised recipes. The first, the rolled pavlova, was a direct import from Australia; the second, sometimes called the Snax pavlova, was an indirect borrowing from North America.

Standardised pavlovas of the 1980s–90s

The pavlova roll, in New Zealand from 1980

In essence the pavlova roll is a thin meringue cake that is cooked in a rectangular tin for just long enough to strengthen the outer skin so that it can be spread with cream and fruit, and then rolled up, like a Swiss roll. Whoever devised the original version in the 1970s appears to have regarded it as a form of pavlova from the outset, for most examples were called Rolled Pavlova or Pavlova Roll, with just two instances of Pavlina (also written as Pavleena) in the 1980s, and one of Pavlova Log in 1990. In 1997 two examples were named Meringue Roulade. As a pavlova (or subversion of one, depending on your point of view), the roll became a very popular type, with fifty-seven examples recorded in my spreadsheet.

Just over 80 per cent of the pavlova roll recipes are made from four egg whites and the most common recipe (fifteen instances between 1982 and 1998) calls for eight tablespoons of sugar. Only four of the fifty-seven recipes call for water. Compared to many other types of pavlova, there is less variation in this relatively new and decidedly different dish, though at present this similarity cannot be attributed to a single source recipe. One characteristic recommendation that suggests such a source might yet be found is to sprinkle coconut over the surface of the meringue before putting it in the oven, or after five or six minutes of cooking.

How to make a Pavlova Roll *(1980–)*

Serves 8–10

This trendy, impressive, and delicious pavlova presents some handling difficulties but with a practice run, on just the family, it becomes easier and quicker to make. It is an advantage to leave it covered in a fridge for 2 to 24 hours before serving, but this is not essential. The roll can also be frozen but allow 2 hours for thawing.

- **225 g can crushed pineapple in natural juice**
- **½ cup coarse desiccated coconut**

- **4 egg whites**
- **pinch salt**
- **½ cup caster sugar**
- **1 teaspoon cornflour**
- **1 teaspoon wine vinegar**

- **¼ cup icing sugar**
- **150 ml cream**

Drain the pineapple. Preheat the oven to 180°C with a rack in the centre position. Spread the coconut in a Swiss roll pan (30cm x 20cm approximately). In the oven toast the coconut for 2–3 minutes until lightly golden, stirring every minute and watching closely. Tip into a cup until required. Line the base and sides of the Swiss roll pan with non-stick baking paper (see Hint 7, p.146).

Beat the egg whites, salt, caster sugar, cornflour, and vinegar until the meringue is very stiff (10–12 minutes with an electric beater or longer by hand). Spread the mixture evenly right out to the sides of the prepared pan. Bake for 15 minutes. Remove from the oven and allow to cool for 10 minutes. Use a knife to ensure the meringue has separated from the sides of the pan.

Use the back of a spoon to push the icing sugar through a small sieve to evenly coat the meringue. Sprinkle with three-quarters of the toasted coconut. Lay another piece of non-stick baking paper over the surface. Hold a rack or board lightly on top and carefully flip over so the coconut side is downwards. Peel off the cooking paper. Whip the cream until stiff. When the meringue is cool, spread the cream evenly over the surface and top with the thoroughly drained pineapple. Carefully roll up like a Swiss roll – use the paper to help roll a long side up and inwards. Leave the paper in place and store in the fridge until ready to serve. Transfer to a long plate and remove the paper. Sprinkle on the remaining coconut to disguise any cracks.

This is included in thirty of the recipes. Sometimes slivered almonds are given as an alternative to the coconut, and occasionally the surface of the meringue is scored diagonally before the coconut is applied. Once the pavlova roll is cooked – it takes about ten to fifteen minutes in a moderate oven – it is turned out of the Swiss roll pan to cool upside down on a sheet of greaseproof paper sprinkled with sugar. Then a layer of fruit is spread over the surface followed by whipped cream. In nineteen recipes pineapple is recommended, but kiwifruit, raspberries, strawberries, and passionfruit pulp are also listed, as in more conventional pavlovas. Then comes the tricky part: rolling the spongy meringue to form a long tube with the luscious filling layers safely tucked inside. The paper helps in this process, just like a sushi mat. The roll is then chilled for at least two hours before the top is decorated, sometimes with more cream but more often with icing sugar or powdered chocolate.

The first two New Zealand occurrences of this pavlova are in 1980, under the names Rolled Pavlova[1] – this particular recipe was soon renamed Pavleena[2] – and Pavlova Fruit Roll.[3] The most common version (with four whites, eight tablespoons of sugar, two teaspoons of vinegar and one teaspoon of cornflour) first appeared in 1982 as Pavlova Roll,[4] and is represented in fund-raising books from Auckland to Invercargill. The first microwaved version of the roll followed in 1984 in a microwave specialist's cookbook.[5]

An Australian origin of the rolled pavlova seems highly likely on present evidence, since I have found it in the second edition of a cookbook originally published in 1976. There it is called Meedo's Pavlova Roll, named after a sheep station in the outback.[6] It is likely to have a longer history, however, because that particular recipe, though close in many respects, is not identical to any yet recorded in New Zealand. We might expect an earlier Australian source, followed by the development of some minor variants, and then perhaps transmission of one or more of these to New Zealand via the Australian women's magazines widely read here.

The Snax torte or pavlova, from 1981

Between 1981 and the present, New Zealand cooks have circulated a distinctive meringue cake recipe characterised by three egg whites, three-quarters to one cup of sugar (or six to eight ounces), half to one teaspoon of baking powder, up to a packet of crushed Snax, water cracker or cream cracker biscuits, vanilla, and half to one cup of chopped walnuts. Although the ingredients are virtually identical in each recipe, the name of this dessert cake has displayed great variability. Of the twenty-nine recorded examples, seven have been called Nut (or Nutty) Torte, two Walnut Torte, two Mystery Torte, two Snax Supreme, and there is one example of each of the following names: Dunstan Pudding, Coconut Torte, Snax Biscuit Dessert, Snax Delight, Snax Delight Dessert, Snax Pavlova, Nuttie Pavlova, 'Snax

Meringue' Dessert, Snax Torte, Saratoga Torte, Meringue Torte, Pavlova (Torte), Nut Cracker Sweet, Party Cake, Ritzy Walnut Pie and Peach Torte Pie.

With only three examples bearing the name pavlova, you might argue that this dish is not really a pavlova. However, as a related cluster of recipes, I added it to the analysis because if I had included only the three examples named pavlova in my data set I would not have discovered the significance of the group as a whole. The Snax dessert cake was conceivably at the same stage in the 1980s and 1990s as the uncooked pavlova was in the early 1960s when a particular recipe for a type of marshmallow or snow dessert was modified and renamed as a pavlova. The name 'pavlova' exerted a powerful attraction, taking over the identity of the earlier uncooked desserts, but in countries where the pavlova was not an iconic dish, this appropriation did not happen. Whether names like 'nuttie pavlova' will replace 'nutty torte' and so on remains to be seen. This recipe type is still being disseminated under other names, such as Alison Holst's Apricot and Almond Cake.[7] I suspect that the pavlova name may be losing some of its magnetic attraction, and that the take-over bid will fail. The recipe will then continue to circulate under all its various aliases, with few people aware of its historical identity.

There can be no dispute that the Snax pavlova developed out of a type of American torte or pie in which the texture of the meringue was modified by adding crushed savoury biscuit crumbs and nuts. An early example was published in the *Hostess Handbook of Party Foods*, issued by the popular American magazine *Ladies' Home Journal* in 1953, and in a second book in 1954.[8] The 1953 recipe was named Meringue Nut Torte and contained finely crushed saltine cracker crumbs, chopped pecan nuts, and baking powder. The New Zealand recipe is essentially the same, but halved in quantity. A similar American recipe named Macaroon Angel Pudding included graham cracker crumbs, flaked coconut and chopped nuts.[9] In the *Harvard Business Wives Cookbook* (c. 1963), the recipe for Ritz Cracker Pie had the same quantities of egg whites, sugar, and baking powder as most of the later New Zealand recipes.[10] The American and earlier New Zealand recipes gave identical cooking temperatures and times, and several of the New Zealand examples stipulated cooking it in a nine-inch greased pie dish as was done in America.

The American recipes specified saltine, graham or Ritz crackers, names not familiar to most New Zealand cooks. Only one New Zealand recipe referred to saltine crackers, and it is likely that the contributor was an American, judging by the mention of corn syrup and 'confectioner's' sugar in other recipes she submitted. Of the twenty-nine recipes I recorded, twenty-three stipulated Snax biscuits, three Cream Crackers, and one water crackers. One anomalous recipe called for wine biscuits. The history of Snax in New Zealand has been supplied by a long-term employee of the manufacturers, Griffins: it was developed by a Canadian (Nick Cody) employed by the company in the mid-1950s, and was adapted from a North American cracker biscuit known as Ritz. Snax have been made in Lower Hutt since the mid–late 1950s, with very few modifications to the formula.[11] Despite this long history, the 'Snax torte/pavlova' has not yet been found in New Zealand cookbooks of the 1960s and 1970s, even though 1950s American books with recipes for Meringue Nut Tortes were in use here (Fig. 9.1).

The Snax version appeared in New Zealand in 1981, and the limited amount of variation in the early recipes indicates that one source, as yet unidentified, had been influential. Even though the first known example was published in the widely read *New Zealand Woman's Weekly*, it is hard to accept this as the pivotal recipe because its name, Dunstan Pudding, was never used again.[12] All other recorded examples occur in localised community cookbooks. We should also rule these out as the main agent of dispersal, since we have found

9.1 The League of Mothers' *Calling All Cooks* recipe book, published about 1967, had an advertisement for Snax biscuits, but no recipes calling for their use in tortes or pavlovas appeared for over a decade.

that they don't travel far outside their province of origin. By 1985 the recipe had been published in the four main centres, as well as the smaller provincial towns. To achieve this rapid spread, it possibly appeared in a national magazine or newspaper in the late 1970s or very early in the 1980s.

Although the core ingredients remained the same for the next two decades, the contributors modified the quantity of biscuits and the cooking instructions. Some counted out the biscuits (opting for 16, 20, 30, or 30–35), while others stipulated half or a whole packet of Snax. Similarly there were two preferences for baking powder: half or a whole teaspoon, varying independently of the quantity of biscuits. From the start there was great variability in the cooking container: pie dish, flan dish, spring-form tin, round tin, Swiss roll tin, or loaf

How to make a Snax Pavlova *(1981–)*

Serves 6–8

Another name for this pavlova is 'Snax torte', as it has a similar appearance, texture and flavour to a traditional German torte made with nuts and breadcrumbs instead of flour.

- **3 egg whites**
- **1 cup caster sugar**
- **1 teaspoon vanilla**

- **½ cup finely chopped walnuts**
- **30 Snax biscuits, chopped in a food processor to resemble coarse breadcrumbs**
- **1 teaspoon baking powder**

Topping

- **200 ml cream**
- **1 tablespoon brandy, sherry or rum**
- **chocolate chips**

Line a 23 cm sponge sandwich pan with non-stick baking paper. Preheat the oven to 180°C with a shelf in the centre position.

Beat the egg whites until stiff. Add the caster sugar and vanilla and beat until very stiff.

In a small bowl, combine the walnuts, crushed biscuits, and baking powder. Stir to mix thoroughly. Fold gently into the egg whites. Spoon the mixture evenly into the prepared pan. Bake for 20–30 minutes, until golden brown and starting to pull away from the sides. Loosen edges with a table knife and carefully invert onto a rack. Remove the pan and baking paper. When cool invert back onto a flat serving plate.

Whip the cream until stiff. Briefly beat in alcohol. Spread evenly over pavlova (torte) and decorate with chocolate chips.

tin. Most were cooked at 160–180 deg. C (or Fahrenheit equivalent) for 20–45 minutes. As for decoration, ten of the recipes suggested chocolate flakes, chips or shavings, and eight called for walnuts or nuts. What stands out is the readiness of the home cooks who contributed these recipes to adapt what probably began as a single recipe in a national publication to their own kitchen practice. Only two pairs of recipes show close matches: two Dunedin-published recipes – one from an undated (probably 1980s) cookbook and one from around 1997;[13] and two recipes from 1986 and 1996, the earlier contributed by Phyllis Aspinall of Wanaka, formerly of Mt Aspiring Station, and the other by Dunedin councillor Ian McMeeking.[14] The rest reflect individual variations within the general concept.

Microwaved pavlovas, from 1983

In North America, the microwave oven went through quite a long development period before it could be manufactured cheaply enough for domestic use. The Radarange, as microwaves were first known, was introduced for commercial use in 1947, but cost several thousand dollars. It wasn't until 1967 that an affordable household model appeared, following the invention in Japan of a compact low-cost magnetron. After a federal report warned that early models could leak microwaves, new standards were adopted and the public embraced microwave technology, initially for reheating food rather than cooking it from scratch. By 1975 more microwaves were sold in the United States than gas ranges.[15] They spread rapidly through New Zealand in the second half of the 1970s. Looking through my cookbook collection, I find that microwave recipe books produced by well-known New Zealand food-writers cluster in the 1980s. Sections devoted to microwave cookery appear in fund-raising cookbooks earlier than this, from the late 1970s, showing how quickly the microwave became a desirable kitchen appliance – but pavlovas are not included in these sections until the 1980s.

This delay is no surprise, since the crisp outer shell, so typical of the conventional pavlova, cannot form in microwave cookery. It is remarkable that microwaved pavlovas were developed at all, given this drastic transformation in their texture. Perhaps the simultaneous emergence of the pavlova roll in Australia in the 1970s and New Zealand from 1980 created a climate of acceptance of a non-crisp pavlova. Indeed we shouldn't forget that the unbaked pavlova, in circulation since 1959, was quite soft and spongy.

Twelve microwaved pavlova recipes have been recorded so far, not including pavlova rolls. The earliest is from the 1983 South Otago High School recipe book (Fig. 9.2). It was cooked on a high-power setting for two minutes then allowed to stand for a further ten minutes (Fig. 9.3).[16] The same recipe reappeared in fund-raising books from Invercargill in 1987 and Christchurch in the 1990s.[17] Apart from one matching pair of recipes printed in community cookbooks around 1987 and in 1990,[18] the other microwaved pavlovas are each a little different. One recipe

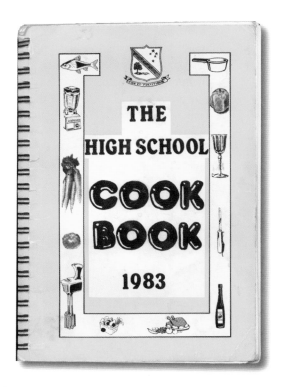

9.2 The cover of the second cookbook produced by South Otago High School in Balclutha in 1983 – their first appeared in 1959 (reissued in 1960).

9.3 *The South Otago High School Cook Book* (1983) included the earliest recipe for a microwaved pavlova so far recorded.

MICROWAVE PAVLOVA: Tracy Fenton

4 egg whites   **1 tsp vinegar**
¾ cup castor sugar   **1 tsp vanilla**

Beat whites stiffly. Add sugar, vinegar and vanilla, beat until very stiff, all sugar dissolved, and it is stiff and shiny. Turn onto a sheet of greased and slightly dampened greaseproof paper. Shape to a neat round with sides moulded up. Cook for 2 minutes on high. Stand for 10 mins.

published about 1986 was the work of microwave consultant and demonstrator Trish Rountree, while another was issued by the New Zealand Poultry Board.[19] These were the only two microwaved pavlova recipes that I found with commercial origins, indicating that most of the experimentation was taking place in domestic kitchens. The cookbooks issued by the microwave manufacturers were slow to include pavlovas. One originating in Australia in 1986 contains a pavlova recipe that does not seem to have been duplicated in New Zealand community cookbooks, though New Zealand cooks may well have tried it.[20]

An early recipe for a microwaved pavlova roll appeared in food-writer Glennys Raffills' instruction book in 1984.[21] The microwaved pavlova roll from a Timaru kindergarten fund-raising cookbook, first printed in 1986, provides a good

How to make a Microwaved Pavlova *(1983–)*

Serves 6–8

In the 1980s many home cooks purchased their first microwave oven. Keen to make full use of this new appliance, many attended classes offered by the experts in the new technology. Some then attempted to make 'everything' in their new toy. The pavlova was no exception! Now that we are more discerning when it comes to knowing what does or does not cook well in a microwave oven, we have to ask 'is there still a place for this recipe?' The cooking method makes it possible to have a pavlova ready in less than 30 minutes – the perfect solution for unexpected overseas guests expecting to sample a Kiwi pavlova. The crisp shell is missing but the sweet and smooth marshmallow is a good foil for fresh seasonal fruit.

- **4 egg whites**
- **¾ cup caster sugar**
- **1 teaspoon malt vinegar**
- **1 teaspoon vanilla**

Topping

- **200ml cream**
- **a selection of one or more types of fresh berries or other fruit**

Remove the glass turntable from the microwave oven. Cover it with a piece of non-stick baking paper. Draw a 23 cm circle in the centre.

Beat the egg whites until stiff. Add the caster sugar, vinegar, and vanilla. Beat again until very stiff, shiny, and the sugar dissolved. Spoon onto the circle and spread evenly into a neat round with the sides mounded up. Position the turntable and cook pavlova on high (650W) for about 2 minutes. The pavlova is cooked when it just begins to crack. Cooking times will vary with different ovens. Remove the turntable and leave the pavlova to stand for 10 minutes. Carefully slide onto a flat plate.

Whip the cream until stiff and spread over the pavlova. Top with the fresh berries.

example of the process of adaptation.[22] The recipe had been modified from one in circulation by 1982, cooked in a conventional oven.[23] Another, called 3-Minute Pavlova Roll, was printed in a Lions Clubs' recipe book in 1990, and repeated in a church fund-raising book in 1995.[24] Of all the different sorts of pavlova, the roll was best suited to the microwave method, since there was no danger of it becoming crisp. It could, however, be overcooked, and the cooking time of all microwaved pavlovas was tightly constrained: three to four minutes for the pavlova roll, and from one minute ten seconds to two minutes for the pavlova cake. Cracking was a sign that the microwaving should cease.

The existence of twelve different microwaved pavlova or pavlova roll recipes in fifteen cookbooks, four originating in the 1980s and three in the 1990s, suggests that experimentation was on-going from the introduction of this new technology, and much of this was taking place in domestic kitchens.

Another new development

Pavlovas for diabetics, from 1981

I have recorded four pavlova recipes for those with diabetes, dating from 1981 to 1997, each of which represents a different attempt to find a solution to a sugarless meringue. The first of these, Diabetic Mock Pavlova, was published in 1981 in a Catholic Women's League cookbook from Dunedin.[25] The four egg whites were sweetened with a liquid sugar substitute and stabilised with vinegar and cornflour. Another recipe used saccharin tablets and relied on cornflour to stabilise the whipped whites,[26] while a third added three tablespoons of skim milk powder.[27] The fourth recipe was a form of the uncooked pavlova suitable for diabetics, where gelatine gives body to the dish.[28] It is remarkable that these sugarless pavlovas were independently developed by home cooks, considering that sugar has been one of the two essential ingredients of meringues for several hundred years, added not just for its sweetness but also for its ability to make watery egg whites more viscous.[29] These cooks must have been highly motivated to produce a pavlova for diabetics, and their experiments emphasise how important an icon the pavlova had become by the 1980s.

Toppings and fillings

Of the pavlova toppings and decorations specified in recipes from the 1980s and 1990s, chocolate was the most popular, recommended for 33 per cent of the recipes in the 1980s, and 39 per cent in the 1990s. The cooked lemon and egg yolk topping that had peaked in the 1970s declined sharply as chocolate toppings became fashionable. Many forms of chocolate were tried as decoration: grated, powdered, shavings, curls, chips, and hail. When taken together with the melted chocolate toppings, chocolate emerges as the most popular form of finishing for pavlovas and meringue cakes.

Fruit was still important and cooks chose from a wide variety. Orange segments, raspberries, bottled peaches (a good choice in winter), cherries, passionfruit, and of course kiwifruit were all mentioned. Of the fresh berry fruits, strawberries had been consistently popular (13–20 per cent of specified toppings per decade) until the 1980s when a decline set in. The only new fruit to make an appearance in pavlova recipes in these decades was the blueberry, reflecting increased commercial production in the 1990s (6 per cent). Though pineapple had disappeared from the top of pavlova cakes in the 1980s and 1990s, it found a new home in the centre of the pavlova roll.

In comparison to chocolate, kiwifruit came a distant second as a finishing choice in the 1990s, mentioned in only 16 per cent of recipes with topping advice. Of course it is possible that recipes that did not include suggestions for finishing – 72 per cent in the 1980s and 56 per cent in the 1990s – were decorated with kiwifruit, but it seems more likely that where the choice of topping was left to the cook, the proportion of those opting for kiwifruit would be similar to that found in the recipes that gave topping advice. The idea of the iconic pavlova with its pristine cream covered in cool green kiwifruit does not quite match the facts generated from the data set for this period.

Pavlovas in the twenty-first century

Mini- and micro-pavlovas, from 2000

Muffins and commercial cookies may have become 'supersized' since the 1990s, but one of the latest trends in pavlovas is downsizing. This does not necessarily mean a smaller helping. On the contrary, each diner has an individualised pavlova. For example, using five egg whites, Ray McVinnie's Strawberry Pavlovas recipe makes eight mini-pavlovas seven centimetres in diameter and four centimetres high.[30] The idea of single-serve pavlovas has appeared before – in 1969 Miss C. Clark contributed a recipe for Individual Pavlovas (Meringues)[31] – but the latest fashion seems to have been driven by overseas food-writers and television presenters. I have not seen any mini-pavlova recipes in recent New Zealand fund-raising books, but they are plentiful on internet sites from Australia, the United Kingdom, and the United States. In Britain, Nigella Lawson included a recipe for mini-pavlovas, ten centimetres in diameter, in one of her best-seller books, while Delia Smith offered fail-safe instructions for her Mini Pavlovas with Strawberries and Mascarpone – you start by buying meringue nests from Marks and Spencer's![32]

As for the micro-pavlovas, overseas visitors departing New Zealand can purchase duty-free New Zealand Pavlova Meringue Bites flavoured with hokey pokey, manuka honey or kiwifruit.[33] While Rose Rutherford would probably have been happy to see them called pavlovas, to most contemporary New Zealand cooks they are just little meringues. The promoters and tourists, however, see them as edible national icons and souvenirs.

Mini-pavlovas belong to a globalised and commercialised cuisine, somewhat removed from New Zealand home kitchens. It is true that some New Zealand cooks now buy a pavlova shell when they need to serve a pavlova for a special occasion; however, the persistence of standard pavlova recipes in primary school and play centre fund-raising cookbooks tells us that the pavlova types of the twentieth century are still in demand by the generation that followed the baby-boomers. How long pavlova recipes will continue to be made in our home kitchens is difficult to predict. Reaching iconic status in the 1950s, the pavlova has had a greater longevity than is normal for most fashionable cakes and desserts. The name encompassed and probably gained strength from the many variants, of which there will be probably be more in the twenty-first century. In fact continual innovations might be necessary to keep the dish popular, and at the same time reinforce the power of the name's iconic associations with New Zealand. It does not matter where the new variants are developed – after all the pavlova roll was borrowed from Australia – but they have to be widely adopted and circulated throughout New Zealand communities. They may even need to become embroiled in international disputes and have their association with New Zealand enhanced in response to overseas challenges.

10

Some sticky issues

NOW that we have reached the beginning of the twenty-first century and the eightieth anniversary of the first pavlova, it is time to reflect on two issues concerning the large pavlova. These are best examined over the whole span of the pavlova's existence rather than decade by decade. Like a badly made pavlova, they are sticky – in the first case bound up with myth and controversy, and in the second literally sticky. The first issue concerns marshmallow centres, the role of cornflour, and the true essence of a pavlova. The second deals with the long struggle that cooks have had to stop their pavlovas sticking to the surface on which they are cooked.

What makes soft centres – and do soft centres make pavlovas?

In the naming of large pavlovas, only a few cooks drew attention to an attribute that many people consider to be essential in a 'real' pavlova – a soft, or marshmallow, centre. In recording 667 recipes, I found four published between 1934 and 1951 that were called Marshmallow Cake or Marshmallow Meringue. From 1961 to 1988 there were nine pavlovas called Marshmallow Pavlova or Pavlova with Marshmallow Centre, and from 1961 to 1990 there were eight recipes named Pavlova (Soft Centre) or Soft Centre Pavlova. Another group of six recipes published between 1970 and 1993 include the comment, after giving the mixing instructions, that the resulting cake is soft- or marshmallow-centred. This certainly does not mean that all the remaining recipes were for pavlovas that lacked a soft or marshmallow centre. Many other recipes have the same ingredients in the same proportions as those explicitly described as marshmallow- or soft-centred, but make no mention of this quality, and among those that advertise their soft centres are several different recipes: five standard three-plus-three pavlovas, four four-plus-four, two all-in-one, and eleven are unique. In other words, there is no particular recipe that can be singled out as producing the marshmallow- or soft-centred meringue.

Perhaps there is a distinctive ingredient that makes a pavlova soft-centred. One pavlova contributor to a 1992 fundraising cookbook actually stated in her recipe that 'The cornflour gives the marshmallow softness.'[1] If she is correct, then all the recipes that claim to be soft- or marshmallow-centred should contain cornflour. Six recipes do not include it. This is not a minor issue, because the role of cornflour in making pavlovas soft-centred has been woven into both popular belief as well as academic papers on the origins and identity of pavlovas. Noeline Thomson had to change her mind about its importance when she found her friends achieving a marshmallow consistency in their pavlovas with and without cornflour. In 1996 I stated that the addition of vinegar and/or cornflour to a meringue cake resulted in a softer centre.[2] Jennifer Hillier picked up on my point in 2001, when she argued that one of the New Zealand recipes named pavlova dated to 1934 was not a true pavlova:

> I can't see how this meringue can have a soft-centre as it misses the essential ingredient of cornflour. Surely the name pavlova should represent the distinctive, soft-centred meringue.[3]

It seems we were all wrong about cornflour. The analysis of a much larger number of pavlova recipes has shown that cooks were making soft- and marshmallow-centred meringues both with and without the addition of cornflour. For a while I wondered if it was the inclusion of water that produced this effect, but ten of the recipes that were explicitly soft-centred had no added water, compared with sixteen that did. It was time to find out more about the chemistry of pavlovas.

The scientific analysis of pavlovas

Harold McGee has been one of the pioneers scrutinising the physics and chemistry of kitchen operations. In the most recent revision of his book *On Food and Cooking*, he discussed the roles played by several meringue ingredients:

> The addition of sugar is what makes a fragile egg-white foam into a stable glossy meringue. The more sugar added, the more body the meringue will have, and the crisper it will be when baked.[4]

There is no evidence of reduced quantities of sugar in the pavlova recipes that claim to make soft-centred cakes. Nor, it seems, is water the key to soft centres. According to McGee,

> in small amounts it increases the volume and lightness of the foam. Because water thins the whites, however, it's more likely that some liquid will drain from the foam.[5]

This risk can be partially mitigated by adding cornflour. Finely powdered sugar such as icing sugar contains cornflour to prevent caking, and cooks may have discovered its 'value as moisture-absorbing insurance'.[6] However, icing sugar was recorded in only four pavlova recipes. It is noticeable that most of the standardised pavlovas with water added also include cornflour, for example the four-plus-four, three-plus-three and the all-in-one. However, the coffee-walnut pavlova contains water but no cornflour. Overall only 50 per cent of recipes in the total data set contain cornflour, and only 42 per cent have added water. It would be nonsensical to claim, in either case, that the remainder lack soft centres (Fig. 10.1).

In 2006 an opportunity arose for some controlled experimentation on the role of different ingredients in pavlovas. My colleague and member of our research team, Janet Mitchell, who teaches in the Department of Food Science at the University of Otago, prepared and cooked seven pavlovas including several standardised forms: the first Edmonds' pavlova of 1939, a one-egg pavlova from 1956, two three-plus-three versions from 1961 and 2005, an early all-in-one from 1967, plus

ONE EGG PAVLOVA CAKE:

1 egg white	1 tsp. vinegar
1 tsp. vanilla	2 tbsp. boiling water
1 breakfast cup sugar	

Beat white until stiff, add sugar and beat, then boiling water and essence. Put in shape on greaseproof paper and bake slowly at 250 deg 1 hour approx.

PAVLOVA CAKE—1 A. E. Campbell

Separate 4 egg whites from yolks and put into a large basin. Beat until the whites stand stiffly in peaks. Add pinch of salt. Gradually add 1 cup sugar, folding in carefully without any more stirring than necessary. Add 1 tsp. vinegar. Pile on to greaseproof paper which has been greased then run under the cold tap. Cook for 1¼ hours, oven 300 deg. F, and gradually reduce heat.

PAVLOVA CAKE—2 Noeline Costello

4 eggs	2 tsp. vinegar
¾lb sugar	1 dessp. cornflour
Vanilla	Pinch cream of tartar

Beat egg whites, pinch of cream of tartar well, add ¾lb sugar and beat well then rest of sugar and beat again, lastly add cornflour and vinegar. Bake 1 hour at 350 deg. F.

PAVLOVA CAKE: UNCOOKED R. A. Hutton

1 egg white	½ cup sugar
¼ tsp. vanilla	Pinch salt
¼ cup any fruit juice	1 dessp. gelatine
½ cup boiling water	1 tsp. baking powder

Dissolve gelatine in boiling water, let cool. Put all ingredients except baking powder in bowl and beat 15 minutes. Fold in baking powder and whisk lightly. Butter greaseproof paper and line round tin, turn in mixture, cool until firm and then turn out on flat dish.

10.1 This group of pavlova recipes from the first *South Otago High School Recipe Book* (1959, p. 112) shows the range of variation by the late 1950s – one is the uncooked type, while of the other three, only one contains cornflour and one other calls for water.

two non-standard forms, one from 1939 and the other from 1992.[7] She attempted to replicate the conditions under which they were originally made, such as using a hand beater for recipes in use before 1960. All were cooked in the same oven, and then their characteristics were scientifically recorded. Janet found that the proportion of sugar in each recipe, and the type used, had a major effect on crust formation and stickiness of the interior. Where water was included, the resulting pavlova was light and more porous. The action of cornflour depended on the amount of water available to combine with it, and the temperature reached in the interior. The baking powder added to one of the recipes seems to have whitened the pavlova as well as acting as a source of acid. Brownness was linked to both the proportion of sugar and the method of mixing it in. Folding in the sugar produced a browner crust than beating. Where the sugar failed to dissolve completely, stickiness was a common result.

All of the pavlovas tested by Janet Mitchell included vinegar. A different approach was needed to isolate the particular role of vinegar and of each of the other ingredients. This became a research project undertaken in 2006 by Renée Wilson, a final year BSc Honours student in Food Science at the University of Otago. She took one recipe and systematically altered its ingredients in a way that would not be possible in a domestic kitchen. If you want to know the effect of eliminating the vinegar in a pavlova, or doubling it, you have to keep all the other components the same, and repeat the experiment several times. You also need specialised equipment to objectively measure the acidity/alkalinity, density and stability of the uncooked meringue foam, the temperature reached in the centre of the pavlova as it is cooked, how much moisture it loses during and immediately after cooking, the degree to which the pavlova rises and the amount of air space under the crust, the colour of the crust, and the overall firmness. Renée had to make eighty-one small pavlovas since she was testing nine variations on a single recipe, making three pavlovas from each, and repeating the process three times to ensure consistency.[8]

She started with Elizabeth Pedersen's four-egg-white pavlova published in 1992, which has one cup of caster sugar added progressively, one teaspoon of vinegar, one and a half teaspoons of cornflour, and a pinch of salt.[9] Then she made the same recipe again with one variable altered each time: the second was made with the egg whites in a different form (obtained frozen); the third, without salt; the fourth, with only half a cup of sugar; the fifth, with one and a half cups of sugar; the sixth, with no vinegar; the seventh, with two teaspoons of vinegar; the eighth, with no cornflour; and ninth and finally, she made a version with three teaspoons of cornflour.

Though the science behind egg-white foams is very complex, involving the molecular behaviour of the proteins in relation to the air bubbles they surround,[10]

Renée was able to explain her findings in cooks' as well as food scientists' terms. She showed that leaving out the salt has no measurable effect on the pavlova, because the pinch of salt in the original recipe is too small to alter the behaviour of the egg whites as they are beaten. But halving the sugar produced dire effects: the uncooked foam was significantly less dense, and more unstable – it broke down quickly, forming large air bubbles, and leaked water. When cooked, this pavlova lost height and showed no crust formation nor any airspace. It developed a rather unpleasant-looking brown sticky skin that darkened further after it was taken from the oven. Inside, the foam had a soft texture.

Renée found that adding half as much sugar again as in the original recipe was not so catastrophic. As you might expect, the uncooked foam was denser, and a little more unstable. On cooking, this high-sugar pavlova developed a much thicker, firmer crust above a large air gap. Inside, the foam was little different in firmness from the original recipe. However in texture, it would not have won a prize because liquid sugar was observed marbling the cooked foam.

Omitting the vinegar led to a poor quality pavlova. Egg whites are naturally alkaline and it has been shown that more air can be whipped into them, in the form of tightly packed tiny air bubbles, if their alkalinity is lowered. The uncooked foam is also much more stable if an acid like vinegar (or lemon juice or cream of tartar) is present. Without vinegar the cooked foam was significantly softer. Doubling the quantity of vinegar produced the firmest foam of all the experimental pavlovas. Another contribution made by the acid is to lower the temperature at which the egg-white proteins begin to gel and thereby solidify the foam. In turn this shortens the period when the pavlova is at risk of collapse, and gives it longer to dry out in the oven.

As for cornflour, Renée's research showed conclusively that in the original recipe there was insufficient water in the egg white and sugar mixture to bind with the cornflour: so whether or not cornflour was present, or doubled in quantity to one tablespoonful, it played no significant role in this recipe. If water had been an ingredient in her original recipe, the cornflour might have proved functional, binding the additional liquid and gelatinising when the interior temperature in the pavlova climbed over 75 degrees C. Gelatinisation under these conditions would add to the marshmallow effect. In other words, cornflour does have a role in the soft-centred pavlova, but only if water is added to the egg whites and the right temperature is reached in the interior.

Hints for making pavlovas

1. Use eggs that are a few days old. Very fresh or stale eggs do not beat well.

2. Egg whites are easier to separate from the yolks when cold, but in beating greater volume is achieved with whites at room temperature. The solution is to separate the eggs straight after removal from the fridge, but then to leave the whites in a bowl for an hour before beating. If time is a problem, hurry the process by placing the whites in a small bowl or jug and standing it in a larger vessel containing warm (not hot) water. Leave for just a few minutes.

3. Egg whites will not whip to their maximum volume in the presence of even a small trace of fat or oil. Make sure that your mixing bowl and beater blades have been thoroughly cleaned with hot water and detergent before use – glass or metal bowls are better than plastic bowls, which tend to retain traces of fatty material on their surfaces. Separate each egg over a smaller bowl before transferring to the mixing bowl – if a yolk (which contains some fat) breaks and leaks into the egg white, you can put it aside for another purpose without having to start again from scratch.

4. It is important to dissolve the sugar during the beating process. Undissolved granules give a meringue a gritty texture and can cause beads of syrup to form during baking. Use caster sugar in preference to ordinary white sugar, as it is finer and dissolves more readily. To check that beating has dissolved the sugar, rub a little of the mixture between finger and thumb – it should feel smooth, not gritty.

5. During whipping, the air bubbles become finer and finer. But you need to stop the process before the mechanical action of the beaters damages the proteins and causes the bubble walls to collapse – referred to as over-beating. If hand-beating your whites, whip them until they are stiff and the peaks stand up when you lift up the beater. If they fold over, whip some more. Then start adding your sugar tablespoon by tablespoon, beating until the mixture is glossy and very stiff. You may need to fold in the last portion of sugar. If using an electric mixer, over-beating can be avoided by adding the sugar at the start as in all-in-one pavlova recipes – but the mixing takes longer and a high-speed setting is necessary.

6. If using boiling water, cover the whites with sugar before adding the water, to prevent damage to the egg whites.

7. As they cook, meringues have a tendency to stick to any surface with which they are in contact. Use greased greaseproof paper, butter wrapping paper, a teflon liner, or preferably non-stick baking paper (no need to grease) to cover the oven tray or line the cake pan. Spray a few droplets of non-stick baking oil under the paper to stop it from sliding when spreading the pavlova mixture. If using a pan, spray the sides with non-stick baking oil.

8. Follow the recipe instructions regarding the cooling process – most modern pavlovas are best left to cool in the turned-off oven, over night or for at least an hour.

9. For a low fat pavlova, substitute thickened yoghurt or lemon cream for the traditional whipped-cream topping. To make thickened yoghurt, line a sieve with a piece of muslin or Chux cloth that has been dipped in boiling water. Position the sieve to fit over a jug or deep bowl. Tip the yoghurt into the sieve. Loosely cover the surface with plastic film and stand in a fridge for several hours to drain and thicken. (A recipe for lemon cream is given in Fig. 7.9.)

Cooking times and temperatures

Since we cannot isolate any particular ingredient or recipe as pivotal in making a pavlova soft-centred, perhaps we should ask whether soft-centred meringues of any type are simply undercooked. If cooking temperatures and times were consistent in the recipes, it might be possible to test the argument that very soft marshmallow centres result from significantly shorter cooking times and/or lower temperatures, coupled perhaps with greater meringue thickness. But most recipes leave cooks to judge for themselves when the pavlova is ready, and ovens vary enormously.

The difficulty of demonstrating this correlation from existing recipes means that we have to turn to the long history of meringues for supporting evidence. In nineteenth-century bakers' ovens, the standard egg-shaped meringues began to colour before they had dried out completely. This was the signal to remove them from the oven, and scoop out the soft centre. After a final drying upside down in an oven or drying cabinet, the resulting cavity was filled with cream and fruit. As meringues grew to the size of plates, and especially when they were cooked as a single thick layer, cooking became more difficult and was more likely to lead to a soft centre as the crust insulated the interior and slowed the drying out process. Many early meringue cakes counted on the centre collapsing after removal from the oven, as in the recipe for the Meringue Cake in Aunt Daisy's N.Z. 'Daisy Chain' Cookery Book, which baldly stated: 'Cake drops in centre. When cold fill up with whipped cream and fruit ...'[11]

Viewing the small meringue as inherently crisp and the pavlova as soft-centred is probably too simplistic. When the pavlova cake began to be made as a single layer rather than two or more layers sandwiched together, I suspect it became harder to dry it out completely. In small meringues, the soft centre was turned to advantage when its removal created a cavity for the filling. Similarly the soft centre of the meringue cake or pavlova became an attribute, and the subject of its own mystique. Pavlovas can be fully dried out, given the right oven conditions and plenty of time, but most people now prefer the contrast between a crisp exterior and a softer, more melt-in-the-mouth interior (Fig. 10.2).

After 1950, as pavlovas shifted from the 'cakes' category to that of 'desserts, cold sweets or puddings', we see the growing preference for a soft centre taken to extremes in the uncooked pavlova, pavlova roll, and microwaved pavlova. However, the recipes for the most common type of pavlova, standardised or otherwise, still call for the long, slow cooking that ensures a thick crust, if not a firm interior. Although soft or marshmallow centres may be a contemporary preference, the cooking instructions for most pavlovas in my New Zealand data set usually give no indication that this is the desired outcome. Many are left in the oven after the one and a half to two hours' cooking time or until the oven is cold,

10.2 Though solid fuel and early electric stoves could be managed to provide suitable conditions for drying out meringues, gas stoves were less satisfactory – gas combustion produced water and so gas ovens needed large vents and had little insulation (reproduced from *The Ideal Cookery Book*, 1929, p. 114).

while others are placed in an oven preheated to a high temperature (e.g. 200 degrees C.) that is turned off five minutes later, leaving the pavlova to dry out on stored heat. By contrast the truly soft types, such as the pavlova roll, are cooked for a mere ten to fifteen minutes. To define the essence of the pavlova as being its soft centre fails to take account of the many different types, and the many different instructions for cooking them. The thicker the mass of meringue, the greater is the chance of it having a soft centre when taken from the oven, a fact well known to cooks for over two centuries. A soft centre no more defines a pavlova than the absence of one defines a meringue.

The cooking interface – from white paper to non-stick baking paper

In 1782 Elizabeth Raffald instructed her readers to put their cream cakes (an old name for meringues) on a tin tray covered with a wet sheet of paper, before inserting them into a baker's oven to cook after the loaves of brown bread had been removed.[12] Through the course of the nineteenth century, it became more common to place the paper (usually white) on a board about an inch thick, rather than on a tin or iron sheet. By the end of the century cooks were commonly advised to wet the board. Waxed and 'paraffine' papers were tried out during the 1880s in London and New York, and in London during World War 1, a baking sheet might be rubbed over with wax to provide a non-stick surface. Early in the twentieth century, Fannie Merritt Farmer recommended buttered paper under her Meringues or Kisses.[13] Greased and floured baking sheets were increasingly used under the larger meringues, though paper continued for several decades under small meringues. All of these recipes take great pains to advise cooks how meringues should be prepared for the oven. We can read into their complex instructions an on-going problem: how to stop meringues browning underneath and sticking to the surface on which they are cooked.

With meringue cakes and pavlovas, sticking posed the greatest risk, because efforts to remove the stuck cake might lead to catastrophic fractures. Of the seven meringue cakes I have recorded from New Zealand recipe books of the 1920s (including the first Pavlova Cake), one was cooked on white paper, then split for filling, while five were cooked in greased sandwich tins normally used to cook the layers of sponge cakes. Only the American contributor's Strawberry Basket Meringue was a single layer cake, and it was cooked in an ungreased sandwich tin! I have no idea how it was removed. In the 1930s, most pavlova and meringue cakes (83 per cent) were still cooked in tins, but their recipes frequently stipulated the use of a lining: buttered paper, wetted buttered paper, wet wrapping paper, wet brown paper, and from 1937 greaseproof paper and wetted greaseproof paper. Wetting the paper or board was a technique with a long history in relation to small meringues and so it is not surprising to see its transfer to the larger cakes. Those meringue cakes that were cooked on a tray or slide used paper, buttered paper, or greaseproof paper as their interface. Tin-cooked pavlovas or meringue cakes remained dominant in the 1940s, and their tins or dishes were usually lined with buttered paper, including 'butter paper', the wrapping used for store-bought butter. Nearly half recommended wet or at least dampened paper as extra insurance against sticking.

In the 1950s, tins were increasingly abandoned in favour of greased oven slides covered with greased paper, greaseproof paper and even greased greaseproof paper, wetted for good measure. Only 27 per cent of the large cooked pavlova cakes were made in tins, and this proportion continued to drop steadily for the remaining decades of the century. In 1961 a new product became available, waxed paper, which could be used to line a tin or cover an oven tray. It was first recommended in 1961 by Mrs S.D. Sherriff in her widely distributed GHB Cookery Book.[14] Other food-writers endorsed it during the 1970s and 1980s, including Eleanor Gray, Mary Mountier, and Gordon Dryden.[15] However, home cooks seemed less enthusiastic, with only ten recipes from community cookbooks specifying waxed paper over the period 1960–99. One recipe contributor went so far as to say that her pavlova should be placed on buttered 'lunch paper (not waxed)'.[16]

In contrast, foil was readily adopted when first promoted in Rosemary Dempsey's cooking columns of the New Zealand Herald in the late 1960s, and subsequently endorsed by Tui Flower.[17] Community cookbooks included pavlovas cooked on greased 'tinfoil' (later increasingly referred to as 'foil' or 'aluminium foil') from 1970 onwards. A variation on this method was to use a ready-made tinfoil plate. Foil retained its popularity in the 1990s, despite increasing use of another new product that did not need to be greased or wetted – baking paper, also known as non-stick paper. Again food writers played a role in the introduction of this kitchen aid, starting with Des Britten in 1977 and Jan Bilton in 1981.[18] After a slow start, baking paper took off in popularity from 1990. Rather than compete with foil, non-stick paper led to a sharp fall in the use of greaseproof paper, a decline that is likely to accelerate.

Janet Mitchell's trial of seven historic pavlova recipes included observations of how easily they were removed from their baking surface.[19] Where the recipe specified greasing of both the paper and underlying tray, as in the 1939 Edmonds pavlova, the paper peeled off the pavlova easily; however, ungreased greaseproof paper stuck, especially where syrup had leaked from the cake. Wet greaseproof paper on a tray or lining a tin was no better because the water evaporated before the cake had set. The two most recent recipes that she tested, from 1992 and 2005, called for the use of baking paper and no sticking occurred. Janet's results raise the question why cooks used an unreliable method of preparing the cooking interface. Recipes using wet ungreased greaseproof paper are less common than those where the cooking surface is buttered, but they persist from 1939 through to the 1970s when non-stick paper was introduced. Sometimes cooks would have used (as I did) butter-wrapping paper as a form of greaseproof paper, and the residual grease would have prevented sticking, and sometimes the recipe writers may have simply forgotten to mention greasing the paper. But the fact remains that wet greaseproof paper was recommended for several decades.

Over the nearly eighty-year history of pavlovas, there have been several inventions of special containers or plates to facilitate their cooking. The first was mentioned by Isabella Finlay, demonstrator to the Dunedin City Gas Department. She referred to it as a 'special Pavlova cake tin',[20] but no illustrations have been found to aid identification of any surviving examples, and questions as to where was it made, and how long was it on sale remain unanswered. Much later, in a fund-raising book first published in 1978, reference is made to a 'pavlova ring'.[21] A 'hinged pavlova ring' placed on damp greaseproof paper on a cold tray is mentioned in 1984.[22] Though not referred to in any of the recipe books studied, a porcelain plate (made in Japan but printed with what reads like a New Zealand pavlova recipe) was sold as a dual-purpose cooking and serving surface in 1978 (Fig. 10.3).[23] In theory, using the same plate for cooking and serving should eliminate the risk of fracture during the transfer from one surface to another – but how easy is it to serve the pavlova if it has stuck to the plate during cooking? Other pavlova aids and inventions may exist in New Zealand, given the popularity of the dish and the on-going challenge of cooking it. However, they may not have been widely advertised, and probably now sit in secondhand shops with their original purpose unrecognised. Even flat pavlova serving plates, and their matching china cake trowels, cannot be readily distinguished from conventional cake plates that were made flat to help the afternoon tea hostess transfer helpings of sponge cake to her guests' plates.

Fortunately, ever since the very first meringue cakes and pavlovas were developed, cooks have had a fall-back position in case of emergency. Whipped cream is like snow on a glacier, covering the deepest crevasses with an all-enveloping whiteness. Even when a cake has broken in half, or the crust has ruptured to reveal the airspace beneath, the damage can be concealed by a blanket of cream.

10.3   Jane Teal obtained this dual-purpose oven-to-table pavlova plate in 1978. Though manufactured in Japan, the recipe on the front is for a typical New Zealand pavlova.

Why pavlovas are important

THE FACTS are these: within three years of Anna Pavlova's visit to New Zealand there were three different dishes called pavlova. The earliest was devised in Australia in 1926 by Davis Gelatine, a company of New Zealand origin. Though the layered gelatine pavlova appeared in the New Zealand editions of Davis's give-away cookbook until the 1950s, we have no idea whether it was popular – I suspect not, because of its complicated instructions. However, its name prepared the way for public acceptance of the next type of pavlova: Rose Rutherford's little coffee and walnut pavlovas, bite-sized meringue novelties that she thought up in Dunedin in 1928. These became very popular in the 1930s and were still being made as late as 1966. Within a year of the publication of the recipe for Rose's pavlovas, we find the first known recipe for a large pavlova cake in the *New Zealand Dairy Exporter Annual*, dated 10 October 1929. If you are wedded to the idea of a 'real pavlova', then this is currently the earliest – but who knows how long it was in circulation before 'Festival' submitted it to 'Tui', the lady editor of the cookery section? Festival's pavlova was just one of five meringue cakes, each called Pavlova, that I have found in New Zealand recipe books printed before 1935. Each one was different, and there may be more awaiting discovery.

An important objective of my study was to reveal the complexity of the food items we call pavlovas. By doing so I hoped to correct the simplistic view of the pavlova as a single concept bearing a single name, invented in one place and at one time, a view that permeates public debates about pavlova origins. As I have shown, there have been many sorts of pavlovas in New Zealand since 1927, and many dishes sharing the same concepts but appearing under different names, especially in the early decades. These were incorporated in the study for a good reason: restricting the analysis to recipes named 'pavlova' would have allowed the name to stand for the identity of the dish, whereas the distinctiveness of a dish lies in all its variables: ingredients and method as well as name. By taking the broader view,

The pavlova timeline

Date	Current events	History of the pavlova
1691		First meringue recipe in French cookbook
1702		First meringue recipe in English cookbook
1881	Anna Pavlova born in St Petersburg, Russia	
1926	Anna Pavlova tours Australia and New Zealand	Meringue cakes become popular in New Zealand and Australia
		Davis Gelatine publishes recipe for Gelatine Pavlova in Australia
1927		Davis Gelatine publishes recipe for Gelatine Pavlova in New Zealand
1928		Rose Rutherford (Dunedin) contributes original recipe for little Pavlova Cakes to *The Weekly Press* (Christchurch)
1929	Anna Pavlova tours Australia	'Festival' contributes recipe for large two-layered Pavlova Cake to *The N.Z. Dairy Exporter Annual*
1931	Anna Pavlova dies, aged 49 years	
1933		Laurina Stevens contributes recipe for large single-layer Pavlova Cake to *Rangiora Mothers' Union Cookery Book*
1935		Bert Sachse develops first Australian pavlova cake in Perth
c. 1936		Rose Rutherford's Pavlova Cakes republished in Edmonds' *The 'Sure to Rise' Cookery Book*, sixth ed.
1939		Edmonds publish their first recipe for a large pavlova (seventh ed.), repeated till 1978

I was able to throw light on the origins of pavlova cakes as a form of meringue cake, and of the little pavlovas as a variant of small meringues. I also revealed the power of a popular dish with a distinctive name to appropriate dishes of different origin (such as the uncooked pavlova derived from snows and marshmallow puddings, and the Snax pavlova derived from meringue nut tortes). Not only did they take the name 'pavlova', but they enlarged the range of variation perceived in the pavlova category as a whole, and in doing so expanded its popularity.

Something very similar happened in North America with the angel cake. In the nineteenth century, angel cakes were made by whipping a large number of egg

Date	Current events	History of the pavlova
1942	Wartime rationing of sugar begins in New Zealand, lasts till 1948	
1943	Rationing of butter begins, lasts till 1950, tight controls on access to cream	
1944	Rationing of eggs becomes nationwide, lasts till 1950	
1951		First appearance of three-plus-three and four-plus-four standardised pavlova recipes
c. 1952		One-egg pavlova develops from recipe for one-egg meringues; lemon curd topping/filling introduced
1957	Price of a dozen eggs peaks at twice that of 1945	
1959		First appearance of Coffee Pavlova cake and standard one-egg uncooked pavlova; appearance of chocolate & egg yolk topping
1964		First electric frypan pavlova
1970		First standardised all-in-one recipes for pavlova; appearance of the jelly crystal pavlova
1974	Bert Sachse dies in Australia; New Zealand adopts metric measurements	
1980		First appearance of pavlova roll, borrowed from Australia
1981		First appearance of Snax torte or pavlova; development of first pavlova for diabetics
1983		First known recipe for microwaved pavlova
2000		International appearance of mini-pavlovas

whites, beating in sugar, and then folding in finely sifted flour, cream of tartar and vanilla. The mixture was cooked in an ungreased tin so that it rose high and was less likely to sink.[1] During the twentieth century, angel cakes became an essential item in a good cook's repertoire, and the name 'angel' was extended to dishes that were formerly classified as meringues or tortes. If you want to order the equivalent of a pavlova in the United States, ask for angel pie. It is made from a meringue shell, filled with a cooked lemon, sugar, and egg yolk mixture (the same one introduced to New Zealand by Helen Cox in the early 1950s), and is smothered in whipped cream.[2] The earliest dish that matches the concept is a Kiss Torte, dated to 1903; however, it lacks the lemon filling, being filled instead with whipped cream and berryfruit. The first to be called Angel Pie is from the famous Toll House cookery book, first published in 1936.[3]

Not only were there three different pavlovas in New Zealand by 1929, but over the next eight decades one of them, the large meringue pavlova, spawned multiple standardised variants (at least eleven recognised so far). As well, the name 'pavlova' was transferred to marshmallow gelatine desserts, and less completely to nutty tortes of American origin. Besides these standardised pavlovas, there are several hundred personalised pavlovas, the product of home kitchens throughout New Zealand.

Because I analysed a well-dated body of recipes from cookbooks published in most regions in New Zealand, I was able to identify 'lineages' of recipes linked by ingredients, proportions, and methods, and to reveal their spread over time and space. Some lineages showed little variation over several decades, in particular Rose Rutherford's pavlovas, the three versions of uncooked pavlova, and the rolled pavlova. However, the single-layer pavlova cake branched into several variants, and in the case of the three-plus-three this quickly gave rise to four versions. The four-plus-four underwent progressive modification through time, with a series of offshoots replacing each other in popularity.

Why should some variants branch out while others follow a more or less unilineal course? I suspect that where a recipe is distinctively different, stemming from an obvious innovation, cooks adhere to the original recipe to maintain its separate identity. Thus, cooks who made Rose Rutherford's pavlovas were obliged to include the coffee essence and walnuts since these were the ingredients that marked this dish off from the ordinary meringue. Along the way cooks made no attempt to change the number of egg whites (two) or the method of measuring out the sugar (five tablespoons). Uncooked pavlovas are even further removed from the conventional pavlova or meringue cake. Three versions of uncooked pavlova appeared in the first decade of its existence, but only one became widely adopted and reproduced. Similarly the rolled pavlova is dominated by a four-egg-white version that was established within two years of its first appearance. In contrast, the three-plus-three and four-plus-four variants don't exist as distinct forms of pavlova in the minds of their makers. For a start they have a variety of names, many overlapping between the two variants, for example Never Fail Pavlova and Pavlova (Soft Centre). They can only be recognised as standard types when compared to a very large number of recipes. As such, their continued existence depends entirely on the faithfulness with which they are transmitted. Fortunately they have proved very reliable and busy cooks asked to contribute a recipe to a fund-raising recipe book have passed them on time after time, with only minor modifications.

Chief forms of standardised (large) pavlovas and their variants, with dates of earliest known appearance in New Zealand

Assigned name of pavlova type	Variant	Number of egg whites	Sugar	Water	Vinegar	Cornflour	Baking Powder/ Cream of Tartar
Edmonds' First 1939–1978		3	9 oz caster		1 tsp		
One Egg 1952–1980s		1	1 cup	2 Tbsp boiling	1 tsp		½–1 tsp BP
Three-plus-Three 1951–	#1 1951–	3	1½ cups	3 Tbsp cold	1 tsp	3 tsp	
	#2 1961–	3	1¼ cups	3 Tbsp cold	1 tsp	3 tsp	
	#3 1966–	3	1½ cups	3 Tbsp cold	1 tsp	1 tsp	
	#4 1967–	3	1 cup	3 Tbsp cold	1 tsp	3 tsp	
Four-plus-Four 1951–	#1 1951–	4	4 oz + 4 oz	1 Tbsp cold	2 tsp	1 dssp	Pinch CoT
	#2 1961–	4	4 oz + 4 oz	1 Tbsp cold	1 tsp	1 dssp	Pinch CoT
	#3 1963–	4	4 oz + 4 oz	1 dssp cold	1 tsp	1 Tbsp	Pinch CoT
Coffee-Walnut 1959–		3	1½ cups	2–4 Tbsp boiling			
Uncooked 1959–	#1 1959–	1	½ cup	½ cup	¼–½ cup fruit juice		1 tsp BP
	#2 1960–	3	½ cup	½ cup	½ cup lemon juice		
	#3 (1956) 1961–	2	½ cup	1 cup			
All-in-One (1959) 1970–	#1 1959	2	1½ cups	4 Tbsp boiling	1 tsp	1 tsp	
	#2 1972	3	1 cup	3 dssp	1 tsp		
	#3 1978	3	1½ cups	4 Tbsp boiling	1 tsp	1 tsp–1dssp	
Pavlova Roll (1980) 1982–		4	8 Tbsp		2 tsp	1 tsp	
Snax Pavlova 1981–		3	¾–1 cup (6–8 oz)				½–1 tsp BP

Tbsp = tablespoon
dssp = dessertspoon
tsp = teaspoon
oz = ounce

The three-plus-three type is named after the number of whites and the number of tablespoons of water. The four-plus-four is named after the distinctive practice of adding the sugar – four ounces beaten in then four ounces folded in. The metric equivalent is 125 g plus 125 g.

The evolution of pavlovas

Because I am an anthropologist interested in the evolution of humans as a species, and their increasingly elaborate cultures, I have noticed many parallels between the history of pavlovas and evolutionary processes. Branching and unilineal lineages are frequently discussed in biological evolutionary theory, along with concepts such as extinction, selection, descent with modification, and adaptation. Many of these concepts are also used in writings on cultural evolution. I have found that they can usefully be applied to pavlovas and related dishes in the form of a simple analogy.

Some recipes clearly have common ancestors, although modifications along the way have produced variations, which in turn have their own lines of descent. Each time recipes are transmitted they are subject to selection. The recipe I write out for you may have been *selected for* its reliability or simplicity, while the one I pass over has been *selected against*, just as individuals are selected for or against in natural selection. Whenever dishes are reproduced they may be changed to suit the tastes of the cook and the conditions of the kitchen. This is how variation is introduced and different versions originate. If recipe reproduction (cooking) and transmission (publication or copying) ceases, extinction follows, unless a recipe is revived from a relict cookbook. Unlike biological organisms (prior to genetic engineering), recipes can acquire new ingredients or segments of method from unrelated dishes. Once incorporated, however, these innovations become part of the modified form and contribute to the success or failure of that version. Simplification or elaboration can be seen through time, along with aspects of recipes adapted to earlier conditions (such as cooking pavlovas on wet paper because meringues used to be cooked that way). Overall, the value of the evolutionary analogy is that it focuses attention on evolutionary processes such as selection acting on variation, the means by which variation emerges, different forms of reproduction, the role of competition between varieties, and adaptation to changing environments. These processes link the individual recipes scattered in time and place and provide us with a valuable mechanism for understanding the complex history of pavlovas.

Successful transmission of recipes depends on selection not only by compilers of cookbooks or editors of cookery columns in magazines and newspapers, but on the selection of the particular recipe by the cook who plans the menu. A surprising number of pavlova recipes published in authored recipe books failed to be repeated later in community cookbooks, despite wide circulation of the original work and the reputation of the food-writer as a media personality. They are not even present in plagiarised form! In fact well-known food writers and television chefs played a greater role in promoting products associated with pavlovas, such as foil and baking paper, than in introducing new variants themselves. Publication of a recipe submitted to a national magazine or newspaper, or in a national compiled collection (for example, by Country Women's Institutes, League of Mothers, or Women's Division of Federated Farmers) was more likely to lead to further copying. Rose Rutherford's pavlovas achieved wide distribution through appearance in four nationally distributed publications in the 1930s, and the one-egg pavlova that appeared in the N.Z. Truth Cookery Book about 1956 became the standard version of that variant (Fig. 11.1 and 11.2). Similarly the soft-centred pavlova published by Mrs Sherriff in the GHB Cookery Book in 1961 became the most popular of the three-plus-three pavlovas, and the coffee and walnut pavlova chosen by Thelma Christie for the Triple Tested Recipe Book in 1959 became the standard for that form. Selection by Tui Flower of one version of the three-plus-three pavlova for publication in the 1971 New Zealand Woman's Weekly Cookbook allowed what may be an original Southland recipe to achieve national popularity. The distribution of the standardised all-in-one pavlovas (1970–) was later enhanced by publication in a cookbook by Jan Bilton (1981) and in one edited by Gordon Dryden (1984).

11.1 This *N.Z. Truth Cookery Book* (sold for 6s 0d when first published c. 1956, but repriced in 1967) was one of a long series that began during World War 2, containing recipes originally contributed to *New Zealand Truth*.

ONE-EGG PAVLOVA

ONE eggwhite, 1 cup sugar, 1 teaspoon vinegar, 2 tablespoons hot water, pinch salt, 1 teaspoon baking powder, vanilla. Put eggwhite, sugar, vinegar, salt and water in a basin and beat well over hot water till fluffy. Add baking powder and vanilla and leave a few minutes. Spread mixture on some wet greaseproof paper—this ensures the pavlova coming away cleanly—and cook in slow oven.

11.2 This widely circulated recipe became the standard for the one-egg pavlova (reproduced from *N.Z. Truth Cookery Book*, c. 1956, p. 124).

While publication in a high-profile national recipe book or column often accelerated the spread of the different pavlova types, it was equally possible for recipes to spread steadily and slowly from person to person, both within and between communities. The four-plus-four pavlova, which in the course of five decades appeared in local cookbooks from most regions in New Zealand, is a good example. The length of time involved in its spread, and its progressive modification along the way, argues against an as yet unidentified national source for this variant.

As well as household-to-household transmission, there may have been some interaction between commercial and domestic kitchens, especially in relation to the inclusion of hot water in the meringue mix and the heating of the contents of the bowl over boiling water, evident in the 1950s. Considering that commercial kitchens had food mixers decades before most home kitchens, it is quite possible that some of the experimentation that led to the electric mixer variants took place in New Zealand cake kitchens or restaurants.

Quantitative analysis in a spreadsheet focuses on the identification of patterns in the data, and allows the recognition of standardised types, making it is easy to ignore recipes that fall outside these well-defined groups. Nearly half the recipes for pavlovas are non-standardised. They represent individual interpretations of the pavlova concept and in no sense should be considered as forms that became extinct after a single appearance. They adhere to general principles, such as the fairly consistent ratio of egg whites to sugar, and the quantities of vinegar and cornflour (if used) falling within a confined range. These one-off recipes and those for making the Snax pavlova or torte show the importance of analysing groups of recipes that are held together not by name but by shared concept. In the Snax type, the permitted range of variation in ingredients is narrow – however, ingredient proportions, cooking container, and the name vary significantly. Nevertheless the concept of the Snax pavlova or torte can be circumscribed by a much smaller circle than that required to accommodate all the personalised recipes that make up the body of non-standardised pavlovas. In the mind of the cook, the Snax pavlova or torte is a distinctive form, whereas most customised pavlovas are those that cooks have modified to suit their tastes or equipment. Once contributed to the local fund-raising recipe book, they are tweaked by every cook who makes them.

Turning to the concept of adaptation (which in biological evolution confers differential fitness), pavlova recipes provide excellent examples of adaptation to both the cost of ingredients and to the development of new kitchen technology. It is no coincidence that one-egg-white pavlovas, both the cooked form and the uncooked gelatine variant, appear in the 1950s when eggs were increasingly expensive following World War 2. The addition of water to several other post-1950 types might be interpreted as a way of achieving greater volume with fewer whites.

In contrast, the pavlova roll, which achieved fashionable status in the affluent 1980s–90s, used four egg whites.

In relation to kitchen technology, the spread of food mixers in the 1950s prompted experimentation with pavlova recipes and led to the emergence of several variants with both ingredients and methods adapted to mechanical mixing, especially the all-in-one pavlova. Most of these recipes cannot be made successfully with hand-operated rotary beaters. In just the same way, the arrival of electric frypans and microwaves in New Zealand kitchens encouraged adventurous cooks to adapt pavlova recipes to these appliances. Obviously the frypan and microwave ovens were not purchased to facilitate the making of pavlovas – instead the pavlova was adapted, perhaps to justify the purchase of the appliance.

Pavlovas have also shown a remarkable adaptation to changing patterns of entertaining in New Zealand society. Though they continued to be served as luncheon desserts, the same context in which meringue cakes were served in the United States, in New Zealand they were quickly adapted for use in the formal afternoon tea. I think that the trend away from the two-layered pavlova or meringue cake to the single-layered pavlova is connected to this change of venue and occasion. In contrast to a meal served course by course in the fashion (known as *à la russe*) adopted in Britain in the second half of the nineteenth century and still used today, the afternoon tea was set out on the tea wagon or table as a collection of set pieces, in the way that dinners used to be served *à la française*. Unquestionably, *à la française* service offered greater scope for display. As the centerpiece of an afternoon-tea display, the single-layered pavlova hid none of its luxurious accompaniments inside as a filling, but arranged them artistically on top. The preference for a single layer pavlova continued even after the decline of the formal afternoon tea, perhaps because the meals at which they were served after the 1960s frequently included buffets, which are also occasions for display.

Ancestry and migration are of great relevance to evolutionary studies. My study has looked beyond the immediate ancestor of the early pavlovas, the meringue cakes of the early 1920s, to the history of the meringue itself. In the process it revealed the circumstances under which soft centres were initially scraped out to create a cavity in small crisp meringues, and then as the pavlova evolved were positively valued to the point where completely non-crisp pavlovas would become acceptable, and even popular. The evolution of the pavlova complex has seen the migration of several concepts from overseas sources. Certainly the 1920s New Zealand meringue cake had input from the United States and Australia and probably from Britain. While there is no evidence for an external origin of either Rose Rutherford's pavlovas or the large New Zealand pavlova cake, this does not mean that the later history of pavlovas was purely locally driven. The Snax variety is clearly a borrowing from the United States subjected to re-naming by

New Zealand cooks in the 1980s. The rolled pavlova is recorded in Australia a few years before it appears in a New Zealand cookbook in 1980, so it too probably represents a borrowing. The practice of adding water to pavlovas, uncommon in Australian recipe books, and not seen in American angel pies or meringue tortes, may well have been learned from the hard-pressed cooks of 1940s Britain. But the pavlova complex that I have examined is essentially New Zealand-based.

Comparison of New Zealand recipes with a sample of thirty Australian pavlovas dated between 1950 and 1998 showed a possible borrowing of the one-egg pavlova from east to west across the Tasman and the likely movement of the rolled pavlova in the opposite direction. The rest have only generic resemblances. When an in-depth analysis of Australian pavlova recipes is performed, it may well show the same pattern of local and largely independent evolution, influenced from time to time by external ideas. In the meantime I can add one important observation to the history of Australian pavlovas: I have been unable to match Bert Sachse's recipe with any known New Zealand example, and as I complete this book there are now more than 700 in my data set. There is no evidence to doubt the Perth account of the origin of the Australian pavlova in 1935. It is not an obvious copy of an earlier New Zealand recipe, nor was it copied by New Zealand cooks.

A very simple message can be taken from the recognition of processes like adaptation, selection, and extinction in the history of pavlovas: like species of plants and animals, they evolved – they were not created from scratch. Looking for a creator and an original pavlova will thus always be a fruitless activity. However, I suspect that on the whole Australian and New Zealand journalists are creationists and will go on looking for the pavlova's equivalent of Eve!

From fashionable dish to contested icon

How long will the pavlova survive? A dish will be made for millennia, if it has a significant role to play in a region's cuisine. Dishes that play an integral part in everyday meal structures – especially cooked cereals, such as breads and rice, and staple root crops – go back many thousands of years to the very origins of agriculture ten thousand years ago. I'm not suggesting that the pavlova will last that long under the name pavlova; however meringues, the umbrella category to which pavlovas belong, have already been around in English-speaking countries for three centuries. If we compare meringues to certain other sweet dishes like jellies, plum puddings, blancmanges, rich fruit cakes, tarts, and creams, then persistence over five or six centuries would not be an unreasonable expectation. Within these overarching categories, particular versions rise and fall in popularity; so although it is possible that the pavlova name will be replaced over the next century by something more topical, meringues are likely to be in our repertoire for centuries to come.

What may keep the name 'pavlova' viable is a shift in its associations. A case can be made that this has happened already. In the 1920s meringue cakes were one of the latest food fashions – from London to New York, San Francisco to Sydney – and Anna Pavlova was the most famous ballerina of the era. The combination of the fashionable dessert cake and her name got the pavlova off to a good start, and the early death of Pavlova in 1931 added some pathos. In the 1930s when you made a pavlova, you showed that you were up with the latest trends at the same time as you commemorated the world's greatest ballerina. Today very few New Zealanders have personal memories of her visit, and the history of the arts is not widely taught in schools. So is the passage of time eroding the power of the name? World War 2 could have led to the pavlova's extinction because its key ingredients (eggs, sugar, and cream) were all subject to rationing that persisted for most of the 1940s (Fig. 11.3). Yet in rural New Zealand the pavlova was taking on new roles – as marker of resistance against wartime regulations, and symbol of a land which we believed should flow not just with milk and honey but cream and eggs as well. I think that the 1940s were critical to the rebirth of the pavlova as a recognised national icon in the 1950s.

Iconic dishes have a much greater chance of longevity than passing fashions. As a national icon, the pavlova proliferated from the 1950s. When I first began to make them, I certainly wasn't commemorating a ballerina (in fact, for various family reasons I was very anti-ballet in the 1950s). I prepared pavlovas

11.3 Rationing provided the greatest challenge to the pavlova in the 1940s, yet may have enhanced the rebound effect that led to it becoming a national icon in the 1950s – this *Housewives' Guide [to] Food Prices [and] Food Rationing* was issued in 1944.

because they were a luxurious dish that we were proud to serve to visitors (Fig. 11.4). At that stage I wasn't aware that Australians also made pavlovas. As I argued in Chapter One, growing realisation in the 1970s that our ownership was contested, and the eventual outbreak of the pavlova wars, added extra significance to the dish. So pavlovas have in nearly eight decades moved from fashionable commemorative dish to national icon, and then contested national icon. Each step injected renewed vitality and stimulated new varieties.

11.4 In the 1950s we cooked our pavlovas in a proudly New Zealand-made Neeco stove (reproduced from *700 Neeco Tested Recipes*, c. 1951, p. 5).

This sort of transformation is not unique to pavlovas. Anzac biscuits show many parallels with the pavlova story. They emerged out of a category of biscuit usually known as Rolled Oats Crispies or Biscuits that appeared just before World War I. The dramatic events on Gallipoli in 1915 led to the renaming of several different dishes as Anzac: Anzac Cakes (printed in a Dunedin recipe book in 1915), Anzac Pudding (Invercargill 1917–18), Anzac Biscuits (Sydney 1917, but a completely different recipe), and eventually Anzac Crispies (Dunedin 1919, later renamed Anzac Biscuits). Just as with pavlovas, a highly significant name was applied to a range of different dishes at first, and then eventually settled on just one, which became iconic. Several variants can be traced through the twentieth century. Anzac biscuits are still popular nearly ninety years after they first appeared in recognisable form, and it is probably no coincidence that their origins are also contested between Australia and New Zealand. But just like pavlovas they evolved out of existing biscuits, and no 'creator' was involved. The importance of their namesake, which we are reminded of every Anzac Day, has meant that they have outlasted their original contemporaries like Cockles, Peep Bo's and Cocoanut Delusions.

The people's pavlovas

Unlike Escoffier's Peach Melba, New Zealand pavlovas are not the product of haute cuisine, but evolved within a regional culinary tradition. I had better explain what I mean. In essence, a culinary tradition is a people's cuisine, not the haute cuisine of social leaders, but the foodways of ordinary people. A culinary tradition encompasses the unwritten rules for constructing daily meals as well as feasts, of combining dishes in menus, and of preparing, cooking and serving those dishes in ways that sometimes come to mark that particular people and their region. A people may be aware that some of their dishes are distinctive to them, but a culinary tradition is much more than a collection of national dishes (which like Chop Suey or Hungarian Goulash often turn out to lack authenticity or antiquity in their homeland). A real culinary tradition has to be observed in home kitchens, local markets, and community recipe books. That is why cookbooks compiled from contributed recipes are a much better guide to a people's foodways than the recipe books written by famous chefs.

At the present time, New Zealand's mainstream culinary tradition contains some dishes that go back many centuries in the parent British tradition (like pea soup and barley broth which go back to the seventeeth century if not earlier),[4] as well as larger numbers of dishes that have been around for decades rather than centuries. Many of these are borrowings from other culinary traditions adjusted to our local tastes and fully assimilated – chiffon pies are a good example, borrowed in the 1950s from the United States where they were highly fashionable from 1929.[5] A few dishes have been simplified from originals developed by practitioners of haute cuisine – like Peach Melba. Another group of dishes are currently fashionable items that have been promoted in magazines or on television. They are on trial and may, or may not (like fondues), gain a place in our tradition.

Food writers, chefs, and television cooks generally work on the edges of their own culinary traditions. To succeed they are under pressure to adopt an international perspective – we probably wouldn't take much notice of them if all they could offer us were our own dishes. Some derive much material from overseas chefs and fashionable ethnic cuisines that they then reinterpret for their audience to make the dishes locally acceptable. Sometimes they are very successful, as Graham Kerr was in 1963 when he introduced zabaglione to his New Zealand television audience. It was adopted by sufficient numbers of home cooks for the recipe to make occasional appearances in fund-raising cookbooks between 1964 and 1983. Helen Cox was even more successful in her transference of the lemon and egg-yolk filling from the American angel pie to the New Zealand pavlova.

If I had tried to write the story of New Zealand pavlovas from cookbooks written by well-known cooks and chefs, or by food or appliance manufacturers, there would barely have been enough information to fill one chapter. As I have shown, the *Edmonds "Sure to Rise" Cookery Book* published its first recipe for a large pavlova in 1939, ten years after the dish began to circulate. Before the Edmonds' recipe appeared, only Isabella Finlay, the Dunedin City Gas Department demonstrator, had published a pavlova recipe in a commercial cookbook, about 1935. The early history of pavlovas is to be found not in these trade books but in fund-raising cookbooks, and in the magazine and newspaper food columns that published readers' recipes. Compiled cookbooks remain the primary source of pavlova recipes right through the twentieth century. They predominate because both the little pavlovas and the large pavlova cakes were developed by New Zealand home cooks, and fund-raising cookbooks and reader's recipe columns are the chief outlet for their ideas. I have stressed just how ready home cooks were to experiment, adapting their pavlovas to new appliances, and even to the dietary restrictions of those with diabetes. In fact most of the pavlova variants I have identified appear to have started in home kitchens.

Fund-raising cookbooks play a key role in passing on the recipes that make up our culinary tradition. They are a form of publication where the concepts of copyright or plagiarism have little meaning. Contributors hand on their favorite recipe for the public good. They expect no monetary payment, just the pleasure of seeing their name in print or receiving an acknowledgement from their friends. Wherever each recipe originated, it was seldom repeated word for word. Sometimes cooks simplified the method, at other times they added or deleted ingredients, or modified the proportions. Such flexibility is essential if a culinary tradition is to survive in a rapidly changing world.

So why are pavlovas important? They are a product of the people, fashioned by all the cooks who ever made them and passed on the recipes. Their story reveals just how adaptable, practical, generous and disrespectful of authority home cooks can be. They remind us that domestic kitchens are sites of creativity and individualism.

Notes

1: The Pavlova Wars

1. *The Press* (Christchurch), 28 January 1999, p. 6
2. *Sydney Morning Herald*, 29 January 1999, 'Stay in Touch', p. 20
3. New Zealand Press Association, 2 February 1999
4. e.g. *The Press*, 3 February 1999
5. *Evening Post*, 3 February 1999, p. 2
6. *The Press* (Christchurch), 28 January 1999, p. 6
7. *Evening Post*, 3 February 1999, p. 2; New Zealand Press Association, 2 February 1999; *Dominion*, 2 February 1999, p. 1
8. *The Press* (Christchurch), 28 January 1999, p. 6; *Sydney Morning Herald*, 29 January 1999, 'Stay in Touch', p. 20
9. *Dominion*, 2 February 1999, p. 1.
10. *Illawarra Mercury*, 4 February 1999, p. 8
11. *Evening Post*, 3 February 1999, p. 2
12. *Evening Post*, 3 February 1999, p. 2
13. Leach, H.M. 1997 'The Pavlova Cake: the evolution of a national dish', pp. 219–23 in H. Walker (ed.) *Food on the Move; Proceedings of the Oxford Symposium on Food and Cookery 1996*. Prospect Books.
14. Fulton, M. 1999 *I Sang For My Supper: memories of a food writer*. Sydney, Landsdowne, pp. 237, 260.
15. *Sydney Morning Herald*, 11 February 1999, 'Letters', p. 14
16. Osborne, C. 1999 'Pavlova Wars', *Saveur* 36, pp. 17–18
17. Oldham, J. 'The Pavlova is Ours', *Sunday Times* Perth, 4 July 1999
18. New Zealand Press Association, 10 March 2000
19. *Evening Post*, 28 April 2000, p. 2
20. *Evening Post*, 1 June 2002, p. 3
21. Symons, M. 1982 *One Continuous Picnic: a history of eating in Australia*. Adelaide: Duck Press.
22. *New Zealand Dairy Exporter Annual*, 10 October 1929, p. 101
23. *Southland Times*, 2 September 2004, 'Opinion Story'
24. Bristow, R. 'Just dessert as NZ claims pavlova', *The Press*, 16 July 2005, p. A3
25. *Cairns Post*, 19 July 2005, pp. 1–3; *The Gold Coast Bulletin*, 19 July 2005, p. B7; *Geelong Advertiser*, 19 July 2005, pp. 1–16
26. *Courier Mail*, 19 July 2005, pp. 1–3
27. BBC News, Tuesday 19 July 2005: http://news.bbc.co.uk/2/hi/asia-pacific/4696575.stm, accessed 15 December 2006
28. *Otago Daily Times*, 22 September 1950, p. 6
29. Howe, R. 1958 *Cooking From the Commonwealth*. London: Andre Deutsch, pp. 255, 297
30. Barnes, A. (ed.) *Home Management*, Vol. 2. London: George Newnes Ltd, pp. 439, 443
31. Correspondence between Mrs M. Ratley, President Otago University Association of Home Science Alumnae, and Mrs S. Sharpley for the Secretary of External Affairs, 17 January 1961, 12 February 1961
32. Anon. [Otago University Association of Home Science Alumnae] 1960 *New Zealand Dishes and Menus*. Wellington: Price Milburn, p. 35
33. Correspondence between Mrs M. Ratley, President Otago University Association of Home Science Alumnae, and Mrs S. Sharpley for the Secretary of External Affairs, 10 June 1961, 16 June 1961
34. Mitchell, A. 1972 *The Half-Gallon Quarter-Acre Pavlova Paradise*. Wellington: Whitcombe and Tombs, p. 164
35. Personal communication from Les Gibbard, 16 July 2007
36. *Otago Daily Times*, 6 April 1974, p. 4
37. *Otago Daily Times*, 24 April 1974, 'Talk of the Times', p. 4
38. *Otago Daily Times*, 2 May 1974, 'Mainly for Women', p. 18
39. *Otago Daily Times*, 2 May 1974, 'Mainly for Women', p. 18
40. Munro, N. and J. 1977 *A Taste of New Zealand in Food and Pictures*. Wellington: A. H. & A. W. Reed, p. 61
41. *The Globe and Mail*, Toronto, 2 September 1981, p. SB2
42. *The Globe and Mail*, 16 June 1982, p. SB9
43. Symons, M. 1982 *One Continuous Picnic: a history of eating in Australia*. Adelaide: Duck Press, p. 149

44 Symons, M. 1982 *One Continuous Picnic: a history of eating in Australia*. Adelaide: Duck Press, p. 150

45 *Sydney Morning Herald*, 30 May 1988, 'Stay in Touch', p. 32

46 *Otago Daily Times*, 27 November 1995

47 [Basham, M.] [1934] *The N.Z. 'Daisy Chain' Cookery Book*, pp. 48–9

48 [Basham, M.] [1934] *The N.Z. 'Daisy Chain' Cookery Book*, p. 180

49 Letter from Noeline Thomson to Helen Leach, 6 December 1995

50 Letter from Noeline Thomson to Helen Leach, 6 December 1995

51 Letter from Noeline Thomson to Helen Leach, 15 December 1995

52 Letter from Noeline Thomson to Helen Leach, 27 December 1995

53 Letter from Noeline Thomson to Helen Leach, 22 February 1996

54 Letter from Noeline Thomson to Helen Leach, 16 April 1997

55 *Otago Daily Times*, 7 March 2001, p. 43; an obituary was published in the *Otago Daily Times*, 17 March 2001, p. 21.

56 Leach, H.M. 1981 'Cooking without pots: aspects of prehistoric and traditional Polynesian cooking', pp. 312–321 in A. Davidson (ed.) *National and Regional Styles of Cookery* (Oxford Symposium Proceedings 1981), London: Prospect Books

57 Anon. 1927 *Davis Dainty Dishes*. Sixth ed. Christchurch: Coulls Somerville Wilkie Ltd, p. 11

58 McKay, K. 1929 *Practical Home Cookery Chats and Recipes*. Christchurch: Simpson and Williams Ltd

59 Futter, E. c. 1926 *Home Cookery for New Zealand*. Christchurch: Whitcombe and Tombs Ltd, p. 141

60 [Basham, M.] [1934] *The N.Z. 'Daisy Chain' Cookery Book*, p. 180

61 Finlay, I. [1934–6] *Cookery* [Dunedin City Gas Dept.]. Dunedin, p. 125

62 Leach, H. M. 1997 'The Pavlova Cake: the evolution of a national dish', in H. Walker (ed.) *Food on the Move; Proceedings of the Oxford Symposium on Food and Cookery 1996*. Prospect Books, p. 221

63 Davidson, A. 1999 *The Oxford Companion to Food*. Oxford: Oxford University Press, pp. 584, 587

64 Airey, M. 'The great pavlova controversy', *The Press*, Christchurch, 2 January 1997, p. 13

65 Leach, H. 'Evolution of the pavlova', *Otago Daily Times*, 11 January 1997, p. 17

66 Anon. 1933 *Rangiora Mothers' Union Cookery Book of Tried and Tested Recipes*. Rangiora: Wilson Brothers Printers, p. 17

67 Letter from Harry Orsman to Helen Leach, 18 January 1997

2: Why pavlova?

1 Davidson, A. 1999 Entry for 'Peach', *Oxford Companion to Food*, Oxford University Press, p. 589

2 Montagné, P. 1961 *Larousse Gastronomique; the encyclopedia of food, wine and cooking*. London: Paul Hamlyn, p. 535

3 Escoffier, A. 1909 *A Guide to Modern Cookery*. London: William Heinemann, pp. 851–91

4 Davidson, A. 1999 Entry for 'Escoffier', *Oxford Companion to Food*, Oxford University Press, pp. 282–3

5 Willan, A. 1977 *Great Cooks and Their Recipes; from Taillevent to Escoffier*. London: Elm Tree Books, p. 176

6 Escoffier, A. 1909 *A Guide to Modern Cookery*. London: William Heinemann, pp. 853–54; Montagné, P. 1961 *Larousse Gastronomique; the encyclopedia of food, wine and cooking*. London: Paul Hamlyn, p. 534

7 Lake, N. 1915 *Menus Made Easy: or how to order dinner and give the dishes their French names*. Twenty-fifth ed. London: Frederick Warne and Co., p. vi

8 Davidson, A. 1999 Entry for 'Escoffier', *Oxford Companion to Food*, Oxford University Press, p. 282

9 Willan, A. 1977 *Great Cooks and Their Recipes; from Taillevent to Escoffier*. London: Elm Tree Books, pp. 176, 179

10 Montagné, P. 1961 *Larousse Gastronomique; the encyclopedia of food, wine and cooking*. London: Paul Hamlyn, p. 535

11 Basham, M. [1934] *The N.Z. 'Daisy Chain' Cookery Book*. Auckland: Harvison & Marshall Ltd, p. 130

12 Willan, A. 1977 *Great Cooks and Their Recipes; from Taillevent to Escoffier*. London: Elm Tree Books, p. 53

13 Willan, A. 1977 *Great Cooks and Their Recipes; from Taillevent to Escoffier*. London: Elm Tree Books, p. 74

[14] [Glasse, H.] 1995 *The Art of Cookery Made Plain and Easy*. Facsimile of first ed. 1747. Blackawton, Totnes, Devon: Prospect Books

[15] Beeton, I. 1869 *The Book of Household Management*. London: Ward, Lock, and Tyler

[16] Soyer, N. 1912 *Soyer's Standard Cookery*. London: Andrew Melrose.

[17] Gillies, H. T., Anderson, A. D. and E. J. Stewart (eds) 1921 *South Auckland Queen Cookery Book*. Second ed. Hamilton: Bonds' Ltd, pp. 33, 71, 83

[18] Anon. [c. 1917–18] *Southland Red Cross Cookery Book*. Invercargill: The Southland Times Company, pp. 96, 113, 128, 149, 154, 155, 157

[19] Anon. 1917 *Town and Country Patriotic Women Workers' Cookery Book*. Palmerston North: H. L. Young, Limited, pp. 25, 92, 100

[20] *Otago Witness*, 22 June 1926, p. 64

[21] *Otago Witness*, 15 June 1926, p. 72

[22] Pavlova, A. 'Anna Pavlova: pages of my life', p. 1 in Magriel, P. (ed.) 1977 *Nijinsky, Pavlova, Duncan*, [Part 2]. New York: Da Capo Press

[23] Pavlova, A. 'Anna Pavlova: pages of my life', pp. 5–6 in Magriel, P. (ed.) 1977 *Nijinsky, Pavlova, Duncan*, [Part 2]. New York: Da Capo Press

[24] Franks, A. H. (ed.) 1956 *Pavlova. A biography*. London: Burke Publishing Co. Ltd, p. 26

[25] Franks, A. H. (ed.) 1956 *Pavlova. A biography*. London: Burke Publishing Co. Ltd, p. 31

[26] *Otago Witness*, 24 June 1926, p. 14

[27] *Otago Witness*, 6 July 1926, p. 27

[28] Lazzarini, J. and R. Lazzarini 1980 *Pavlova: repertoire of a legend*. New York: Schirmer Books, p. 163

[29] Lazzarini, J. and R. Lazzarini 1980 *Pavlova: repertoire of a legend*. New York: Schirmer Books, pp. 89, 90–91, 210

[30] *Otago Daily Times*, 2 July 1926, p. 15

[31] Olivéroff, A. 1932 *Flight of the Swan. A memory of Anna Pavlova*. New York: E. P. Dutton and Co., p. 257

[32] Franks, A. H. (ed.) 1956 *Pavlova. A biography*. London: Burke Publishing Co. Ltd, p. 39

[33] Franks, A. H. (ed.) 1956 *Pavlova. A biography*. London: Burke Publishing Co. Ltd, p. 42

[34] PIC P348/AP/35 LOC Album 810/4, from Geoffrey Ingram archive of Australian ballet [picture], 1926–1980, National Library of Australia

3: The first pavlova

[1] In the 1920s when the gelatine pavlova first appeared, carmine and cochineal were derived from a species of scale insect cultivated on cactus in the Canary Islands, while saffron yellow was more likely extracted from safflower inflorescences than from the expensive stigmas of the true saffron flowers. Sap green was derived from bitter buckthorn berries. See Beeching, C.L.T. c. 1931 *Law's Grocer's Manual*. Third ed. London: William Clowes and Sons, Limited, pp. 93, 123–4, 135–6; Grieve, Mrs M. 1980 *A Modern Herbal*. [first published 1931]. Harmondsworth: Penguin Books, pp. 134–135

[2] Lushus advertised in the *New Zealand Exporter Annual* 10 October 1938, p. 122; originally made by Shirriff's, by the 1960s these jellies were manufactured by N. W. Stevens & Co. Ltd

[3] Brears, P. 1996 'Transparent Pleasures – the story of the jelly. Part One'. *Petits Propos Culinaires* 53, p. 9

[4] Wyman, C. 2004 'Jell-O', pp. 732–4 in A. F. Smith (ed.) *The Oxford Encyclopedia of Food and Drink in America*, Vol. 1. Oxford: Oxford University Press

[5] e.g. http://www.madmartian.com/food_jello. htm, accessed 17 July 2007

[6] e.g. http://www.chefandy.com, accessed 17 July 2007. See LeBesco, K. 2001 'There's always room for resistance: Jell-O, gender, and social class', pp. 129–49 in Inness, S.A. (ed.) *Cooking Lessons. The Politics of Gender and Food*. Lanham: Rowman & Littlefield Publishers, Inc.

[7] McGee, H. 2004 *On Food and Cooking. The science and lore of the kitchen*. Rev. ed. New York: Scribner, p. 597

[8] Anon. 1927 *Davis Dainty Dishes*. Sixth NZ ed. Christchurch: Coulls Somerville Wilkie Ltd, p. 11

[9] Anon. 1927 *Davis Dainty Dishes*. Sixth NZ ed. Christchurch: Coulls Somerville Wilkie Ltd, pp. 5, 13, 16, 21

[10] Jack, R.I. 2005 'Davis, Sir George Francis (1883–1947)', pp. 94–6 in *Australian Dictionary of Biography*, Supplementary Volume. Melbourne: Melbourne University Press.

[11] The recipe calls for raw papaya and the presence of a protein-digesting enzyme within this fruit might be expected to prevent the gelatine setting

– so was this recipe ever tested? See McGee, H. 2004 *On Food and Cooking. The science and lore of the kitchen*. Rev. ed. New York: Scribner, p. 607

12 Mabel Leith's illustration of a woman pouring tea for her afternoon tea guest, resplendent in fur stole and cloche hat, appeared on the back cover of *The Australian Woman's Mirror*, July 13, 1926

13 Anon. c. 1910 *Jell-O: America's Most Famous Dessert*. Leroy, New York: Genesee Pure Food Co., p. 1

14 Anon. 1927 *Davis Dainty Dishes*. Sixth NZ ed. Christchurch: Coulls Somerville Wilkie Ltd, p. 1

15 Anon. 1927 *Davis Dainty Dishes*. Sixth NZ ed. Christchurch: Coulls Somerville Wilkie, p. 45, cf. Anon. 1915 *Knox Dainty Desserts for Dainty People*. Johnstown, New York: Charles B. Knox Company, p. 18. Both recipes have identical quantities of raisins, dates or figs, currants, sugar and chocolate. The Davis recipe uses more milk and more lemon peel and nuts. Both recipes provide very similar instructions.

16 Wyman, C. 2004 'Jell-O', pp. 732–3 in A.F. Smith (ed.) *The Oxford Encyclopedia of Food and Drink in America*, Vol. 1. Oxford: Oxford University Press; LeBesco, K. 2001 'There's always room for resistance: Jell-O, gender, and social class', in Inness, S. A. (ed.) *Cooking Lessons. The Politics of Gender and Food*. Lanham: Rowman & Littlefield Publishers, Inc., p. 131

17 *Otago Daily Times*, 6 November 1924, p. 2

18 Personal communication from Elizabeth Driver, 25 July 2006

19 Brears, P. 1996 'Transparent Pleasures – the story of the jelly. Part One'. *Petits Propos Culinaires* 53, pp. 9–10

20 Flummery was made from bitter and sweet almonds ground with rosewater and set with sweetened calf's foot jelly. See Raffald, E. 1970 [1782] *The Experienced English Housekeeper*. Facsimile of eighth ed. London: E & W Books Ltd, pp. 186, 191, 193, 194

21 Brears, P. 1996 'Transparent Pleasures – the story of the jelly. Part Two'. *Petits Propos Culinaires* 54, pp. 25–37

22 Miller, E.B. 1890 *Technical Classes Association Cookery Book*. Dunedin, p. 79; cf. Parloa, M. 1882 *Miss Parloa's New Cook Book: a guide to marketing and cooking*. New York: C.T. Dillingham, pp. 275–6. Elizabeth Raffald called her dish 'a pretty decoration for a grand table'. See Raffald, E.

1970 [1782] *The Experienced English Housekeeper*. Facsimile of eighth ed. London: E & W Books, Ltd, p. 199

23 Price, R. 1974 *The Compleat Cook or the Secrets of a Seventeenth-Century Housewife*. London: Routledge & Kegan Paul, pp. 170–1

24 Anon. 1927 *Davis Dainty Dishes*. Sixth NZ ed. Christchurch: Coulls Somerville Wilkie, p. 8

25 Smith, E. 1734 *The Compleat Housewife: or, accomplish'd gentlewoman's companion*. London: J. Pemberton, p. 154

26 Leys, T.W. (ed.) 1883 *Brett's Colonists' Guide*. Auckland: H. Brett, pp. 598–9

27 Anon. [1901] *Colonial Everyday Cookery*. First ed. Christchurch: Whitcombe & Tombs Limited, p. 146

28 Price, R. 1974 *The Compleat Cook or the Secrets of a Seventeenth-Century Housewife*. London: Routledge & Kegan Paul, p. 171

29 Smith, E. 1734 *The Compleat Housewife: or, accomplish'd gentlewoman's companion*. London: J. Pemberton, p. 154

30 Smith, P. I. 1943 *Glue and Gelatine*. Brooklyn, New York: Chemical Publishing Co., p. 33; Anon. c. 1880 *Cassell's Dictionary of Cookery*. London: Cassell Petter & Galpin, pp. 246, 331

31 Felter, H.W. and J.U. Lloyd 1898 'Ichthyocolla (U.S.P.) – Isinglass'. In *King's American Dispensatory* eighteenth ed. [on-line copy at http://www.henriettesherbal.com/eclectic/kings/ichthyocolla.html, accessed 17 July 2007]

32 Beecher, C.E. 1850 *Miss Beecher's Domestic Receipt Book*. New York: Harper, p. 178

33 Anon. c. 1880 *Cassell's Dictionary of Cookery*. London: Cassell Petter & Galpin, p. 335

34 Wall, W. 2006 'Shakespearean Jell-O: mortality and malleability in the kitchen'. *Gastronomica* 6(1), p. 42

35 Beecher, C.E. 1850 *Miss Beecher's Domestic Receipt Book*. New York: Harper, pp. 172, 174; there is a possibility Peter Cooper's gelatine was not the first available in Britain, for Cathrine Waite has drawn my attention to the statement in Charlotte Yonge's novel *Abbeychurch* (1844), 'Mrs. Turner is going to give me a receipt for making *blanc-manger* with some cheap stuff which looks quite as well as isinglass. It is made on chemical principles, she says, for she heard it all explained at the Mechanics' Institute' (quoted

from Yonge, C.M. *Abbeychurch. The Castle Builders.* New York: Garland Publishing, p. 3 of facsimile)

36 Beeton, I. 1869 *The Book of Household Management.* Second ed. London: Ward, Lock, and Tyler, p. 731

37 Anon. 1889 *Economic Cooking Lessons* [Women's Christian Temperance Union]. Dunedin: Mills, Dick & Co., p. 33

38 Murdoch, Mrs F. (ed.) 1888 *Dainties; or how to please our lords and masters.* Second ed. Napier: Dinwiddie, Walker & Company

39 Leys, T. W. (ed.) 1883 *Brett's Colonists' Guide.* Auckland: H. Brett, p. 634

40 Leys, T. W. (ed.) 1883 *Brett's Colonists' Guide.* Auckland: H. Brett, p. 633

41 Boyd, M. 1993 'Nelson, William 1843–1932', pp. 349–350 in *The Dictionary of New Zealand Biography Volume Two 1870–1900.* Wellington: Bridget Williams Books Limited and the Department of Internal Affairs; Moss, M. 1999 *Historic Outline of the Hastings District,* section 1.1, available at http://www.hastingsdc.govt.nz/hastings/hastingshistory.pdf, accessed 17 July 2007. Nelson's prime interest was in meat refrigeration. According to *Wise and Co's New Zealand Directories* New Zealand was still importing gelatine from Nelson G. Dale in London in 1890.

42 Jack, R. I. 2005 'Davis, Sir George Francis (1883–1947)', pp. 94–96 in *Australian Dictionary of Biography,* Supplementary Volume. Melbourne: Melbourne University Press

43 McKay, K. 1929 *Practical Home Cookery Chats and Recipes.* Christchurch: Simpson & Williams Ltd, p. 57

44 McKay, K. 1929 *Practical Home Cookery Chats and Recipes.* Christchurch: Simpson & Williams Ltd, pp. 107–110

45 *New Zealand Dairy Exporter Annual,* October 9 1930, p. 156; *New Zealand Dairy Exporter Annual,* October 8 1935, p. 151

46 Basham, Mrs D. c. 1935 *Aunt Daisy's Book of Selected Special Recipes from California, Canada, France, Australia and New Zealand.* Auckland: Whitcombe and Tombs Ltd, pp. 137–138

4: Rose Rutherford's little pavlovas

1 *Timaru Herald,* 27 September 1879, p. 2

2 *Clutha Leader,* 18 May 1883, p. 5

3 The Kaitangata Old Cemetery has a gravestone commemorating various members of the family, from William to Rosina.

4 Personal communication from Jane Teal, 2006

5 The movements of Rosina and her mother can be traced in the *New Zealand Post Office Directories* and *Stones' Otago and Southland Directories* from 1892. The late Mrs Phyl Robinson of Lawson Street, who moved to an address near the Rutherfords in 1944, told me that Rose lived at the Eventide Home at Company Bay, Dunedin after James and Elizabeth died. She described Rose as a tiny old lady who, by the late 1940s, no longer cooked.

6 Leach, H. (ed.) 2003 'Introduction to the Facsimile first Edition of the St Andrew's Cookery Book (1905)', pp. i–xiv in *St Andrew's Cookery Book Facsimile Edition* Dunedin: Hamel Publishing

7 Leach, H. (ed.) 2003 *St Andrew's Cookery Book Facsimile Edition.* Dunedin: Hamel Publishing, p. 133; Vienna icing appears to be an Australian and New Zealand specialty, made from icing sugar, butter, sherry, and vanilla or chocolate flavouring.

8 Anon. 1919 *St. Andrew's Cookery Book.* Eighth ed. Dunedin: The Evening Star Company Ltd, pp. 132–3,136; the word 'Mode' always preceded the instructions in Mrs Beeton's recipes

9 Anon. 1928 *Dainty Recipes* [North-East Valley Presbyterian Church]. Third ed. Dunedin: Mills, Dick & Co. Ltd, pp. 82, 88

10 McKay, K. 1929 *Practical Home Cookery Chats and Recipes.* Christchurch: Simpson & Williams Ltd, pp. 133, 155, 171, 173

11 Rosina H. Rutherford died in Dunedin on 4 March 1963. James and Anne predeceased her in 1954 and 1955 respectively. City of Dunedin Website Cemeteries Database, accessed 3 September 2006

12 *Weekly Press,* 5 September 1928, p. 23 col. 3; McKay, K. 1929 *Practical Home Cookery Chats and Recipes.* Christchurch: Simpson & Williams Ltd, p. 155

13 Anon. 1927 *Dainty Recipes* [North-East Valley Presbyterian Church]. Second ed. Dunedin: Mills, Dick & Co. Ltd

14 Anon. c. 1930 *New Zealand Women's Household Guide* [The Women's Division of the New Zealand Farmers' Union]. Wellington: Lankshear's Ltd, p. 36

15 Mrs E.P. L. of Springhill, South Canterbury supplied her recipe for Pavlova Cakes in response to a reader's request, *New Zealand Truth*, 9 July 1931, p. 17

16 *New Zealand Woman's Weekly*, 8 March 1934, p. 26

17 Basham, Mrs D. c. 1934 *The N.Z. 'Daisy Chain' Cookery Book*. Auckland: Harvison & Marshall Ltd, p. 49

18 Rickerby, B. (compiler) 1935 *Tried Recipes* [Ever Ready Committee, the Victoria League, Auckland]. Sixth ed. Auckland: Newmarket Printing House, p. 284

19 Anon. c. 1936 *The 'Sure to Rise' Cookery Book*. Sixth ed. Christchurch: Whitcombe and Tombs Ltd, p. 22

20 Anon. c. 1956 *Favourite Recipes of St Andrew's Auxiliary*. Invercargill: Times Print, p. 71

21 Anon. 1964 *What's Cooking* [Oamaru Intermediate School Parent Teacher Association]. Oamaru: Comet Print, p. 47

22 O'Connell, S. (compiler) 1966 *Napier Intermediate School Recipe Book*. Napier: Martin Printing Company Limited, p. 113

23 Montagné, P. 1961 [1938] *Larousse Gastronomique*. English ed. London: Paul Hamlyn, p. 620

24 *Oxford English Dictionary Online* (2006) gives the earliest example of the word meringue in English as 1706; it is clearly derived from the 1702 translation of Massialot's book.

25 Price, R. [compiled by M. Masson] 1974 *The Compleat Cook or the Secrets of a Seventeenth-Century Housewife*. London: Routledge & Kegan Paul, pp. 255, 259

26 Ranhofer, C. 1894 *The Epicurean*. Part 2. New York: Charles Ranhofer, p. 966

27 Massialot, F. 1702 *The Court and Country Cook* [translated into English by J.K.]. London: W. Onley

28 This term may have later been shortened to 'camp-oven'; so instead of a derivation of the camp oven as 'an oven for use when camping', it may have originated as 'an oven used on military campaigns'.

29 Massialot, F. 1702 *The Court and Country Cook* [translated into English by J.K.]. London: W.

Onley, p. 154

30 Massialot, F. 1702 *New Instructions for Confectioners* [translated into English by J.K.]. London: W. Onley, pp. 102–3

31 Raffald, E. 1970 [1782] *The Experienced English Housekeeper*. Facsimile of eighth ed. London: E & W Books (Publishers) Ltd, p. 272; Holland, Mrs M. 1843 *The Complete Economical Cook and Frugal Housewife*. London: Thomas Tegg, pp. 331–2. Mary Holland's recipe for cream cakes is a badly written version of Elizabeth Raffald's.

32 Hale, S.J.B. 1839 *The Good Housekeeper, or the Way to Live Well and to Be Well While We Live*. Boston: Weeks, Jordan & Company, p. 86

33 Anon. 1945 *Practical Cookery and the Etiquette and Service of the Table*. Twenty-first ed. Kansas State College of Agriculture and Applied Science, p. 306

34 Farmer, F.M. 1896 *The Boston Cooking-School Cookbook*. Boston: Little Brown and Co., p. 401

35 Ranhofer, C. 1894 *The Epicurean. A complete treatise of analytical and practical studies on the culinary art...* New York: C. Ranhofer, p. 966; Kirkland, J. (ed.) 1908 *The Modern Baker Confectioner and Caterer*. Vol. III. London: The Gresham Publishing Company, p. 401

36 Anon. 1927 *Terrace Tested Recipes* [Terrace Congregational Church, Wellington]. First ed. Auckland: Whitcombe & Tombs Ltd, p. 107

37 MacInnes M. (ed.) 1896 *Cookery Book of Good and Tried Receipts* [Women's Missionary Association of the Presbyterian Church of New South Wales]. Third ed. Sydney: S. T. Leigh & Co., Printers and Publishers, p. 69

38 Soyer, A. 1847 *The Gastronomic Regenerator: a simplified and entirely new system of cookery...* Fourth ed. London: Simpkin, Marshall, & Co., pp. 512–513

39 Leys, T. W. (ed.) 1883 *Brett's Colonists' Guide*. Auckland: H. Brett, p. 619; Brandon, L. E. and C. Smith [compilers] 1905 *'Ukneadit'* [Home for Incurables Bazaar, July, 1905]. Wellington: Geddis and Blomfield, pp. 54, 80

40 Basham, Mrs D. c. 1934 *The N. Z. 'Daisy Chain' Cookery Book*. Auckland: Harvison & Marshall Ltd, p. 49; this is the earliest New Zealand recipe book that I know of which mentions greaseproof paper.

41 Palmer, A. 1984 [1952] *Movable Feasts. A*

Reconnaissance of the origins and consequences of fluctuations in meal-times with special attention to the introduction of luncheon and afternoon tea. Oxford: Oxford University Press, pp. 132–133

42 Mason, L. 1994 'Everything Stops for Tea', pp. 71–90 in C. A. Wilson (ed.) Luncheon, Nuncheon and Other Meals: Eating with the Victorians. Stroud: Alan Sutton Publishing Ltd

43 Devereux, G. R. M. 1920 Etiquette for Women. A book of modern modes and manners. Revised ed. London: C. Arthur Pearson, Ltd, p. 32

44 Palmer, A. 1984 Movable Feasts... Oxford: Oxford University Press, p. 133

45 Bell, B. 1976 Notes of Life in Olveston. Typescript copy supplied to author by Mrs Margery Blackman, President of The Friends of Olveston, 1999

46 Otago Witness, 6 July 1910, 'The Ladies' Page, Table Talk'

47 Murdoch, Mrs F. (ed.) 1888 Dainties; or how to please our lords and masters. Second ed. Napier: Dinwiddie, Walker & Company

48 Anon. 1921 St. Andrew's Cookery Book. Ninth ed. Dunedin: The Evening Star Company, Limited

5: The first large pavlovas

1 Printed in The N.Z. Dairy Exporter Annual (Inc. Tui's Annual), 10 October 1929 (Fig. 5.1); recipe reprinted elsewhere in 1931 and 1935

2 'Tui' (ed.) 1929 The N.Z. Dairy Exporter Annual (Inc. Tui's Annual), 10 October 1929, p. 101

3 'Tui' (ed.) 1929 The New Zealand Dairy Exporter Annual (Inc. Tui's Annual), 10 October 1929, p. 99

4 New Zealand Truth, 23 July 1931, p. 17; New Zealand Truth, 17 April 1935, p. 22

5 from Rangiora Mothers' Union Cookery Book of Tried and Tested Recipes, 1933

6 Anon. 1933 Rangiora Mothers' Union Cookery Book of Tried and Tested Recipes. Rangiora: Wilson Bros., Printers, p. 17

7 Teal, J. 2004 'Recipes for the Renovations: Laurina Stevens and the Pavlova Cake'. History Now. Te Pae Tawhito o te Wa 9(4), pp. 13–16

8 Teal, J. 2004 'Recipes for the Renovations: Laurina Stevens and the Pavlova Cake'. History Now. Te Pae Tawhito o te Wa 9(4), p. 14

9 from The New Zealand Woman's Weekly, 8 March
1934, reprinted in The N.Z. 'Daisy Chain' Cookery Book, late 1934

10 The New Zealand Woman's Weekly, 8 March 1934, p. 26

11 Basham, Mrs D. [1934] The N.Z. 'Daisy Chain' Cookery Book. Auckland: Harvison & Marshall Ltd, pp. 26–7, 48–9

12 From Blue Triangle Cookery Book [Wellington Y.W.C.A.], 1934

13 Anon. [1934, dated by handwritten inscription] Blue Triangle Cookery Book [Y.W.C.A. Wellington]. Wellington: Hutt and Petone Chronicle, p. 109

14 Anon. [1934, dated by handwritten inscription] Blue Triangle Cookery Book [Y.W.C.A. Wellington]. Wellington: Hutt and Petone Chronicle, p. 117

15 From Dunedin City Gas Department's Cookery, between 1934 and 1936

16 Symons, M. 1982 One Continuous Picnic: a history of eating in Australia. Adelaide: Duck Press, pp. 149–50

17 Finlay, Miss I. c. 1934 [dated by Edmonds' advertisement, p. 82] The Osborne Cook Book [Dunedin City Gas Department]. Second ed. Dunedin: [?]John McIndoe, p. 125

18 Finlay, Miss I. c. 1934–6 Cookery [Dunedin City Gas Dept.]. Third ed. Dunedin: John McIndoe, p. 125

19 The recipes were reproduced in Leach, H. 1997 'The Pavlova Cake: the evolution of a national dish', in H. Walker (ed.) Food on the Move. Proceedings of the Oxford Symposium on Food and Cookery 1996. Blackawton, Totnes, Devon: Prospect Books, pp. 222–3

20 These changes appear in a coverless copy of what has been determined on internal evidence to be a sixth or seventh edition of Miss Finlay's Cookery, printed about 1937 or 1938.

21 Finlay, Miss I. c. 1939 Cookery [Dunedin City Gas Dept.]. Eighth ed. Dunedin: Stanton Bros. Ltd, p. 125

22 Miss Finlay's long-running Cookery outlived her. Though she died in Dunedin in 1942, aged 63 years, the Gas Department issued several further editions. The last that I have seen is the fourteenth, published in the early 1950s.

23 Anon. 1926 The Manawatu Red Cookery Book. Revised and enlarged edition. Palmerston North: Keeling & Mundy Ltd, p. 59

24 Futter, E. c. 1926 Home Cookery for New Zealand.

Christchurch: Whitcombe & Tombs Ltd, p. 141; Futter's book *Australian Home Cookery* was published about 1924.

25 Anon. 1927 *Terrace Tested Recipes* [Terrace Congregational Church, Wellington]. First ed. Auckland: Whitcombe & Tombs Ltd, p. 70

26 Cameron, E. M. [compiler] 1929 *The Ideal Cookery Book*. First ed. Wellington: Watkins Print, p. 93

27 Cameron, E. M. [compiler] 1929 *The Ideal Cookery Book*. First ed. Wellington: Watkins Print, p. 89

28 Cameron, E. M. [compiler] 1929 *The Ideal Cookery Book*. First ed. Wellington: Watkins Print, p. 69

29 Gouffé, J. 1869 *The Royal Cookery Book*. London: Sampson Low, Son, & Marston, p. 529

30 Ranhofer, C. 1894 *The Epicurean. A complete treatise of analytical and practical studies on the culinary art ...* New York: C. Ranhofer, p. 943

31 Henderson, M.N.F. 1877 *Practical Cooking and Dinner Giving*. New York: Harper & Brothers, p. 303

32 Corson, J. 1886 *Miss Corson's Practical American Cookery*. New York: Dodd, Mead & Co., pp. 512–13

33 Anon. c. 1905 *Los Angeles Times Cook Book No. 2*. Los Angeles: Times-Mirror Co., p. 73

34 Anderson, J. 1997 *The American Century Cookbook*. New York: Clarkson Potter Publishers, p. 382

35 Conley, E. c. 1914 *Principles of Cooking. A textbook in domestic science*. New York: American Book Company, p. 186

36 Greenbaum, F.K. 1918 *The International Jewish Cook Book*. New York: Bloch Publishing Co., p. 391

37 e.g. a Schaum Torte was listed for light refreshments accompanying a June wedding in Parker, M.J. [1920s] *Selected Recipes and Menus for Parties, Holidays, and Special Occasions* [Calumet Baking Powder], p. 15

38 Adams, L. 1925 *Spark Lid-top Gas Stove Cook Book 1925* [Hammer-Bray Co., Oakland, California]. Santa Rosa: Press Democrat Print, pp. 34, 46

39 *The Times*, 15 April 1922, p. 15

40 Jekyll, A. [c. 1922] *Kitchen Essays with Recipes and their Occasions*. London: Thomas Nelson & Sons Ltd, pp. 252–3

41 *Auckland Weekly News*, 26 December 1934, 'Aunt Daisy's Mail-Bag', p. 26

6: Pavlovas from 1935 to 1950

1 Leach, H. and R. Inglis 2006 'Cookbook collections – from kitchen drawer to academic resource'. *The New Zealand Library and Information Management Journal* 50(1), pp. p. 69–81

2 Macdonald, Mrs M. (compiler) 1938 *What's For Lunch?* [The Waikouaiti Children's Health Camp Association]. Dunedin: Coulls Somerville Wilkie Ltd, pp. 42, 45

3 The American equivalents to pavlovas were the Kiss Cake, Meringue Torte, Schaum Torte, and Angel Pie. Lovegren, S. 2005 *Fashionable Food. Seven decades of food fads*. Chicago: University of Chicago Press, p. 72

4 Todhunter, E. N. c. 1935 *Creamoata Recipes*. Gore: Fleming & Company Limited, p. 3

5 Anon. [1939] *'Milkmade' Cook Book* [issued by New Zealand's Leading Milk Vendors]. Levin: Kerslake and Billens, Ltd, p. 41

6 Letter from Noeline Thomson to Helen Leach, 26 April 1998, pp. 3–4

7 Letter from Noeline Thomson to Helen Leach, 26 April 1998, p. 4. According to the *Oxford English Dictionary Online* 2006, this use of the word 'curate' was a shortened form of curate's delight, comfort or friend, first used by playwright George Bernard Shaw in 1914.

8 Anon. c. 1933 *New Zealand Women's Household Guide* [The Women's Division of the New Zealand Farmers' Union]. Second ed. Wellington: Lankshear's Ltd, pp. 5–29

9 Orr-Walker, Mrs C. R. [convenor] 1941 *The Diner's Digest* [Auckland Travel Club]. Auckland: Wright & Jacques Ltd, p. 96

10 *New Zealand Truth*, 13 August 1947, 'Answers to Women Correspondents', p. 34. The same recipe was supplied to another correspondent on 3 January 1951, but with the mock cream changed to cream.

11 Crawford, F.M. and M.J. Lousley [compilers] 1940 *The Southland Patriotic Cookery Book*. Invercargill: Whitcombe & Tombs Limited, p. 139

12 Carter, U. c. 1944 *Una Carter's Famous Cookery Book*. Ninth ed. Wellington: Hutcheson, Bowman & Johnson Ltd, pp. 162–3; Anon. c. 1944 *The Red Cross War-time Rationing Cookery Book*. Wellington: Roycroft Press Ltd, entry for June 16th

13 Taylor, N.M. 1986 *The New Zealand People at*

War. The Home Front. Wellington: Historical
Publications Branch, Department of Internal
Affairs, pp. 789–90

14 Taylor, N.M. 1986 The New Zealand People at
War. The Home Front. Wellington: Historical
Publications Branch, Department of Internal
Affairs, p. 791

15 Taylor, N.M. 1986 The New Zealand People at
War. The Home Front. Wellington: Historical
Publications Branch, Department of Internal
Affairs, p. 796

16 The New Zealand Official Year-Book, 1950. Fifty-sixth
issue. Wellington: R.E. Owen, Government
Printer, p. 830; Taylor, N.M. 1986 The New
Zealand People at War. The Home Front. Wellington:
Historical Publications Branch, Department of
Internal Affairs, pp. 778–9

17 Taylor, N.M. 1986 The New Zealand People at
War. The Home Front. Wellington: Historical
Publications Branch, Department of Internal
Affairs, p. 820

18 May, M.W. 1973 Freshly Remembered: half a century
of school. Christchurch: Whitcombe and Tombs,
p. 108

19 May, M.W. 1973 Freshly Remembered: half a century
of school. Christchurch: Whitcombe and Tombs,
p. 109

20 Geering, L. 2006 Wrestling with God. The story of
my life. Wellington: Bridget Williams Books in
association with Craig Potton Publishing, pp.
76–7

21 Brasch, C. 1980 Indirections. A memoir 1909–1947.
Wellington: Oxford University Press, p. 408

22 Taylor, N.M. 1986 The New Zealand People at War. The
Home Front. Wellington: Historical Publications
Branch, Department of Internal Affairs, pp. 796,
819–20; The New Zealand Official Year-Book, 1951–52.
Fifty-seventh issue. Wellington: R. E. Owen,
Government Printer, p. 905

23 Anon. 1948 Approved Recipes and Household Hints
[Grocers' United Stores Ltd]. Christchurch:
Simpson & Williams Ltd, p. 5

24 New Zealand Truth, 14 April 1948, p. 27

25 New Zealand Truth, 26 February 1947, p. 31

26 New Zealand Truth, 3 September 1947, p. 35

27 New Zealand Truth, 27 August 1947, p. 35

28 Carter, U. c. 1944 Una Carter's Famous Recipe Book.
Ninth ed. Wellington: Hutcheson, Bowman &
Johnson Ltd, p. 93

7: Pavlovas come of age, 1950–59

1 In 1945 the average price of a dozen eggs was
2s 5½d, in 1947 2s 8¾d, in 1949 3s 2d, in 1951
3s 10½d, in 1953 4s 7d, in 1955 4s 10d, peaking
at 5s 1½d in 1957. Sources: New Zealand Official
Yearbooks and New Zealand Statistical Reports on
Prices, Wage-rates … 1945–57

2 Palmer, M. 1976 Easy as Pie. Wellington: Reed
Home Economics Series, p. 58

3 Herbert, Mrs O.M. 1956 St Mary's School Stratford
Recipe Book. New Plymouth: Taranaki Herald Co.
Ltd, pp. 36–7; Anon. 1958 'Gala' Cookery Book
[Taieri High School Parents' Assoc.]. Dunedin:
Disabled Servicemen's Re-establishment
League, pp. 74–5; Henley, M., M. Harding and
V. Foster (editors) 40th Birthday Recipe Book.
Old Girls' Recipes. Wellington: Queen Margaret
College Old Girls' Association (Inc.), pp. 67–8,
80; [Burnett, J. and E.M. Roy (compilers)]
1959 South Otago High School Recipe Book 1959.
Balclutha: Clutha Leader Print, p. 112

4 Anon. c. 1936 Edmonds 'Sure to Rise' Cookery Book.
Sixth ed. Christchurch: Whitcombe & Tombs
Ltd, pp. 21-2

5 Anon. c. 1939 Edmonds 'Sure to Rise' Cookery Book.
Seventh ed. Christchurch: Whitcombe & Tombs
Ltd, p. 25

6 Anon. 1978 Edmonds Cookery Book. Centennial
Edition. Christchurch: Whitcoulls Ltd, p. 45

7 Anon. 1992 Edmonds Cookery Book. New Revised
Edition. Auckland: Bluebird Foods Ltd, p. 179;
however, the 1978 recipe is found again in the
forty-sixth edition of 1999 and in the most recent
from 2005.

8 Anon. 2005 Edmonds Classics. New Zealanders'
Favourite Recipes. Auckland: Hodder Moa, p. 121

9 Anon. c. 1952 Recommended Cooking. A recipe book of
proven country recipes [Springs-Ellesmere Plunket
Society]. Leeston: Ellesmere Guardian, p. 70

10 Kirkland, J. (ed.) 1908 The Modern Baker
Confectioner and Caterer. Vol. III. London: The
Gresham Publishing Company, p. 401

11 Allen, I. C. B. 1924 Mrs Allen on Cooking, Menus,
Service. New York: Doubleday, Page & Company,
pp. 657–8

12 Craig, E. c. 1940 Cooking with Elizabeth Craig.
London: Collins, p. 267

13 Woolley, G.B. 1947 A Practical Recipe Book for

Bakers, Pastrycooks and Caterers: the most concise and up-to-date handbook for the baking trade published in New Zealand. Napier: Swailes Print Co., p. 95

14 Craig, E. 1947 1000 Household Hints. Rev. ed. London: Collins, p. 11

15 Anon. 1950 The Wellington East Girls' College Silver Jubilee Cookery Book Nelson: R. W. Stiles & Co. Ltd, p. 41; Anon. 1950 Khandallah Cookery Book [Khandallah Presbyterian Church]. Wellington: A.H. & A.W. Reed, p. 102

16 Anon. 1952 Abbotsford Kindergarten Mothers' Club Cookery Book. Dunedin: Budget Ltd, p. 48

17 Anon. c. 1955 Reliable Tested Recipes [Hora Hora Kindergarten Association]. Whangarei: The Northern Publishing Co., Ltd, p. 84; Anon. 1960 W.D.F.F. Maungaturoto Cookery Book. Wellsford: Campbell Press, p. 58

18 Anon. 1964 Recipe Book [The Hawkesdale Auxiliary of the Warrnambool Hospital]. Victoria, pp. 6, 9

19 Anon. 1952 Roslyn Presbyterian Church Jubilee Cookery Book. Second ed. Dunedin, p. 30. These recipes occur in the first part of the book, not in the additions made for the second edition. They therefore can be confidently dated to the unseen first edition of 1951.

20 Sherriff, Mrs S.D. 1961 GHB Cookery Book. Christchurch: Bascands Ltd, p. 23

21 Britten, D. 1977 The Des Britten Cookbook. Auckland: Woolworths (NZ) Ltd, p. 159

22 e.g. Anon. c. 1966 Our Favourite Recipes [Helen Deem Centre for Pre-School Education]. Dunedin: S.N. Brown Ltd, p. 11

23 Bishop, J. 'Pavlova easy, inexpensive and popular; definite NZ flavour', Otago Daily Times, 20 May 1992, 'Simply Entertaining', p. 18

24 Anon. c. 1967 Tried Recipes. Gordon Cub Pack. Gore: Gore Publishing Company Ltd, p. 83

25 Flower, T. (ed.) 1971 The New Zealand Woman's Weekly Cookbook. Auckland: Paul Hamlyn, p. 145

26 Anon. 1978 Edmonds Cookery Book. Centennial Edition. Christchurch: Whitcoulls Limited, p. 45; Simpson, T. 1985 An Innocent Delight. The art of dining in New Zealand. Auckland: Hodder and Stoughton, p. 235

27 Hendry, A. [convenor] 1990 Lions Clubs International District 202B 'Partners in Service' Recipe Book. Carterton: Roydhouse (1986) Ltd, pp. 100–1

28 Anon. 1952 Roslyn Presbyterian Church Jubilee Cookery Book. Second ed. Dunedin, p. 30.

29 Anon. 1965 Cookery Book [The Women's Division of Federated Farmers of New Zealand]. Fourteenth ed., revised. Levin: Kerslake, Billens & Humphrey Ltd, p. 150

30 Anon. 1961 S. Hilda's Recipe Book. Dunedin: Laing & Matthews, p. 21

31 Anon. c. 1967 Tried Recipes. Gordon Cub Pack. Gore: Gore Publishing Company Ltd, p. 83; Anon. c. 1974 The Cooking Pot [fund-raising for New Zealand Nurses Association (Inc.) Otago, North Otago and South Otago]. Hamilton: Oakmore Publishing Co. Ltd, p. 93

32 e.g. Anon. 1983 Fordell School & District Centennial Cookery Book 1883–1983. Fordell, p. 40

33 Anon. 1963 The Silver & Green Jubilee Cookery Book [The Solway Old Girls' Association]. Masterton: Masterton Printing Co., p. 56; Anon. 1972 Martinborough Cook Book [Women's Fellowship, First Church, Martinborough]. Palmerston North: Swiftcopy Centre Limited, p. 113; Anon. 1986 The Good Harvest Cook Book [Puketapu Women's Fellowship]. Hawke's Bay: Stanton Speedprint, p. 34

34 Christie, T. 1959 Triple Tested Recipe Book [Lower Hutt Plunket Society]. Wellington: A. H. & A. W. Reed, p. 111

35 Anon. 1963 The Silver & Green Jubilee Cookery Book [The Solway Old Girls' Association]. Masterton: Masterton Printing Co., p. 56

36 Flower, T. (ed.) 1971 The New Zealand Woman's Weekly Cookbook. Auckland: Paul Hamlyn, p. 145

37 Anon. 1956 The New Home Cookery Book [Country Women's Institutes of N.Z.]. 1956 'Reprint' with 100 additional recipes. Levin: Kerslake, Billens and Humphrey Ltd, p. 221

38 Anon. 1961 S. Hilda's Recipe Book. Dunedin: Laing & Matthews, p. 29

39 Anon. c. 1960 New Zealand Dishes and Menus [Otago University Association of Home Science Alumnae]. Wellington: Price Milburn, p. 35

40 Burton, D. 1982 Two Hundred Years of New Zealand Food & Cookery. Wellington: A.H. & A.W. Reed Ltd, p. 132

41 [Burnett, J. and E. M. Roy (compilers)] 1959 South Otago High School Recipe Book 1959. Balclutha: Clutha Leader Print, p. 112; Henley, M., M. Harding and V. Foster (editors) 40th

Birthday Recipe Book. Old Girls' Recipes. Wellington: Queen Margaret College Old Girls' Association (Inc.), p. 80

[42] Anon. c. 1997 Jonathan Rhodes Kindergarten Recipe Book. Dunedin: U-Bix Copy Centre, p. 45

[43] Schauer, A. and M. 1952 The Schauer Australian Cookery Book. Tenth ed. Brisbane: W. R. Smith and Paterson Pty. Ltd, p. 427

[44] McGee, H. 1986 On Food and Cooking. The science and lore of the kitchen. London: Unwin Hyman, p. 75

[45] The New Zealand Food and Drug Regulations of 1946 prohibited the addition of any compound of aluminium to baking powder. This regulation was revoked in 1973 when sodium aluminium phosphate was specifically permitted.

[46] Mc Gee, H. 2004 On Food and Cooking. The science and lore of the kitchen. New York: Scribner, p. 533

[47] Beeching, C.L.T. (ed.) c. 1930 Law's Grocer's Manual. Third ed. London: William Clowes and Sons, Limited, p. 25

[48] Ron Hooker quoted by Charmian Smith in 'Still rising to the occasion', Otago Daily Times, 20 October 2004, p. 19

[49] e.g. Snow Pudding in Anon. 1934 Knox Cookery Book. Christchurch: H.W. Bullivant & Co. Ltd, p. 51

[50] Kent-Johnston, Mrs W.F. c. 1938 Everyday Recipes. Tried and tested by Mrs Kent-Johnston. Christchurch: Willis and Aiken Ltd, p. 62; Kent-Johnston, Mrs W.F. (comp.) 1939 Christchurch Boys' High School Cookery Book. Christchurch: Whitcombe and Tombs Ltd, p. 93

[51] Anon. 1937 Davis Dainty Dishes. 12th ed. Christchurch: Coulls Somerville Wilkie Ltd, p. 19

[52] Anon. 1947 Papanui Parish Cookery Book [St Paul's Church]. Christchurch: Bascands, p. 12

[53] Anon. 1952 Nelson Intermediate School Cookery Book. Nelson: R.W. Stiles & Co. Ltd, p. 78

[54] Cox, H. 1952 The Hostess Cook Book. Sydney: Angus and Robertson, p. 145

[55] Perkins, W.L. 1949 The Boston Cooking-School Cook Book, by Fannie Merritt Farmer. Revised ed. London: George G. Harrap and Co. Ltd, p. 581

[56] Scaife, K. and M. Scurr (compilers) 1972 Souvenir Recipe Book. Wanaka: Wanaka Improvement Society, p. 69

8: Pavlovas consolidate, 1960–79

[1] Flower, T. 1972 Tui Flower's Modern Hostess Cook Book. Wellington: A.H. & A.W. Reed, p. 19

[2] Scaife, K. and M. Scurr (compilers) 1972 Souvenir Recipe Book. Wanaka: Wanaka Improvement Society, pp. 68, 69, 81, 82, 83

[3] Dempsey, R. [1967–1973] 1,001 Ways With Food. Auckland: Wilson and Horton Ltd, p. 60

[4] Scaife, K. and M. Scurr (compilers) 1972 Souvenir Recipe Book. Wanaka: Wanaka Improvement Society, p. 83; Anon. 1976 Cookery Book [Roxburgh Play Centre]. First ed. Alexandra: Central Otago News Print, p. 50

[5] Anderson, J. 1997 The American Century Cookbook. New York: Clarkson Potter, p. 281

[6] Anon. 1964 Recipe and Instruction Book Sunbeam Gourmet Large Eleven Inch Frypan. Wellington: Evening Post, p. 31; Mills, K. (compiler) c. 1987 Cooking with Kevin. Kevin Mills shares his favourite recipes. Dunedin: Crown Kerr Printing, p. 34

[7] Phillips, H. 1960 The 'Oak' and 'K' Recipe Book. Auckland: Thompson & Hills Ltd, p. 116

[8] Anon. c. 1953 The Esk Valley Cookery Book [The Country Women's Association]. Melbourne: Southdown Press Pty. Ltd, p. 83

[9] Mills, K. (compiler) c. 1987 Cooking with Kevin. Kevin Mills shares his favourite recipes. Dunedin: Crown Kerr Printing, p. 34; Anon. c. 1995 St. Ninian's Presbyterian Church Family Recipe Book. Christchurch, p. 60

[10] Henley, M., M. Harding and V. Foster (editors) 40th Birthday Recipe Book. Old Girls' Recipes. Wellington: Queen Margaret College Old Girls' Association (Inc.), p. 67

[11] Anon. c. 1967 Calling All Cooks [Recipes reprinted from League of Mothers' Magazine]. Dunedin: Evening Star Co. Ltd, p. 76

[12] Baine, Mrs B. and Mrs V. Stevens (compilers) 1970 Recipe Book [Newlands Home and School Association]. Wellington: Universal Printers Ltd, p. 83

[13] Bilton, J. 1981 New Zealand Kiwifruit Cook Book. Auckland: Irvine Holt, p. 34; Dryden, G. (ed.) 1984 The All-Colour Guide to New Zealand Entertaining. Auckland: The Dryden Johnson Group, p. 136; Anon. 1996 Farmers Cookbook [Farmers Community Support Programme].

First ed. Auckland: Farmers Trading Company, p. 97

14 Anon. n.d.[early 1950s] *Sunbeam Mixmaster Cooking Guide*. Sydney: Blake & Hargreaves Pty Ltd, p. 41

15 Kent-Johnston, Mrs W. F. (compiler) 1939 *Christchurch Boys' High School Cookery Book*. Christchurch: Whitcombe and Tombs Ltd, p. 43

16 Anon. c. 1952 *Recommended Cooking. A recipe book of proven country recipes* [Springs-Ellesmere Plunket Society]. Leeston: The Ellesmere Guardian, p. 80

17 Kent-Johnston, Mrs W.F. c. 1938 *Everyday Recipes. Tried and tested by Mrs Kent-Johnson*. Christchurch: Willis and Aiken Ltd, p. 78

18 Anon. 1970 *Cook It Our Way*. Lovell's Flat: Lovell's Flat Country Women's Institute, p. [13]; Anon. [1991] *The Glenfalloch Cook-Book* [Otago Peninsula Trust]. Dunedin: University of Otago Printery, p. 110

19 Seddon, M. (comp.) 1981 *Catholic Women's League Cookbook* [Dunedin Diocese of the Catholic Women's League]. Dunedin: Allied Press Commercial Print, p. 55

20 Anon. 1985 *Kitchen Carnival* [Eastern Districts South Island Swimming Centre]. Waimate: Waimate Publishing Co. Ltd, p. 86

21 Christie, T. 1959 *Triple Tested Recipe Book* [Lower Hutt Plunket Society]. Wellington: A.H. & A.W. Reed, p. 110

22 Howe, E.J. 1967 *Cadbury's Chocolate Cookery*. Dunedin: Cadbury Fry Hudson Ltd, p. 23

23 Britten, D. 1977 *The Des Britten Cookbook*. Auckland: Woolworths (NZ) Ltd, p. 159

24 Forward, J. 1969 *Lions Recipe Calendar 1969*. Dunedin: Otago Daily Times Ltd, entry for 24 November – like the photographs in this calendar, the pavlova recipe may have originated in Australia.

25 Anon. 1974 *At Home with Metrics*. Wellington: Metric Advisory Board, Ministry of Trade and Industry, p. 1

26 Anon. c. 1967 *Cookery Book* [Karitane Public Hall Building Committee]. Dunedin: Otago Daily Times, p. 35

27 Anon. 1974 *At Home with Metrics*. Wellington: Metric Advisory Board, Ministry of Trade and Industry, p. 8

9: Pavlovas paramount, 1980–99

1 Bell, R. (convenor) 1980 *Ikawai CWI Jubilee Recipe Book 1930–1980*. Ikawai: Members of the Ikawai Country Women's Institute, p. 18

2 Anon n.d. [1982–1986] *Home & Country Cook Book* [New Zealand Country Women's Institutes (Inc)]. Levin: KBH Print [Kerslake, Billens and Humphrey Ltd], p. 31

3 *New Zealand Truth*, 8 January 1980, p. 24

4 Birch, C. (comp.) 1982 *Rally Cook Book* [New Zealand Every Boy's and Every Girl's Rallies]. Arura Souvenir Edition [Eighth]. Palmerston North: G.P.H. Print, p. 100

5 Raffills, G. 1984 *Microwave the New Zealand Way*. Christchurch: Flour Power Press, p. 105

6 Anon 1978 *From Outback Kitchens*. Second ed. Carnarvon: Gascoyne-Ashburton Branch of The Isolated Childrens Parents Association, p. 99

7 Radio NZ, 'Nine to Noon', 2 August 2004

8 Anon 1953 *Hostess Handbook of Party Foods* [Ladies' Home Journal]. U.S.A.: The Curtis Publishing Co., p. 3; O'Connor, H.N. 1954 *Pastry Cook Book*. Greenwich, Connecticut: Fawcett Publications, p. 111

9 Keating. E.M. 1959 *Puddings and Sauces*. Woman's Day Kitchen Collector's Cook Book #34, p. 58

10 Anon c. 1963 *Harvard Business Wives Cookbook*. Cambridge, Massachusetts: Harvard Business School, p. 76

11 Personal communication from S. Littlewood, 5 April 2006

12 *New Zealand Woman's Weekly*, 16 March 1981, p. 134

13 Anon n.d. [1980s?] *Tastefully Yours* [Octagon Senior Citizens' Club]. Dunedin: The Otago Old People's Welfare Council, p. 50; Anon c. 1997 *Jonathan Rhodes Kindergarten Recipe Book*. Dunedin: U-Bix Copy Centre, p. 46

14 Anon 1986 *Golden Jubilee Recipe Book* [Correspondence School Parents' Association]. Te Puke: Te Puke Times, pp. 32–3; Anon 1996 *Divine Desserts* [St Paul's Cathedral Choir]. Dunedin: Dene Waring Photo & Graphics, p. 52

15 Anderson, J. 1997 *The American Century Cookbook*. New York: Clarkson Potter, pp. 233, 247; Smith, A.F. 2004 Entry on 'Microwave Ovens' in A.F. Smith (ed.) *The Oxford Encyclopedia of Food and Drink in America*, Vol. 2. Oxford: Oxford University Press, pp. 89–90

[16] Anon 1983 *The High School Cook Book 1983* [South Otago High School]. Balclutha, p. 103

[17] Anon 1987 *Microwave Cooking* [Lees Street Kindergarten]. Invercargill: John McDowall, p. 54; Anon n.d. [1990s] *Opawa School Microwave Cook Book*. Christchurch: Bascands Commercial Print, p. 35

[18] Anon c. 1987 *Recipe Book*. Gore: St Peter's College, p. 43; Innes, D., A. Guild, and G. Stone 1990 *The Windwhistle Cookery Book*. Timaru: Pope Print Timaru Ltd, p. 37

[19] Rountree, T. c. 1986 *Microwave Cookery*. Christchurch: Infa Print Ltd, p. 58; Anon n.d. [1990s?] *Eggbert Cooks Up a Yummo Summer* [New Zealand Poultry Board]. p. 7

[20] Dunleavy, B. 1986 *Microwave Magic*. Sydney: Watermark Press Pty Ltd for Mitsubishi Electric AWA Pty Ltd, p. 83

[21] Raffills, G. 1984 *Microwave the New Zealand Way*. Christchurch: Flour Power Press, p. 105

[22] Anon 1988 *Glenview Kindergarten Recipe Book*. Second printing. Timaru: Printers & Publishers, p. 66 [first printing recorded as 1986]

[23] Birch, C. (comp.) 1982 *Rally Cook Book* [New Zealand Every Boy's and Every Girl's Rallies]. Arura Souvenir Edition [Eighth]. Palmerston North: G.P.H. Print, p. 100

[24] Hendry, A. (convenor) 1990 *Lions Clubs International District 202B 'Partners in Service' Recipe Book*. Carterton: Roydhouse Print, p. 105; Anon. 1995 *Elim Ladies Christmas Cookbook*. Dunedin: Elim Ladies, p. 55

[25] Seddon, M. (comp.) 1981 *Catholic Women's League Cookbook* [Dunedin Diocese of the Catholic Women's League]. Dunedin: Allied Press Commercial Print, p. 52

[26] Anon 1985 *Kitchen Carnival* [Eastern Districts South Island Swimmers]. Waimate: Waimate Publishing Co. Ltd, p. 86

[27] Cooper, J. (compiler) 1996 *Cookbook*. Bay of Plenty: Gate Pa Bowling Club, p. 46

[28] Anon c. 1997 *Jonathan Rhodes Kindergarten Recipe Book*. Dunedin: U-Bix Copy Centre, p. 45

[29] Wilson, R. 2006 Interaction of Ingredients with Egg White Proteins and their Effects on the Physical Properties of Pavlovas. Unpublished B.Sc Hons research project, Department of Food Science, University of Otago, p. 10

[30] McVinnie, R. 2005 'Strawberry Pavlovas' *Cuisine* 113, pp. 92–3 [recipe available online at http://www.cuisine.co.nz/index.cfm?pageID=34430&r=6, accessed 13 November 2006]

[31] Anon 1969 *Country Cooking* [Amuri Sub-centre The St John Ambulance Association]. Christchurch: Aristo Press Associates, p. 129

[32] Lawson, N. 2000 *How To Be A Domestic Goddess: baking and the art of comfort cooking*. London: Chatto and Windus, p. 239; Delia [Smith] Online, recipes http://www.deliaonline.com/search/?qx=mini-pavlovas, accessed 13 November 2006

[33] Howells, S. 2006 Instore. *Air New Zealand Magazine*, October 2006, p. 29

10: Some sticky issues

[1] Nicholson, J. (co-ordinator) 1992 *Something for Everyone* [St David's Presbyterian Church]. Auckland: Thursday Fellowship Committee, p. 25

[2] Leach, H. 1997 'The Pavlova Cake: the evolution of a national dish', in H. Walker (ed.) *Food on the Move. Proceedings of the Oxford Symposium on Food and Cookery 1996*. Blackawton, Totnes, Devon: Prospect Books, p. 220

[3] Hillier, J. 2001 'The Proof of the Pavlova', in L. Kroetsch and M. Symons (eds) *Proceedings of the Wellington Symposium of Gastronomy 11th Symposium of Australian Gastronomy in Holiday Mood*. Wellington: [the Editors], p. 81

[4] McGee, H. 1986 *On Food and Cooking. The science and lore of the kitchen*. London: Unwin Hyman, p. 106

[5] McGee, H. 1986 *On Food and Cooking. The science and lore of the kitchen*. London: Unwin Hyman, p. 105

[6] McGee, H. 1986 *On Food and Cooking. The science and lore of the kitchen*. London: Unwin Hyman, p. 106

[7] Mitchell, J. 2006 'What's in a Recipe? Pavlovas from selected New Zealand cookbooks 1939–2005'. Paper delivered at the conference 'Cookbooks as History' held at the Research Centre for the History of Food and Drink, University of Adelaide, July 2006

[8] Wilson, R. 2006 Interaction of Ingredients with Egg White Proteins and their Effects on the Physical Properties of Pavlovas. Unpublished BSc Hons research project, Department of Food Science, University of Otago

9 Pedersen, E. 1992 *The Really Reliable New Zealand Cookbook*. Auckland: C.J. Publishing, p. 167

10 Lau, K. and E. Dickinson 2004 'Structural and rheological properties of aerated high sugar systems containing egg albumen'. *Journal of Food Science* 69(5), pp. E232–E239

11 Basham, Mrs D. c. 1934 *The N.Z. 'Daisy Chain' Cookery Book*. Auckland: Harvison & Marshall Ltd, p. 27

12 Raffald, E. 1970 [1782] *The Experienced English Housekeeper*. Facsimile of eighth ed. London: E & W. Books, p. 272

13 Farmer, F.M. 1904 *Food and Cookery for the Sick and Convalescent*. Boston: Little, Brown and Co., p. 216

14 Sherriff, Mrs S.D. 1961 *GHB Cookery Book*. Christchurch: Bascands Ltd, p. 23

15 Gray, E. 1978 *Basic New Zealand Cookbook*. Dunedin: John McIndoe, p. 111; Mountier, M. (ed.) 1984 *Good New Zealand Food and Making the Most of it*. Auckland: Burnham House Publishing Ltd, p. 16; Dryden, G. (ed.) 1984 *The All-Colour Guide to New Zealand Entertaining*. Auckland: The Dryden Johnson Group, p. 136

16 Smith, J.A. (compiler) 1975 *Golden Jubilee Cook Book*. Women's Division Federated Farmers New Zealand, p. 91

17 Flower, T. 1972 *Tui Flower's Modern Hostess Cookbook*. Wellington: A.H. & A.W. Reed, p. 96

18 Britten, D. 1977 *The Des Britten Cookbook*. Auckland: Woolworths (NZ) Ltd, p. 161; Bilton, J. 1981 *New Zealand Kiwifruit Cook Book*. Auckland: Irvine Holt, p. 38

19 Mitchell, J. 2006 'What's in a Recipe? Pavlovas from selected New Zealand cookbooks 1939–2005'. Paper delivered at the conference 'Cookbooks as History' held at the Research Centre for the History of Food and Drink, University of Adelaide, July 2006

20 Finlay, I. c. 1934 *Cookery* [Dunedin City Gas Dept.]. Third ed. Dunedin: [?]John McIndoe, p. 125

21 Birch, C. (comp.) 1982 *Rally Cook Book* [New Zealand Every Boy's and Every Girl's Rallies]. Arura Souvenir Edition [Eighth]. Palmerston North: G.P.H. Print, p. 99

22 Anon 1984 *Cavy Cook Book 1984* National [Garden City Cavy Club]. Christchurch: Halkett Press, p. 5

23 Personal communication from J. Teal, 2006

11: Why pavlovas are important

1 Parloa, M. 1882 *Miss Parloa's New Cook Book*. New York: C.T. Dillingham, p. 317

2 Lovegren, S. 2005 *Fashionable Food. Seven decades of food fads*. Chicago: The University of Chicago Press, pp. 72–3; Perkins, W.L. 1949 *The Boston Cooking-School Cook Book by Fannie Merritt Farmer*. Eighth ed. London: George G. Harrap, p. 581

3 Anderson, J. 1997 *The American Century Cookbook*. New York: Clarkson Potter Publishers, p. 382

4 Leach, H.M. 2006 'From Dunoon to Dunedin—what two distant charitable cookbooks reveal about the British tradition of soups'. *Petits Propos Culinaires* 80, p. 54

5 Anderson, J. 1997 *The American Century Cookbook*. New York: Clarkson Potter Publishers, pp. 164, 364

Index

Cookers, pressure 94

Cookery (Dunedin City Gas Dept.) 27, 76

Cookery Book (Women's Division of Federated Farmers) 104

Cooking from the Commonwealth (1958) 17

Cooking container (meringues and pavlovas), pie dish or plate 132–3, 149, 151; ring 150; tin 18, 28, 70, 74–80, 86, 93, 116, 119, 129, 131, 133, 149–50; tray, oven slide or sheet 18, 28, 75–6, 86, 93, 116, 148–50

Cooking surface (meringues and pavlovas), boards 64, 148–9; foil 119, 149–50, 158; history of materials used 148–51; paper, greaseproof 75, 146, 149–50; paper, non-stick baking 146, 150, 158; paper, plain brown or white 75, 148–9; paper, waxed 148–9

Cooking times and temperatures, role in soft-centred pavlovas 147–8

Cooper, Mrs C. 78

Cooper, Peter 50, 172 fn 3.35

Cornflour, role in soft-centred pavlova, see Ingredients, cornflour

Cornford, Mary 78

Country Women's Institutes (see also individual branches) 159

Courier Mail, The 16

Court and Country Cook, The (1702) 62–3

Cox, Helen 113–5, 155, 165

Cox's Gelatine 51

Craig, Elizabeth 98–9

Creamoata Recipes 87

Creation of recipes, see Recipes, evolution or creation

Cuisine et Vins de France 18

Cuisinier Roial et Bourgeois, Le (1691) 62

Cullen, Vera 100

Dainties; or how to please our lords and masters 51

Dainty Recipes (North-East Valley Presbyterian Church) 57, 59

Dale, David 12

Davidson, Alan 28

Davis Dainty Dishes (Australian editions.) 44–7; (Canadian editions.) 47; (New Zealand editions.) 44–7, 52–4, 69, 112, 153

Davis Gelatine Company 12, 36, 42, 45–7, 52, 54, 153–4

Davis, George 52

Delmonico's (New York) 79

Dempsey, Rosemary 118, 149

Desserts, bombe (ice cream) 32; gelatine 41–3, 45–9, 51–2, 54, 109–12; pavlova and meringue cakes served as 86, 128–9; served in 1950s 41–2; served in 1980s and 1990s 128–9

Devereux, G. 67

Dictionary of New Zealand English 28

Dominion Range Co. (Wellington) 89

Dryden, Gordon 121, 149, 159

Dunedin City Gas Department 27, 76, 150, 166

Edmonds Cookery Book (1978) 103

Edmonds 'Sure to Rise' Cookery Book 61, 96–8, 113, 154, 166

Edmonds' 'Sure to Set' Jelly Crystals 54

Egg, emu, used in pavlova 14

Egg whites, see Ingredients

Egg yolks used in toppings, see also Filling and Topping 113

Electric Refrigeration (N.Z.) Ltd 88

Epicurean, The 78

Escoffier, Auguste 31–4, 165

Etiquette for Women (1920) 66–7

Evening Post (Wellington) 11–12

Evolution of recipes, see Recipes, evolution or creation

Experienced English Housekeeper, The (1769) 63

Farmer, Fannie Merritt 64, 148

Farmers Cookbook (1996) 121

Favourite Recipes from the United Nations (1956–) 17–18

Fenton, Tracy 136

'Festival', pseudonym of early pavlova contributor 70–1, 73, 153–4

Filling ingredients (for multi-layered meringues and pavlovas), almonds 71, 131; apricots 80; bananas 80; cherries (glacé) 60–1, 63, 68, 70–1, 73, 77–8, 80; coconut 129–31; coffee essence 77; cream 60–1, 63, 70, 73, 77–9, 129–31, 147; grapes 80; kiwifruit 131; liqueur 77; loganberries 27, 76; mock cream 90; mulberries 24; nuts, chopped 70, 73; passionfruit 77, 131; peaches 79–80; pineapple 77, 79, 131, 139; raspberries 27, 76, 131; raspberry jam 63; strawberries 77–9, 131; walnuts cooked in milk 106–9, 115

Finlay, Isabella 21, 23, 26–8, 76, 150, 166

Flower, Tui 9, 103, 109, 116, 149, 159

Freer, Warren 125
Freezer, introduction of home 118
Frypan, electric 119, 161
Fulton, Margaret 11–14
Futter, Emily 12, 23, 26, 77

Gasparini 62
Gateau(x) 84, 117, 124
Geering, Lloyd 92
Gelatine (see also Jelly), derived from collagen 43,
    50; development of commercial 50; granulated
    42, 54; pre-mixed fruit-flavoured 42–3, 54
Gems, gem scones 17, 87
Genesee Pure Food Company (USA) 46
Gepp, Nancy 17
GHB Cookery Book 101, 149, 159
Gibbard, Les 9, 19
Girls' Auxiliary Recipe Book (Invercargill) 24
Glasse, Hannah 34
Good Harvest Cook Book (Puketapu Women's
    Fellowship, Hawkes Bay) 104
Good Housekeeper, The (1839) 63
Gouffé, Jules 78
Gray, Eleanor 149
Greenbaum, Florence K. 79
Gregg's (Dunedin) 54
Griffins, biscuit manufacturers 132–3
Grocers' United Stores 92–3
Grocott, Mrs A.D. 99
Guide to Modern Cookery, A (Le Guide Culinaire) 32–3

Hale, Sarah Josepha 63
Half-Gallon Quarter-Acre Pavlova Paradise, The (1972)
    18–19
Hamilton Beach, appliance manufacturer 123
Hartshorn 50
Harvard Business Wives Cookbook 132
Helensville Primary School 73
Henderson, Jean (Deaconess) 112
Henderson, Mary N.F. 79
Hillier, Jennifer 142
Hinds, Elizabeth 23
Hints for making pavlovas 146
Hocken Collections (Hocken Library, Dunedin) 9,
    23
Holst, Alison 132
Home Cookery for New Zealand (c. 1926) 77
Home Management (c. 1956) 17
Hooper, M.M. 57

Hora Hora Kindergarten 100
Hostess Cook Book, The (1952) 113–15
Hostess Handbook of Party Foods (1953) 132
Hotels, Carlton (London) 32; Esplanade (Perth)
    14, 22; Midland (Wellington) 36; Savoy
    (London) 32–3
Housewives' Guide [to] Food Prices [and] Food Rationing
    (1944) 163
Howe, Robin 17

Icon, Jell-O as American 43; pavlova as New
    Zealand 11–15, 19, 112, 116, 128, 132, 138–40,
    162–4
Icons, Australian 12–15
Ideal Cookery Book, The (1929) 78, 80, 89, 148
Illawarra Mercury 12
Ingredients of meringues and pavlovas (see also
    Filling and Topping), baking powder 85, 99–
    100, 109–10, 112, 131–3, 144, 157; coffee essence
    or granules 58–61, 64, 77–8, 84–5, 106–7, 156;
    cornflour 24–5, 28, 58–9, 61, 64, 70–2, 74, 76–
    8, 81, 82, 85–6, 96, 98, 101–5, 109, 112–13, 120,
    122, 130–1, 138, 141–5, 157, 160; cream of tartar
    60, 79, 100–1, 103–5, 109–10, 112, 145, 155, 157;
    egg whites 60, 70–2, 74–80, 85–6, 90, 92–3,
    94, 96–114, 117–20, 122–4, 126, 129–32, 134,
    136–9, 142–6, 154–7, 159–61; food colouring
    43–5, 53; gelatine 109–12, 138; jelly crystals
    124; lemon juice 109, 111–2, 145; milk powder
    138; nuts 58–61, 85, 132; Snax biscuits (or other
    crackers) 131–4; sugar 70–2, 74–8, 85, 90, 93,
    94, 99–104, 106–7, 113–4, 120, 126, 129, 131–2,
    142–6, 155–7, 159–60; sugar (caster) 28, 60, 75,
    94, 96–7, 101–2, 104–5, 108, 111, 117, 118, 122–3,
    126, 129, 134, 136–8, 144, 146; sugar substitutes
    138; vanilla essence 71, 75–6, 86, 96–7, 101–2,
    104–5, 113, 119–20, 122, 131, 134, 136–7, 155, 159;
    vinegar 24–5, 75–6, 78–81, 85–6, 93, 94, 96–9,
    101–6, 109, 113–4, 119–20, 122–3, 130–1, 136–7,
    142–5, 157, 159–60; walnuts 58–61, 85, 131, 134,
    156; water 85, 96, 98–112, 116, 119–20, 122, 129,
    142–4, 146, 157, 159–60
Innocent Delight, An (1985) 103
International Jewish Cook Book, The (1918) 79
Isinglass 50–2
Ivory dust 50

Jekyll, Agnes 80
Jekyll, Gertrude 80